MONTY'S HIGHLANDERS

MONTY'S HIGHLANDERS

51ST HIGHLAND DIVISION IN THE SECOND WORLD WAR

Patrick Delaforce

Pen & Sword
MILITARY

First published in Great Britain in 1997 by Tom Donovan Publishing Ltd
Reprinted in 2000 by Octopus Publishing Group Ltd

Published in this format in 2007 by
Pen & Sword Military
An imprint of
Pen & Sword Books Ltd
47 Church Street
Barnsley
South Yorkshire
S70 2AS

Copyright © Patrick Delaforce

ISBN 978 1 84415 512 5

A CIP catalogue record for this book is
available from the British Library

Printed and bound in England
By CPI UK

Pen & Sword Books Ltd incorporates the Imprints of Pen & Sword Aviation,
Pen & Sword Maritime, Pen & Sword Military, Wharncliffe Local History,
Pen & Sword Select, Pen & Sword Military Classics and Leo Cooper.

For a complete list of Pen & Sword titles please contact
PEN & SWORD BOOKS LIMITED
47 Church Street, Barnsley, South Yorkshire, S70 2AS, England
E-mail: enquiries@pen-and-sword.co.uk
Website: www.pen-and-sword.co.uk

Contents

1

Monty's Highlanders
51st Highland Division

Shortly after the end of WWII Field Marshal Sir Bernard Montgomery addressed many of the senior officers of 51st Highland Division:

"After St Valéry another Highland Division was formed. This Division I got to know very well. In fact it did the whole of its fighting in World War Two under my command, and I do not suppose there is anyone more qualified to speak about it than I am. As far as I am concerned that re-born Highland Division will always be linked with the name of Douglas Wimberley. If ever a General laboured to turn his division into a first class fighting formation, Douglas Wimberley did. And he succeeded. I am proud to tell you that of all the many fine Divisions that served under me in the late war, *none was finer than the Highland Division - none*. When I arrived on 13th August 1942, to take command of the Eighth Army, the Highland Division had also just arrived. It was not with the Eighth Army, but back in the Delta, digging trenches round Mena House Hotel, putting the bar at Shepherd's in a state of defence and planning the defence of Cairo. I knew very well that the safety of the Delta and its cities lay in holding the Alamein position. I knew that well, and so I got the Division sent out from Cairo to join the Eighth Army in the Desert. I feel it was then that my education in matters Scottish began. My tutor was Douglas Wimberley. Until that moment, I had never been to Scotland in my life. That is a dreadful thing to say. My education was taken in hand, as was the education of practically everyone in the Eighth Army. That very fine Division merely wanted to be properly launched in battle and given a fair 'do', and the rest was certain. I put the Division into battle; it received its baptism of fire in the defensive battle of Alam Halfa, which began on 31st August. Then came Alamein. I sensed in the Division before Alamein a very definite anxiousness; no lack of courage; it was an anxiousness to do well and avenge the tragedy of St Valéry: but it never had any cause to be anxious. I put the Division into battle between two veteran Divisions, the 9th Australian and the 2nd New Zealand. It has always been an interesting thing to me how the Scottish soldier very quickly makes friends with the Dominion soldier. It may be because both of them are slightly uncivilised. It does pay, though, to know that fact in battle, and when you put the Division alongside two Dominion Divisions, you need not bother about it. The Division advanced to the attack in the bright moonlight of the Desert at Alamein in October 1942, to the skirl of the pipes. St Valéry was avenged, well and truly, I believe that night. The re-born Highland Division had found its soul. From that day, the Division never looked back. Led by Douglas Wimberley, it went from success to success, and never made a mistake. Tripoli on 23rd January 1943 - three months to a day after Alamein. The Gordons were first into the city, riding on the tanks, and early in February I staged a ceremonial parade for Mr Churchill, who came to visit the Eighth Army. As long as I live, I will never forget the Highland Division on parade that day in Tripoli. Officers and men had the pride of victory in their eyes; every man an emperor. After Tripoli came the Mareth battle, and then Wadi Akarit, where the Division fought one of its finest battles. Then came the end in Africa, in Tunisia.

The Division played a leading part in Sicily. Then Douglas Wimberley, or 'Big Tam', as he was called by his men, left the Division to go as Commandant of the Staff College. Then came Normandy; and as we advanced across the Seine, I gave instructions that the lay-out of the battle was to be such that the Highland Division would be directed on St Valéry, so that it could liberate that place. This was done; but I always feel that St Valéry, 1940, was avenged at Alamein, 1942. Then, the Division was gallantly led from Normandy to the Rhine by Thomas Rennie another very fine officer, and under him they fought that magnificent fight in the Reischwald Forest and suffered severely in officer casualties. Then Thomas Rennie was killed. However, the Division was ready for that great day in March, 1945, when we crossed the Rhine, the Black Watch being the first over the river. Some hard fighting followed, but the end was in sight, and it came on 5th May, on

Luneberg Heath, when I had the pleasure of taking the surrender of some two million men of the once renowned German Army.

I regard it as an immense honour to be asked here tonight. I know very well how, in Scotland, things revolve round the clan and the family, and I suppose this gathering is essentially a great family gathering of the Highland Division. To be included in it is a great honour, a very great honour. But not only Highlanders are here tonight; it is a great pleasure to see the Artillery here.

I have never had an opportunity of saying this: during the course of the war it has fallen to my lot to receive from the nations taking part the highest decorations and orders that they can give, and when one wears them, one feels that they were really won by the officers and men of the regimental units of the army. They won them. I may wear them, Archie Wavell may wear them, but you, gentlemen, won them; and I say that straight from the heart. I have a very great affection for the Highland Division. It was the only infantry Division in the armies of the British Empire that accompanied me during the whole of the long march from Alamein to Berlin. No other Division came all the way; and during the whole of that long journey it never once put a foot wrong. It is at once a humiliation and an honour to have had such a Division under one's command. I shall always remember the Highland Division with admiration and high regard. It is, therefore, with pride, with gratitude and with affection that I give you the toast of the Highland Division."

2

Early History
WW1: "Valiant Scots lying on soil of France"

In May 1915 the 1st Highland Territorial Division crossed the Channel and on arrival in France their designation was changed to the 51st (Highland) Division. 152 Brigade was composed of 5th and 6th Seaforths, 6th and 8th Argyll and Sutherland Highlanders. In 153 Bde were 5th and 7th Gordons and 6th and 7th Black Watch, and in 154 Bde were temporarily four Lancastrian battalions. By December, 154 Bde was reconstituted as 4th Seaforths, 4th and 5th Black Watch and 4th Camerons. They were in reserve for the second battle of Ypres but at Richebourg in May 1915 were heavily engaged at Festubert suffering badly with 1500 casualties. Lt General GM Harper took over command at Mercourt on the Somme in September. The Divisional mark on their vehicles was HD. Rather unfairly they were soon nicknamed 'Harper's Duds,' after their failure to capture High Wood, despite five days of bitter fighting. In March of the following year they occupied the line from Roclincourt to Neuville St Vaast, known as 'the Labyrinth.' For over four months they were harassed day and night, losing many casualties to mines under their trenches. But worse was to come. During the battle of the Ancre and the storming of Beaumont Hamel and Y Ravine they lost 2500 men.

Captain D Sutherland, 5th Bn Seaforth described the Beaumont Hamel attack on 13th November 1916: "The Division took over the front facing Beaumont Hamel, a ruined village a mile north of the Ancre which the Germans had, by two years steady work, converted into a most formidable stronghold. The southern side was flanked by the 'Y' ravine with steep banks in which were numerous deep dug outs where thousands of men could safely withstand the heaviest bombardment. In front of the village were three main trench systems, well connected up with deep dug outs and barbed wire entanglements, machine gun posts and trench mortar emplacements. In the village, reinforced concrete backings to the ruined walls concealed powerful MG posts. It rained persistently converting the (canvas) camps into quagmires, the trenches into impossible sloughs." When the attack went in, "The morning was dark and misty. Long before zero hour the first waves had climbed out of the knee-deep trenches and lay upon the parapet. At 5.45am, 13th November the signal, the exploding of a mine was given, our artillery opened a terrific barrage on the German front line and over went the infantry, not doubling, not even walking, but wading knee-deep and sometimes waist-deep, through the morass of sticky mud and water and neck-deep shell holes which constituted 'No Man's Land.'" By the afternoon the battalion strength was down to 90 men. By 4pm the Division had captured the village with 1700 prisoners, of which the Seaforths claimed 600.

The 6th and 7th Black Watch spent 13 months out of a 2½ year period in the labyrinth of trenches in the French sector at Arras. Mines were the greatest danger but the Black Watch had many coal pitface workers from Fife. From their listening galleries they picked up the noise of the German miners and drove in counter mines. Altogether in 1916 in the Somme fighting HD lost over 8000 casualties. In the spring of 1917 they took part in the battle of Arras on a twelve mile front from Lens and Arras. General Allenby wrote 'Convey to 51st Division my congratulations on their great gallantry at Roeux and the Chemical Works.' During this battle a further 3000 men became casualties. At the end of May, they moved north to the River Lys and took part in the Third Battle of Ypres against the enemy's pill boxes. Round Cambrai they captured Havrincourt, Flesquieres, Cantaing and Fontaine-Notre-Dame, losing 2500 casualties. On 31st July 6th Black Watch had two officers and 50 men cut off on the far side of the river Steenbeeke. A survivor wrote: "Ammunition was running short and the enemy were massing for another assault, when we received the order to fall back on the [already captured] German gunpits beyond the river. Those who came through bear witness that it was one of the most exciting moments of their lives. Stumbling through the mud, falling, rising, pressing on, while the enemy barely one hundred yards away stood up and took deliberate aim, one of the memories of the Great War which no length of time will ever blot out."

On 20th November the Division took part in the joint operation with tanks at Cambrai. A massive attack by six divisions with 400 lozenge shaped Mk IV tanks with a top speed of 4mph. For security reasons HD did not wear kilts. 'Uncle' Harper distrusted these new fangled machines but nevertheless trained his men to follow 150 yards behind the tanks in a close order spearhead formation which closed as they passed through gaps in the wire and opened out again afterwards. 5th Argylls and 6th Black Watch led their brigade and by 0815 had reached the Grand Ravin, a shallow river bed, a perfect operation. But German field guns knocked-out many tanks in the second phase attack. Nevertheless on the first day of Cambrai, four miles of enemy ground had been gained in the formidable Hindenberg line. Sadly ten days later on St Andrews Day all the ground was recaptured by counter-attacks.

In March 1918 their GOC 'Uncle' Harper was promoted to be Corps Commander and was succeeded by Major General Carter-Campbell. In three days defending the Bapaume-Cambrai road defences against massive German attacks, they fought stubborn rearguard actions losing a further 5000 casualties (of which 2714 were missing). King George V visited them and said: "We all know The Fifty First." It seems almost incredible how they could survive these shattering losses, but unbelievably worse was to come. At the Aubers Ridge they lost 3000 and in July near Epernay in the Champagne area around the River Ardre lost another 3500, and finally in late October just before the Armistice between Cambrai and Valenciennes in the final Allied offensive suffered another 2872 casualties.

Monsieur Poincaré, the French President said in 1919, "How many valiant Scots are there lying on the soil of France after fighting for the common ideal of both our nations. To the mothers and widows of those heroes I give the assurance that their image will ever be engraved in the memory and the heart of my country."

The Highland Division won five Victoria Crosses in WWI, three by Seaforth battalions, one by the Gordons, one by the Argyll and Sutherland Highlanders. The Germans had great respect for their Highland opponents and christened them the 'Ladies from Hell' because of their kilted fury.

3

Outbreak of WW2
"No pants under the kilt"

In the autumn of 1938 after Chamberlain's visit to Munich the decision was taken to double the strength of the Territorial Army. A recruiting drive was then started and the Highland regiments were very soon brought up to strength. By the spring of 1939, for instance, the 7th Argyll and Sutherland Highlanders were able to form two complete infantry battalions.

By late August, General Mobilization was well on the way and all TA and Regular Army reservists were advised to report to their respective units. Army Form E518 Reserve and Auxiliary Force Act, 1939 or 'Calling Out Notices' worded, 'You are called out for Military Service' were sent out across the United Kingdom. On 1st September all the regiments and battalions of 9th Scottish and 51st Highland Divisions were duly embodied, usually with a strength in the infantry of 32 officers and 630 other ranks. Almost immediately however men were released to industry and soldiers under 19 were posted to second line units. By the 16th the 51st Highland Division had left Scotland and travelled by troop trains to Aldershot for final equipping and completion of training preparatory to joining the newly formed British Expeditionary Force in France. Drafts of men arrived, battle equipment poured in, and inoculations were carried out. And embarkation leave followed, fortunately for many, over the New Year. The King and Queen reviewed most formations before embarkation at Southampton. Unfortunately, the traditional uniform of Highland regiments was not considered by the War Office as suitable for modern war and the soldiers handed in their kilts. Lt Col Douglas Wimberley, then CO 1st Bn Cameron Highlanders, wrote: "An attack was to be made on the Highland Regts as to their wearing their kilts in battle in Europe... the kilt as a battledress was being attacked from three angles. On grounds of [unit] security, on grounds of its inadequacy in case of gas attack and on grounds of difficulty of supply in war. There was also the tinge of jealousy - why should the kilted regiments be given preferential treatment to wear a becoming kilt. The thickness of the kilt and its seven yards of tartan was extra protection. It was traditional in all Highland regiments never to wear any garments in the way of pants under the kilt. But anti-gas pants were issued."

Major General Victor Fortune, the GOC was a distinguished fighting soldier. He had commanded the 1st Bn Black Watch in 1916, then the 1st Seaforth in 1927 and the 5th Infantry Brigade in 1930. As Major General he commanded 52nd (Lowland) Division in 1935-6 and became GOC the Highland Division in 1937. When the Highlanders arrived at Le Havre in mid January 1940 they were welcomed by 'Lord Haw-Haw' (on German radio). This despite removal of HD signs from battle dresses and vehicles. St Andrew's crosses and stags heads on a background of green and purple were possible clues. General Fortune however continued to wear the HD signs on his uniform!

The Highlanders left Southampton in chilly but sunny weather and arrived to find the coldest, most bitter winter for many a long year. It was not an auspicious start to their first visit to French soil since 1919.

Order of Battle
51st (Highland) Division, 1940

Major General V.M. Fortune, CB, DSO

1st Bn. The Lothians & Border Horse (Yeomanry)

152nd Brigade: Brigadier H.W.V. Stewart, DSO
2nd Bn. The Seaforth Highlanders
4th Bn. The Seaforth Highlanders
4th Bn. The Queen's Own Cameron Highlanders

153rd Brigade: Brigadier G. T. Burnet, MC
4th Bn. The Black Watch
1st Bn. The Gordon Highlanders
5th Bn. The Gordon Highlanders

154th Brigade: Brigadier A.C.L. Stanley-Clarke DSO
1st Bn. The Black Watch
7th Bn. The Argyll & Sutherland Highlanders
8th Bn. The Argyll & Sutherland Highlanders

Royal Artillery: C.R.A., Brigadier H.C.H. Eden, MC
17th Field Regiment, Royal Artillery
23rd Field Regiment, Royal Artillery

75th Field Regiment, Royal Artillery
51st Anti-tank Regiment, Royal Artillery

Royal Engineers: C.R.E., Lt Col H M Smail, TD
26th Field Company, Royal Engineers
236th Field Company, Royal Engineers
237th Field Company, Royal Engineers
239th Field Park Company, Royal Engineers

Royal Corps of Signals: Lt Col T.P.E. Murray
51st Divisional Signals Company

Royal Army Medical Corps: A.D.M.S., Lt Col D.P. Levack
152nd Field Ambulance
153rd Field Ambulance
154th Field Ambulance

Royal Army Service Corps: Lt Col T. Harris-Hunter TD
Divisional Ammunition Company.
Divisional Petrol Company
Divisional Supply Column.

Attached troops
51st Medium Regiment, R.A.
1st R.H.A. (less one Battery)
97th Field Regiment, R.A. (one Battery)
213th Army Field Company, R.E.
1st Bn Princess Louise's Kensington Regiment (Machine-Gunners)
7th Bn The Royal Northumberland Fusiliers (Machine-Gunners)
6th Bn The Royal Scots Fusiliers (Pioneers)
7th Bn The Norfolk Regiment (Pioneers)
Sections of the R.A.O.C. and the R.A.S.C.

4

With the BEF in France: "Entente Cordiale?"

There are two excellent accounts of the Highland Division's epic but short-lived campaign during the first half of 1940; Eric Linklater's (HMSO 1942) and Saul David's (Brasseys 1994). They were the first

territorial division to join the BEF and initially were placed in reserve
south-west of Lille. For six weeks intensive training and digging of
anti-tank ditches ensued in alternate freezing weather, followed by
thaw. The division was well trained with indifferent weaponry, but
apart from a sprinkling of senior officers who had seen action in WWI,
green and inexperienced. On 28th March the Supreme War Council of
Britain and France made a solemn declaration of unity. The intention
was for the two countries to fight as one, and then live as one when the
fighting was finished. It is certain that this key political decision did not
percolate very far down the line from Whitehall but it was to prove a
matter of life or death to the Highlanders. British brigades were
attached for periods of 15 days to the French Army in front of the
Maginot line. The French Army was then regarded as being the largest,
probably the most professional in Europe and the Maginot line,
constructed over the years at vast expense, as being impregnable. The
purpose of attachment was of course to 'blood' the BEF to front line
patrol activity. On 13th April orders came for the Highlanders to
become the first British division to perform a tour of duty under French
High Command, in the Saar area of Lorraine. The Division was now
re-organised with the arrival of three regular battalions. The 1st Black
Watch went to 154 Bde, 1st Gordon Highlanders to 153 Bde and 2nd
Seaforth to 152 Bde. At the same time 6th Black Watch, 6th Gordons
and 6th Seaforth were withdrawn and transferred to the 5th Division.
Moreover, two Pioneer battalions (7th Royal Norfolks, 6th Royal Scots
Fusiliers), two machine-gun battalions (1st Kensington and 7th Royal
Northumberland Fusiliers) plus additional RA and RE support brought
the total strength of the Division up to a formidable 21,000. The French
Command had continued their Maginot line westwards along the
Belgium-France frontier, known as 'The Small Maginot Line.' It had
never been completed since the Belgian government had protested that
it was an open invitation for the Germans to violate their neutrality!
The allotted sector was Hombourg-Bulange, 18 miles north-east of
Metz. The first outpost layer of defence, 'Ligne de Contact' was seven
miles in front of the Maginot forts and about six miles from the
Siegfried line forts. It was green fertile countryside with forests,
beechwoods, many streams, orchards and undulating hills. In 'No Mans
Land' farms and even small villages had been evacuated by the
military. Lorraine had been under German control until 1918 and had
always been a much disputed area. By the end of April 154 Bde had

arrived, with 1st Black Watch and 7th Argylls HQs in the village of Waldweisstroff. The ground was very wet and the French had built log cabins, certainly not bullet-proof. The pioneers were kept busy with mules to improve the dug-outs and huge quantities of sandbags, 'A' frames, revetting material, coils of barbed wire and wiring pickets were needed. Major E Hitchcock's RIASC Coy did sterling work bringing ammunition up by mule 'trains.' The German patrols were very aggressive, mainly local men, using trained dogs, and the Bouzonville woods, full of wild pig and barking deer were also often full of German intruders.

When 4th Camerons arriving in early May at Ising in the Saar found the Brisants (V-shaped defence works) to consist of a few shallow pits and the Ligne d'Arret a series of isolated light MG posts. The Camerons needed 80,000 sandbags, 2000 'A' frames, 2000 sheets of revetting material, 600 coils of barbed wire and 1200 wiring pickets as the minimum requirement to put their line in a fit state of defence. Lt John Boustead, a Seaforth platoon commander spent a night and a day with a French unit to study conditions and positions to be taken over the next day. At about 0100 hrs he heard and saw the French MGs belting out fire. "I said to the French Officer, 'Les Allemands sont-ils içi?' (Are the Germans here?). 'Non non,' he replied airily. 'Mais pourquoi avez-vous tirez?' (But why have you fired?) I asked pointing to the French MG just visible a few yards away. The French Officer shrugged his shoulders. 'C'est notre dernière nuit içi, et cela les amusent' (It is our last night here, and that amuses them). Entente cordiale?"

2/Lt Parnell 7th Argylls: "On patrol we wore the absolute minimum, just our weapons, so we could move quickly and get through fences. Later on the Somme, I discovered how useless a revolver was and used a rifle instead. We always went out at night, slowly, carefully on foot. If you started to crawl you would never get anywhere. We bumped a German patrol one night fired like blazes and scarpered as quickly as possible." The 4th Black Watch were around Remeling 'Ligne de contact' with 154 Bde on their right.

In the early hours of 10th May, the long-awaited German offensive, 'Fall Gelb,' Operation Yellow, the major onslaught on the Low Countries was unleashed. Paratroopers landed in Holland and the Panzers poured across the Belgian and Luxembourg frontier.

The Division was manning the front line, with from right to left, 4th Camerons (had relieved 2nd Seaforths on 8th May), 1st Black Watch (had relieved 8th Argylls on 9th May) and 4th Black Watch (had relieved 1st Gordons on 7th May). On 11th May General Fortune's Divisional Direction: "Patrolling must be active. Any attack by the enemy must at once be exploited by the Tank troops (1st Lothian and

Border Horse) immediately."

Two days later before dawn came a heavy attack on 153 and 154 Bde sectors around Spitzwald wood, Hartsbuch wood, Grossenwald and Winkelmerter woods in what became known as the 'battle for Remeling.' First of all a heavy barrage of 8" shells fell along the four-battalion divisional front followed by infantry with MG, grenades and flame-throwers. They made progress to the right of the Grossenwald.

Private J McGready 1st Black Watch: "Price and Fisher had an excellent time with a Brengun and a rifle, their bag of the enemy was put down as 44 in an afternoon. It was all storm troopers in that action but the Black Watch was more than a match for them - good target practice."

The 1st Lothians had their tanks ditched and knocked-out but Brigadier George Burney's 153 Bde held fast. The next day the 5th Gordons received 3600 shells in a ferocious 90 minute barrage. The guns of 17 Field Regt RA replied in kind, but 1st Black Watch lost 23 casualties. The next day the German attack intensified and in a fierce day-long attack 'D' Coy 5th Gordons took 70 casualties at Heydwald and had to withdraw. General Condé, GOC French 3rd Army ordered the two French divisions on either side of 51st (and the Highlanders) to abandon the villages of Betting and Wolschen, the Grossenwald and Heydwald. They withdrew the whole line back to the 'Ligne de Recueil', three miles in front of the Maginot line, but on a forward slope. In the battle of Remeling Sgt Sidney Newman and CQMS Samuel Taylor both won the DCM.

Holland surrendered five days after the German offensive, and seven Panzer divisions crossed the river Meuse between Sedan and Dinant. On 15th May Paul Reynaud, the French premier telephoned Churchill and told him, "The front is broken near Sedan, they are pouring through great numbers with tanks and armoured cars. We are defeated: we have lost the battle." From that moment onwards Churchill was desperate to keep the Grand Alliance going and to ensure that France went on fighting - at all costs.

On the 20th the Division went into reserve towards Etain, 20 miles north-west of Metz, 154 Bde going to Varennes, north-west of Verden. They had now left General Condé's Third Army and were under direct control of the French High Command. Condé sent them a nice message: "For five months the Third French Army has had the honour of counting British soldiers in her ranks, five months of fighting side by side..." The Highlanders were now lent to the French 2nd Army and reached Grandpré-Varennes on 25th. Meanwhile the Guards Brigade had been driven out of Boulogne and the Rifle Brigade was fighting desperately to keep Calais open. It was a time of orders, counter-orders and very nearly disorder, an instruction came to move to the Sedan to stem the Panzer breakthrough, then plans to evacuate from Cherbourg, and finally to move up to the Somme WWI battlefields. So 3000 divisional vehicles (troop carriers, Bren carriers, cooking, blanket, water, utility trucks, LAA MG trucks) moved about 300 miles on French roads from the Forest of Argonne to Gisors and Haute Forêt d'Eu. The train parties took a longer circuitous route south of Paris, Orleans, Le Mans to Rouen and thence by old French omnibuses 60 miles towards the river Bresle to rejoin the division. Belgium had now surrendered. On 26th May General Fortune was ordered by General Georges, the French Deputy C-in-C to hold the line of the rivers Aisne and Somme with the remaining French forces. So 51st Division came under direct command of General Besson's 3rd Army Group, and in turn of General Robert Altmayer's Groupement A. Their task was to hold the extreme left of the Somme position extending to the Channel.

A new British formation now appeared on the scene. Major General Evans commanded 1st Armoured Division which had been rushed out to France, under strength, under-equipped, barely two weeks earlier. The Germans had crossed the Somme and forced bridgeheads over it at Abbeville. On the 29th General de Gaulle and his tanks of 4th Armoured Division with the 1st Armoured Division counter-attacked the bridgeheads without infantry or artillery support and with little success. Evans told Fortune that his formation needed a period out of the line for drastic overhaul. Eventually the Highlanders were left with one composite regiment of tanks, a sapper company and a light A/Tk and LAA Regt. The other new arrival was Brigadier Beauman DSO who had scrambled together three improvised infantry brigades (Beauforce or the Beauman Division). He told Fortune that Le Havre was almost evacuated and that Rouen would be the supply point for the HD Division. Dieppe was heavily mined, and the port was seriously damaged by air attacks. Beauman and Fortune planned how to fall back on Le Havre, leapfrogging formations in turn. Meanwhile General Fortune loaned 1st Black Watch and 4th Seaforths as a reserve for one final tank attack on 30th May on the Abbeville bridgehead. By the 2nd June the Division was holding part of the river Bresle defences; 152 Bde on the right holding Villers, Huchenneville and Bienfay, 153 Bde (plus 1st Black Watch) the line from Gouy to Moyenneville and in the coastal sector, 154 Bde from the sea to Saigneville. This was a 20 mile front; moreover two enemy bridgeheads had to be contained. Meanwhile 70 miles away the bulk of the BEF and over 30,000 French troops were being evacuated from Dunkirk.

The French 31st Division, a mountain formation, had now arrived on the scene to link up for a joint counter-attack on the Abbeville bridgehead. Despite the fact that the attack would be mainly carried out by French troops, Fortune, as senior general in the sector was put in command! To allow maximum tank pressure in the centre attack on the Marevil ridge and the Mont de Caubert, both flanks were to be protected, on the left by a battalion from 153 Bde, and on the right by one from 152 Bde. 154 Bde was to play no active role, holding the sea line inland to Saigneville. It was a total failure. The French heavy tanks were nearly all wrecked by mines or anti-tank fire. The 4th Camerons on the right attacked Caubert and the wooded ridge called the Hedgehog; they met intense machine-gun fire from cornfields in front of the Hedgehog and along the Route Nationale. The 4th Seaforths following-up in the centre approached the Mont de Caubert with French light tanks which were all put out of action by deadly anti-tank fire. The Seaforths ran into withering machine-gun fire and were mown down like grass. A few survivors reached their first objective 600 yards up the slope. The 2nd Seaforths captured one of the Bienfay woods and by 2100 hrs 1st Gordons had reached the Grand Bois west of Cambron. 152 Brigade lost 20 officers and 543 other rank casualties during the day, exposed to Stuka dive bombing, close machine-gun fire, artillery and mortars. The following day an enemy thrust fell on 154 Bde spread so thinly on the eight miles between Quesnoy, Le Hourdel and the sea.

Eric Linklater admirably describes the situation that the Highlanders now confronted: "The German stream was driving the Division back along its whole front. As the incoming tide advancing over flattish sand comes in by sudden trickles or runnels - a channel here, a channel there - then drowning the islets it has surrounded, goes on with never-deviating purpose... so the Germans found gaps and entry in the 20 miles of hill, hedgerow, village, wood and rolling field from Limeux to the sea. The front was too long, its defenders too few. It was a physical numerical impossibility to hold so long a line with only one division, but nowhere was it abandoned without fighting."

154 Bde had the 8th Argylls holding Ault-Tully-Escarbotin, the 4th Black Watch Fressenville-Feuguières. Several bridges over the river Bresle had been blown. On their right the remains of 152 Bde had fallen back to the main Abbeville-Blangy road. At Martainville 4th Camerons were dive-bombed by Stukas and the 7th Argylls fought desperately to hold Franleu. Despite help from the Kensington's machine-guns, each company was surrounded and besieged throughout a constant shower of mortar bombs. By the end of the day only 'D' Coy survived and they were captured on 7th June. Lt Col EP Buchanan and many others were captured, and only B Echelon, 135 of them, survived. The 8th Argylls also had many of their outposts over-run; 1st Gordons and 1st Black Watch were forced to withdraw. 154 Brigade was down to half its fighting strength. Withdrawal over the Bresle was decided and the new

ten-mile front was from Blangy to the sea.

The CRASC 2i/c, Lt Col MHG Young noted: "General Fortune called a meeting of his brigadiers and senior staff officers and now told them, 'Gentlemen, I know you would not wish us to desert our French comrades. We could be back in Le Havre in two bounds. But they have no transport. They have only their feet to carry them. We shall fight our way back with them, step by step.' French criticism of the British withdrawal may well have influenced the General. Up to this stage the planned port of evacuation was Le Havre. Only a last minute piece of contingency planning that hit upon St Valéry as the only other port on the coast into which ships could come. The GOC was in an impossible position."

A new improvised reinforcement 'A' brigade arrived south of the river facing the Foret d'Incheville, composed of 5th Sherwood Foresters, 4th Border Regt and 4th Buffs. 152 Bde had been so reduced by the last two days of fighting that they were withdrawn into reserve and relieved by the French 31st Division. Early on 7th June 900 reinforcements arrived from Rouen. The Panzer divisions had broken through the French at Amiens and their IX Corps was being torn apart from the rest of X Army. The Highland Division would almost certainly be cut off from its supply base at Rouen. The line of the Bresle was held until the evening of the 8th. The Luftwaffe was very active despite brave sorties by the RAF from aerodromes in England. But most of the casualties were inflicted by the German mortars. On the 8th two Panzer Divisions, the 5th and 7th, were reported at Buchy, 15 miles north-east of Rouen and 30 miles *behind* the Highland Division.

The French IX Corps were now ordered to retire to the general line of the river Bethune, running south-east from Dieppe to St Vaast. On the morning of the 9th Royal Navy officers arrived at Div HQ, the Chateau La Chaussée to discuss evacuation from Le Havre for the 20,000 men of 51st HD and 'A' Brigade. That night nine destroyers plus transport had assembled off Le Havre. Brigadier Stanley-Clarke was now ordered to defend Le Havre with the remains of 154 Bde (4th Black Watch, two Argyll Bns, 6th Royal Scots Fusiliers and supporting RA and RE plus 'A' Bde). Christened 'Ark Force' they moved at night to avoid the Stukas back to the Fecamp-Lillebonne line of defence.

The mountain troops of the French 31st Division had little transport and that was mainly horse-drawn. It is possible that the bulk of the Highland Division could have withdrawn rather quicker but General Fortune decided not to abandon his Allies. Lt Col Harris Hunter, CRASC: "The sad truth of the matter is that had the Division withdrawn on the 10th, the ships were available off St Valéry and they could have got away. The cost to the reputation of British arms however would have been incalculable. The French at that stage had no reputation to protect when eventually on the evening of 11th June, the order was given 'every man for himself,' it was too late. The ships could not get into St Valéry and a ring of German armour prevented what was left of the Division from escaping through Le Havre. The unthinkable was about to become reality." Major CPR Johnston arrived at Ark Force HQ and reported the HD were now cut off from Le Havre. The Ark Force line of defence was now Lillebonne-Godeville with 'A' Bde and 17 Field Regt RA in front, the rest of 154 Bde and 75 Field Regt RA on the inner line.

The Prime Minister, Winston Churchill, wrote in his memoirs: "We had been intensely concerned lest this division [HD] should be driven back to the Havre peninsular and thus be separated from the main armies, and its commander Major General Fortune had been told to fall back, if necessary, in the direction of Rouen. This movement was forbidden by the already disintegrating French command. Repeated urgent representations were made by us but they were of no avail. A dogged refusal to face facts led to the ruin of the French IX Corps and our 51st Division. On 9th June when Rouen was already in German hands, our men had but newly reached Dieppe, 35 miles to the north. Only then were orders received to withdraw to Havre... It was a case of gross mismanagement for this very danger [of being cut off] was visible a full three days before."

The Buffs fought well at Fécamp but suffered heavily. Whilst the bulk of HD were falling back to St Valéry into a box perimeter, the German tanks had reached the river Durdent, six miles beyond St Valéry. General Fortune's Order of the Day after discussions with naval officers at his HQ: "The Navy will probably make an effort to take us off by boat perhaps tonight, perhaps in two nights. Men may have to walk five or six miles. The utmost discipline must prevail. Vehicles will be rendered useless. Carriers should be retained as the final rearguard." The 1st Black Watch fought on at St Pierre-le-Vigier taking 50 casualties, the Seaforth were cut up in the woods at Le Tot but they and 1st Gordons fought on practically to the end.

The defensive box around St Valéry followed the general line of the river Bethune, with four battalions forward, three in the rear. In front were 4th Seaforths, 5th Gordons, 1st Black Watch from Veules-les-Roses to Fontaine-le-Dieu. The western side of the box along the river Durdent was held by 1st Gordons, 4th Gordons and 2nd Seaforths. When Div HQ moved into St Valéry at 1100hrs on 11th June they were shelled and local roads bombed. The only troops in the town besides Div HQ were RASC, 51st Anti-Tank Regt, the Norfolks (from Beauman Division) and a company of Kensingtons with Vickers guns.

The Navy were doing their best. The destroyer *Ambuscade* was hit by shellfire, the *Boadicea* was heavily engaged at Veulettes, taking off 60 troops. Eventually the *Codrington* and *Restigouche* took off about a thousand troops. German batteries had their guns on the top of the cliffs, the Luftwaffe was very active and thick fog prevented large-scale evacuation. Lt John Wells RN sailed in a small Dutch coaster, the *Pascholl*, in a Navy convoy from Poole to take part in the evacuation. He had been doing the same on the beaches of Dunkirk a week earlier. "We carried food, water, 250 lifebelts, a Lewis gun and a White Ensign. My first command. I was very proud." Early on the 11th at Veules-les-Roses, two miles to the east, Wells and his RN crew of ten took off the St Valéry RN beach party together with 350 British and French troops, many of 385 Bty RA. Wells was awarded the DSC.

Major James Grant, now in command of 2nd Seaforths in St Sylvain, with little ammunition and few anti-tank guns, with his depleted, exhausted battalion faced a Panzer tank attack:

> Within a few minutes the tanks had arrived all round Battalion HQ and were firing into us from three sides whilst mortar and machine-gun fire came in from the fourth side. The fire was intense and we suffered between 30-40 killed and wounded in this position within a few minutes. The knocking-out of [three] tanks saved us from being completely over-run, because over a few minutes, which seemed like hours, the main part of the attack swept on to St Valéry.

The German tanks under General Rommel broke into the defensive box from the west. The Camerons, Seaforth and Norfolks were forced back. Lt FA Lochrane, a Seaforth platoon commander:

> For a short month which seemed a hell of a lot longer, we had the all embracing aim of destroying the enemy, of stopping him break through. At any rate that was the original idea. Later on most of us, I'm afraid thought only of holding him off until we could get out of the ever narrowing circle.

> The clear notes of a bugle sounded in St Valéry's smouldering pit - 'Cease Fire.' It couldn't be! Only two hours before I had heard the General threaten to shoot a Frenchman if he didn't take his white flag down from the Church. Then I saw the Brigade Major. 'Does this apply to us, Sir?' I saluted smartly. One had to salute in the field but things were breaking up. One had to keep discipline going in oneself. 'I'm, afraid it does.' Tears, floods of tears, rage and bloody fury. The enemy appeared. Schemes of escape were ended by a polite German officer who said cheerfully, 'for you the war is over!' God, what a damn silly remark. They separated us from the men. We were herded into a field and left to lie there. Unbelievably tired but with no wish to sleep. More officers arrived. We were just rubbish, no use to anyone but our own futile selves. Organisation was broken. Half an hour earlier the 51st Division had held St Valéry. Now there was just a lot of poor fools, masquerading in khaki. The enemy was so bloody cocky. 'London on 15th August - war over in two months.' 'No,' you said 'six years. You'll never beat us!' They looked crestfallen. Odd.

About 6am a French brigadier who wanted to be shipped off the beach told Lt Col Harris Hunter (CRASC) that the commander of the French Corps General Ihler under whose command the 51st HD had been fighting, had capitulated and that white flags had been put out in St Valéry. CRASC ordered the removal of these flags and sent an officer to Div HQ. At about 10pm this officer returned with the shattering news that following the French action, the GOC had agreed to surrender the Division. CRASC was instructed to fall his men in and march them into the town. He went up the beach leading the survivors and through the town much of which was still blazing furiously. There were German troops everywhere, a German broadcasting van blaring out military airs and a noticeable atmosphere of excitement. The victorious panzer troops were in fine fettle. CRASC saw General Rommel standing on a truck in the main square, with the tanks of 25 Panzer Regt. His 7th Panzer Division took prisoner General Fortune, 8000 HD troops and 4000 French at the capture of St Valéry.

> As we drove into St Valéry there were all sorts of vehicles, lorries and jeeps, a tremendous number, machine gunned and burned out. They were everywhere - just left derelict. On our last night in the town we [Pte Robert Kennedy, 1st Gordons] were shelled, bombed and machine gunned. We replied as best we could but we were vastly outnumbered. When we were captured there were only about a dozen of us together at the time. But after we were searched and marched out of St Valéry up the hill to a field overlooking the sea, I was amazed by the hundreds of men gathered together under guard in that field. On arriving there I saw General Fortune, our Divisional Commander being spoken to by Rommel the German General. I realised then that it was all over for us. It was a sad day.

General Victor Fortune had scorned Rommel's first written demand to surrender and at 2100 on the 11th 1500 shells fell on the centre of St Valéry. In the early hours of the 12th, 25th Panzer Regt. and 6th and 7th Infantry Regts. pushed into St Valéry and made surrender inevitable. Some units, including 1st Bn Black Watch and Major Grant's 2nd Seaforth fought on despairingly for several hours. Many officers and men simply could not believe that HD was surrendering. Eric Linklater wrote: "The Division was a division till the end. It had no luck - the dice were loaded outrageously against it - and so it failed to maintain the legend that its predecessor had made in the first German war, for a legend needs a little luck to help it grow." Up to the last moment Churchill was desperate to keep France fighting. Two more British divisions, 3rd and 52nd Lowland were landed at Cherbourg. He sent across the Channel as many squadrons of the RAF as could be spared from the defence of Britain. He had ensured that the maximum of French troops were evacuated at Dunkirk. But finally on 17th June the Petain government asked for an armistice and General Allanbrooke was ordered to withdraw the remainder of the BEF. 135,000 British and

20,000 Polish troops were finally evacuated. Tragically 3000 perished when the *Lancastria* was bombed, set on fire and sank. Most of Ark Force were evacuated from Le Havre on 11th June. The survivors of 4th Black Watch, 7th Argylls, 8th Argylls, plus 'A' Brigade and support gunners, sappers and RASC sailed on 15th on SS *Duke of Argyll* from Cherbourg for Southampton.

"In an attempt to save stores and transport, I [Private Eric Atherton, LAD 154 Bde] volunteered to ride motorcycle and to guide the vehicle convoy through towns and villages. Lillebonne was in ruins and burning. At a crossroads we had to turn right to get to the ferry at Quilleboeuf. I was the last UK soldier on the first and last ferry trip." Atherton and his unit moved back to St Malo via Le Mans and sailed for home on the *Princess Juliana*.

On their way back to captivity to POW camps in Germany and Poland a few brave (and lucky) individuals managed to escape, including Major DB Lang, Camerons, Major Thomas Rennie, Black Watch and Major Macintosh-Walker of the Seaforth. Capt Geoff Collie, RASC, was wounded in the face, captured, taken to various hospitals and escaped in April 1942 via Paris, Angouleme, Andorra to Gibraltar.

Two years later in Edinburgh, General de Gaulle made a speech:

> I can tell you that the comradeship in arms experienced on the battlefield of Abbeville in May and June 1940 between the French armoured division which I had the honour to command and the valiant 51st Highland Division under General Fortune, played its part in the decision which I took to continue fighting on the side of the Allies unto the end, no matter what may be the course of events.

And Winston Churchill wrote:

> The fate of the Highland Division was hard, but in after years not unavenged by those Scots who filled their places, re-created the Division by merging with the 9th Scottish and marched across all the battlefields from Alamein to final victory beyond the Rhine.

5

Re-forming: "51st was the Division"

Of the battalions taken prisoner at St Valéry, 1st Black Watch, 1st Gordons and 2nd Seaforth were re-raised. The 4th Seaforth ceased to be. The 5th Gordons were reconstituted from the 7th Battalion to form 5/7th Gordons. The 4th Camerons were re-raised but became the 2nd Bn when the original 2nd Camerons were taken prisoner at Tobruk. 4th Black Watch embarked for Gibraltar where it garrisoned the Rock for two-and-a-half years. The 7th Argylls amalgamated with the 10th to form 7/10th but changed back to the 7th when the reformed HD set sail for the Middle East in June 1942. 8th Argylls were sent to Plymouth and came under command of 1st Royal Marine Bde.

The Territorial 9th (Scottish) Division was a duplicate of the 51st and was formed in 1939. After the outbreak of war it commenced coastal defence duties and supplied drafts to the 51st. The Brigades were numbered 25, 26 and 27 and 9th Div was commanded in 1940 by General Sir Alan Cunningham. Under Operation Cycle most of the survivors of Ark Force plus the 1350 who escaped by sea from St Valéry filtered back to join 9th Scottish, including 7th Argylls.

Lt Col Douglas Wimberley fought with the Cameron Highlanders in 51st Highland Division in WWI, became a major aged 21 and was awarded the MC. He commanded the 1st Bn and took it to France in 1939. He wrote in his journal:

> After Dunkirk came the tragedy of St Valéry and naturally that surrender affected me much the most (like I'm sure all Highlanders). In my nightly prayers I petitioned, whatever else happened to me, the Almighty would save me from that particular fate. Some of the remnants of the 51st were sent to an Artillery Depot near Devizes. I went over with two or three Highland regiment officers, telling them the Division would come into its own again.

In July Wimberley was promoted to Brigadier in 5th Division stationed at Crieff:

> Orders came through to command the Seaforth and Cameron Brigade in Caithness. In my new brigade were Lochiel's 5th Camerons; the re-raised 78th Seaforth Highlanders, Havelock's Saviours of India and the 5th Sutherland Bn, I had admired in WWI. It was the one brigade in the Army, I would first have chosen.

His Bde HQ in September 1940 was at Halkirk, with the Camerons at Wick, 2nd Seaforth north of Tain and 5th Seaforth near Thurso.

> We trained hard and I enjoyed it all very much. It was grand to see the Brigade improve month by month. Never have I seen better and keener men. Our discipline and turnout went up by leaps and bounds, and the battalions were the keenest rivals at work and play.

Div HQ was at Rothes, Banffshire. "Soon after I joined [General] Cunningham managed to get our Division's name changed from the 9th to the 51st, to everyone's delight, not least my own. Soon we were once more to use our famous Div sign of the 1914-18 war, the 'HD.'" When Cunningham was posted to Egypt he was succeeded by General Neil Ritchie. Wimberley had command of 152 Bde. 5th Black Watch from Angus joined 1st and 5/7 Gordons in 153 Bde. 1st and 7th Black Watch and 7th Argyll and Sutherland Highlanders formed 154 Bde. Of

Ritchie, Wimberley wrote: "A grand fellow to work for who I liked exceedingly, with a very high sense of duty."

One of the captured formations at St Valéry was the Divisional Concert Party, originally formed in 1915 and known as 'The Balmorals.' In October 1940 General Ritchie sponsored the 'new' concert party.

They gave their first performance in Aberdeen the next month under Sgt Felix Barker. Thereafter, through thick and thin, they entertained the HD during the rest of the war. General Ritchie's successor made sure (a) that they retained a very Scottish flavour to their talents and (b) that their humour was not too basic!

The training emphasis in late 1940 was on road discipline, mobility and physical fitness. There were field firing and marching competitions. Each Brigade held piping competitions. 5th Camerons moved from Halkirk to Thurso and erected coastal defence works in the Fraserburgh-Peterhead area. They held competitions for small arms and cross-country teams, and for night patrolling.

Lt John McGregor author of *The Spirit of Angus*: "News of great importance came on 7th August. The Bn was to join 153 Bde in the 51st Highland Division. To the Highland soldier, the 51st was *the* Division and next only to the Regt, it commanded the same pride and loyalty." Lt Col Keir Wedderburn arrived to command 5th Black Watch then stationed near Aberdeen. Veterans of the BEF campaign were distributed throughout HD. Survivors of 7th Argylls joined the 10th Bn now commanded by Lt Col Lorne Campbell who had fought with 8th Bn in France where he was awarded the DSO. Major AF Henry gained the MC serving with the 'old' 7th Bn, and Capt Charles Mackie from Montrose had earned a Mention in Despatches in France. Private Eric Atherton RAOC evacuated from St Malo, arrived at Dumfries where 154 Bde were housed in the 'Big Hoose': "At that time I don't think I even thought whether we could win/lose/continue the war." He modified old Leyland Albion Thorneycroft platform wagons for the defence of Edinburgh airport, "popping off rifles against the 'invading' paratroops 'Dads Army' was not far from reality!"

Gunner Geoff Durant was a Gun Position Office assistant with 128 Field Regt RA. From 4.5 Howitzers they graduated in 1940 to French 75mm guns and the next year to the famous 25-pounder guns: "The 'Seaforth Country' of Invernesshire was the perfect setting for a Highland regiment, such as ours, as we settled into the little towns of Fortrose and Rosemarkie on the Black Isle for our winter billets [Oct 1940]." The station hotel suited 307 Bty and,

> the ancient cathedral provided a theatrical backcloth to their parade ground... Across the water of the Beauly Firth, high on the cliffs could be seen Fort George, barracks of the Seaforth infantry regiment to whom we gave support in the many battle campaigns which followed.

New technical equipment for Signallers, Surveyors, Driver Mechanics etc. improved the quality of courses and accelerated the process of our training. Army 'Drill' methods ensured immediate response to orders and full knowledge of what to do in any given situation. Mistakes couldn't exist. We acted automatically, according to 'The Drill.' Good routine habits like early rising, washing, shaving, dressing properly and parading on time, were firmly established, the drill for 'Misfires' on the guns, fault finding on Radio Sets, M/C Gun stoppages etc, became automatic, saving time on later occasions, when we went into action. This constant drilling produced efficiency-plus, throughout all categories. Officers and NCOs obtained only immediate response to orders which, in the end, produced a new spirit within us.

In the years to come the three Field Gun Regts RA, 126, 127 and 128 provided magnificent close support in attack - and defence.

In January 1941 a new formation was created in all the infantry divisions in the UK. A reconnaissance regiment was formed from the brigade anti-tank companies of the division. 'A' Sqn was made up of Camerons and Seaforths from 152 Anti-Tank Coy; 'B' Sqn from Black Watch and Gordons from 153 Anti-Tank Coy; and 'C' Sqn from Black Watch and Argylls from 154 Anti-Tank Coy. Their CO was Lt Col E H Grant. The unit wore the Tam O'Shanter with the Hunting Stewart flash worn below the right shoulder with the HD sign in white against blue worn below the left shoulder.

Lt Leslie Meek (11Tp, B Sqn) recalls early days of 51st HD Recce Regt, in February 1941:

> After the loss of equipment at Dunkirk, Armadillos (known as Roll-and-Gos) were used in place of light Reconnaissance Scout Cars, slow, cumbersome vehicles, top-heavy and dangerous. Later replaced by Beaverettes, which were too light, then by Humberettes. Only the Bren carriers stood the test of time and did sterling work.

In the autumn of 1941 the Regt was concentrated in Nairn. General Wimberley had ordered RSM 'Paddy' Morrison, "to knock the Regt into shape within three months." In January 1942, 117 Geordie recruits arrived in time to take part in a Divisional exercise to 'capture' the small coastal town of Buckie.

In February 1941, 5/7th Gordons and other units fired for the first time the American Thompson sub-machine gun and the 2" mortar. The next month they worked on coastal defences near Aberdeen. On 9th April they embarked at sea for an unknown destination and the following day were ordered ashore again.

The Division's role was still that of coastal defence in the north-east of Scotland from Buchan-Aberdeen. When Major General Neil Ritchie was posted out to the Middle East, he asked the CIGS General Allanbrooke if Brigadier Wimberley could take his place as GOC 51st

Highland Division. Wimberley was in May 1941 acting Major General of 46 Division. So musical chairs! Wimberley handed over 46 to 'Bimbo' Dempsey and was delighted at his new command:

Divisional mess at Abelour House close to the Spey. George Murray (Seaforth), had 152 Bde, Douglas Graham (Camerons) with 153, and Harry Houldsworth (Seaforth) with 154. The CRA was Brian Wainwright. They were all a grand team to work with. The GSO1 was still Ken Davidson of the Gordons, Angus Ferguson was ADC.

152 was in Banffshire, 153 in Aberdeenshire, 154 in Moray.

We fought many schemes, travelling long distances by MT. It was fascinating to see the Div steadily improving as officers and men gained experience. General 'Bulgy' Thorne HQ Scottish Command set interesting schemes fighting the Poles. They never obeyed the umpires, either because they could not understand them or because they thought the scheme went better without umpiring!

Capt Charles Barker 1st Gordons:

I was wounded before the division was encircled at St Valéry and was caught up in a massive medical evacuation from Rouen to La Baule, finally running the gauntlet of Stukas on the SS *Batory* out of St Nazaire destined for Plymouth.

In the reformed Division every officer and man was imbued with a tremendous pride in the achievements of the past and a desire to avenge St Valéry, fostered wholeheartedly by a new dynamic chieftain, Douglas Wimberley. He was not endeared over much to the English.

Training was now fundamental. **Geoff Durand 126 Field Regt RA:**

We had been on trial and we had responded well. We had taken part in about thirty schemes or exercises ranging from Regimental to Brigade and Divisional in four of five months. We had applied the use of our guns in all kinds of ways - Troop, Battery and Regimental targets, Predicted Fire, Anti-tank shoots, Barrages, Use of Smoke and so on and were proud of our achievement.

And **Eric Atherton:**

After something like 9/10 months we moved to the Inverness-Dingwall-Golspie area, the LAD being stationed in Tain. All this time with the 'new' Division it was intensive training over the moors and peat bogs of the Highlands. A busy time for the LAD rescuing Bren carriers and other vehicles from the peat bogs, ditches and snow drifts.

Traditions were maintained. Lt John McGregor wrote in his *Spirit of Angus*:

All officers below field rank assembled five minutes after Reveille for Scottish dancing... the Bn Piper and Drums were encouraged to attain a high standard of performance. The Pipes and Drums were a show piece of the Bn and were much in demand for local events. Pipers were attached to each of the Rifle companies. Each company had its own pipe tune always played as the company marched back into camp after a route march or exercise.

Major General Wimberley wanted the Division to be comprised - if possible - only of Highlanders. Possibly Lowlanders, but not Sassenachs. Lt Colonel 'Wallaby' Bruton was a candidate for CRASC. A succession of CRASC Commanding Officers had come and gone. When he went for interview with the GOC (now known as 'Tartan Tam'), the Field Ambulance commander, also new, went in first. He was English. He was sacked. Being an Australian he knew that if he did not do or say something special he was 'out' too. He went into the GOCs office, saluted and said "Good morning, Sir. My name is 'Wallaby' Bruton. I'm an Australian." The General looked at him sharply, and said "Sit down." Bruton remained as CRASC until April 1944. On 15th November worse was to follow. It was the arrival of 1st/7th Bn the Middlesex Regt with their carrier-borne medium Vickers machine-guns. The Die Hards were of course a Sassenach unit, the only one in HD. 'A' Coy from Highgate supported 7th Black Watch (and 23rd Armoured Bde in the campaigns to come); 'B' Coy from Enfield supported 154 Bde; 'C' Coy from Hornsey, 153 Bde and 'D' Coy from Tottenham, 152 Bde. They were commanded by Lt Col Rackham for 15 months after Dunkirk.

Their historian, PK Kemp wrote:

> The posting of a Sassenach battalion, to the Highland Division was certainly not greeted with a 'feu de joie' or with any other signs of delight, by the Scotsmen. But soon the cockneys made themselves appreciated and became friends for life with the Highlanders civilian and military alike.

Three months later a 'Sassenach' light Ack-Ack regiment was threatened. 'Tartan Tam' obtained after a stiff fight, and interview with General Tim Pile, 40 Regt LAA which had two territorial batteries recruited in the north of Scotland! Eminent visitors poured in to inspect the Division, the Queen, General 'Budget' Lloyd from Home Forces, General Alanbrooke the CIGS (the GOC took him salmon fishing), General 'Bulgy' Thorne, General Sir John Dill and others. A young officers' Battle School was set up to improve leadership with compulsory Highland dancing after dinner and a commando-type training course at Loch Ailort in Moidart with one platoon from each of the nine infantry battalions, commanded by Major James Oliver, 5th Black Watch.

General 'Tam' Wimberley was born in Aberdeen and was a Highlander through and through. He was now asked by Lt General 'Bulgy' Thorne C-in-C Scotland how he thought the people of Scotland would react to the Highland Division going into action again with the possibility of heavy casualties, after the disaster at St Valéry. Wimberley's answer was that he was sure the people of Scotland would like to see the new HD revenge the 1940 disaster. His views were then passed on to the War Office. The GOC also set up a system whereby young, dedicated liaison officers had as their task that of quickly identifying the situation of a forward unit in battle (or on a training exercise) and report back in person that same evening. The mortality rate was quite high. Although this was often resented by unit COs, it provided General Wimberley with another pair of eyes at the 'sharp end.' History does not relate whether Wimberley or General Montgomery was the first to operate this LO system.

At the end of March 1942 HD moved 'en bloc' south to Aldershot under South-East Command whose GOC was General Bernard Montgomery. Concentrated exercises co-operating with infantry, tanks and even more extensive training followed. At the end of April 'Monty' visited his Highlanders. General Paget C-in-C Home Forces, and PI Grigg, Secretary of State for War, came in May to make their farewells to the Highlanders. When HM the King and Queen came on 1st June to say goodbye over 100 Pipers played Retreat in the Command Sports Ground. The King's kilt was Cameron Highlander, the Queen's a Black Watch tartan. Gunner Geoff Durand 128 Field Regt RA:

> When Retreat was played the Marching Display was immaculate. Can one forget the Senior Pipe Major when in a 'good Scots accent' gave the command, 'Bands: By the Centre: Quick March.' It must have sent a shiver down the backs of many Englishmen present, far less any foreigner watching the parade.

The Middlesex under Lt Col J W A Stephenson (a famous cricketer) were in Mandora barracks. Private F Blowers had been a footman at Royal Lodge, Windsor and was duly recognised. The Die Hards spent much time firing their machine-guns over the heads of the Division at night. Canadian tanks ran over the Middlesex while lying in their trenches. A hair-raising affair, no accidents and every man in 1/7th Middlesex underwent the experience.

5th Camerons received in mid-May ten drafts of reinforcements from the Liverpool Scottish, the Royal Scots, 40 from the 6th Royal Scots Fusiliers, but also Sassenachs from the South Staffs, Royal Warwicks, Leicesters, Green Howards and Royal Berkshires! The 5/7th Gordons took in drafts of 175 men but oddly enough there were only 43 Scots amongst them.

Several changes in command took place. Lt Col Thomas Rennie, a prisoner but also a survivor at St Valéry took command of 5th Black Watch and their 2i/c Major James Oliver took command of 7th Black Watch who rejoined HD after a stint in the Shetlands. Now stationed at Ash, they trained in battle-drill, route marches and intense physical training. They fired blanks on the Common which started some very satisfactory heath fires. In May the batttalion went to Eastbourne where

141 RAC gave them instructions in tank warfare and in due course deliberately 'ran over' every man in the battalion. The 5th Black Watch in Camberley were attacked by swarms of ants. The issue of pith helmets indicated that they must be going to India. There were aircraft recognition courses with appropriate action to send .303 bullets whistling after a Messerschmidt (surely not a Spitfire) pilot. Lt Col Rennie told his men about being in action and facing enemy fire for the first time. They must face the possibility of being wounded or killed in action. His final words were: "As a soldier, I can expect to die in battle and I do not ask for any other fate." Lt John McGregor wrote in *The Spirit of Angus*, "prophetic words indeed." Just before HD sailed on 20th June 1942 the GOC wrote to his wife: "There is no doubt we are a fine formation. We have first class men. We have the picked officer leaders that congregate in the Highland Regiments and we have the tremendous tradition of the Highland Brigade and the WW1 Highland Division at our backs."

6

All at Sea: "a stinking old ship"

The Division sailed - variously - from Clydeside, or Liverpool or Southampton and joined a large convoy of 22 ships with eight destroyers as escorts which sailed from the Clyde on 20th June.

"I enjoyed that voyage," recalled the GOC,

> We were off to Active Service at last. I had an easy time on board ship [SS *Strathedon*] and plenty of time to read. I had a luxury cabin and private bathroom. I read everything I could about Desert and Jungle warfare. At our first port of call at Sierra Leone, I visited all the ships in the Divisional convoy. I was solemnly piped by our bagpipes on board each ship which quite impressed the matelots. HMS *Malaya* as escort joined the convoy on 26th June. At sea, heard of the sad surrender of Tobruk. On board were 7th Black Watch under James Oliver and the Div Recce Regt under 'Prof' Grant of the Argylls. Early in July anchored off Freetown. Most of the convoy was heading for Cape Town but on 18th July the *Strathedon* sailed for Durban.

There were 4000 Highlanders on board including 1/7th Middlesex, RASC and Div Signals. The Black Watch organised a training 'circus', with specialist instructors holding 45 minutes classes, not only of PT, individual training but 'spelling bees,' and a Regimental History Competition. After crossing the line, the temperature dropped and battledress took the place of shorts and shirt sleeves. Ship's sports were popular including medicine ball 'tennis.'

Among the famous liners in the convoy were the *Empress of Russia*, *Orion*, *Strathmore*, *Arundel Castle*, *Stirling Castle*, *Duchess of Richmond*, the Belgian *Leopoldville*, the Norwegian *Bergensfjord* and the French *Cuba*.

On board the 22,000 ton CPR *Empress of Australia* sailed 3500 Highlanders including 153 Bde HQ, 1st Gordon Highlanders, 126 Field Regt RA and 5th Black Watch plus eighty Queen Alexandra's Nursing Sisters of 91st General Field Hospital! The strength of 5th Black Watch was 40 officers and 914 ORs. Lt JD McGregor noted that at sea, beer was only a few pennies per pint and whisky and gin a modest five shilling per bottle! Lecturers included the CO, Lt Col TG Rennie (North-East Frontier, Burma and Desert Conditions) the 2i/c Major CN Thomson (Iran and the Caucasus), Major Blair Imrie (Cyrenaica), RSM Wilkie (Soldiers Conditions in India), Capt Stephen, the MO (First Aid and Hygiene), 2/Lt Guthrie (Compass navigation and stars), 2/Lt Forfar (Message writing) and Lt McGregor (AA recognition and action). Special classes were arranged for Highland Dancing and the Pipes and Drums played at regular times in the ship's aft well. The ship's Purser produced equipment for deck tennis, deck quoits, deck hockey, shuffle board, ludo, chess, draughts, shove ha'penny, darts and 400 packs of playing cards. The latest films were shown, concerts, Tug o'War contests even Pie Eating competitions. It was a luxury cruise, but the senior Colonel RAMC protected his flock of Nursing Sisters aboard. At the crossing of the Equator on 8th July the (Scottish) King Neptune held Court.

On board the 14,000 ton Belgian Cargo liner, the *Leopoldville* were the 7th Argylls. Captain Ian Cameron wrote:

At Freetown the 'White Man's Grave,' the atmosphere was heavy, humid and oppressive. In the officers' cabins it was bad enough where six officers slept in a cabin meant for two, but the troops decks were simply unbearable. Hammocks were slung wherever there was a corner. Some troops slept on their own mess tables...

Until the convoy reached Cape Town,

...the weather had been glorious, the sunsets a vast variety of beautiful colour. At night the Southern Cross and Constellation of Orion were ever present in the sky. The ships at night appeared to resemble a number of large greyhounds bounding over a limitless expanse of ocean. Various denizens of the deep such as whales, sharks, dolphins, porpoises and flying fish were often sighted.

Geoff Durand, 128 Field Reg RA was one of 3500 troops aboard the 20,000 ton CPR *Duchess of Richmond*. He was a member of the Regimental Dance Band formed by Lt Bill Smith a first class drummer: "The quality of the music was not bad. We 'busked' our way to stardom through Quickstep, Waltz and Tango. Eat your heart out, Glen

Miller." They played on board during the officers' dinner in the 1st class lounge, gems of musical comedy, light opera etc. in the evenings. Off Sierra Leone they were dosed with Quinine, given Mepacrine tablets and issued with anti-mosquito cream. Sgt McGoldrick and Gunner Collins won all their fights in the 152 Brigade boxing tournaments. The CO of 128 Field Regt RA, Lt Col Jerry Sheil noted in his diary:

> Drill uniform this morning, 29th June. It is a pleasant change. Crossed the tropic last night. The sun is getting very hot. News from Middle East is very bad. Tobruk has fallen, Mersa Matruh evacuated. Can we hold the Canal? What is our destination? Our job is to keep the men and ourselves fit and occupied. The long drinks in the bar are simply great. A 'Duchess and gin' is a big favourite.

On board were 2 Seaforth and 5th Cameron's on a voyage which would take 52 days to complete.

Driver Andy Johnston who had escaped from Le Havre with 627 Coy RASC sailed with 152 Brigade Coy on the *Duchess of Richmond*, which in the Bay of Biscay was christened 'The Rolling Duchess.' Major Roy Mumford, OC 154 Bde Coy RASC, another survivor from the BEF sailed on the SS *Cuba* and was mildly disconcerted as the ship sailed to the strains of 'For those in peril on the sea!' Driver Neil Campbell of 153 Bde Coy RASC described the SS *Moltan* as a 'stinking old ship.'

Cape Town was reached on 18th July after 31 days at sea. The Highlanders disembarked and marched seven miles from the quayside with the Pipes and Drums announcing their arrival. All the troops were cheered, showered with fruits, cakes, cigarettes and every man returned to the ship laden with goodies. After two days, general leave was granted.

Lines of private cars arrived to whisk all the Jocks out for parties where wine flowed, dances were organised with pretty partners. Geoff Durand: "For most men it will always be a memorable visit. With all this 'Wonderland Treatment', we became human beings again. The food, drinks, fruits and sweets [taken aboard] helped us survive the remainder of the voyage." Capt Ian Cameron 7th Argylls: "We knew that Cape Town would be the last town of the British Empire we would see before going into action. We had a good view of the peaks called 'The Twelve Apostles' and the Indian Ocean was as smooth as a mill pond." Meanwhile the GOC left the convoy on 20th July by flying boat to Cairo via Lourenço Marques, Lake Victoria/Nyasa, Mombassa and Entebbe. The third night was spent in Khartoum, with an extra night at Luxor, with a expedition to see the tomb of the Egyptian Kings. On 25th July he reached Cairo.

On 26th July the convoy was re-united off Durban, later re-entered the tropics and crossed the Equator again on 3rd August. The final destination was still not generally known. India was the favourite and the Middle East in second place provided the Afrika Korps, after capturing the Tobruk garrison were not in Cairo and Alexandria! On 6th August the coast of Saudi Arabia was sighted and on arrival at Aden the pipes and drums of 7th Argylls played the 'Barren Rocks of Aden.' The convoy then split up, some ships going to India, Basra and some to Suez. The ship's company of HMS *Frobisher*, lined their decks to wish the *Duchess of Richmond, Stratheden* and the others carrying the Division, a ceremonial farewell, raised their caps in three hearty cheers.

On board the SS *Empress of Australia* 5th Black Watch on the 12th gave an enormous party for the ship's officers and crew, with music and dancing. The next day anchor was dropped off Port Tewfik at the entrance to the Suez Canal after 59 days and 15,000 miles of ocean travel. Alastair Borthwick, 5th Seaforth: "The *Bergensfjord* dwindled astern, for all its discomfort a last symbol of home; and Suez grew ahead. It was 14th August 1942."

7

North Africa at Last
"Tahag was a hell-hole"

The GOC, on arrival in Cairo, went up to the front to meet General Auchinleck: "I remember that first night sleeping in the open in the Desert, the first of many more. The wonderful canopy of the Heavens overhead and then as one woke up, the sunrise, the cold early morning air till the heat of the sun made itself felt."

And Lt KEA Wilson 276 Field Coy RE:

> The country and the native life where it exists is absolutely amazing. Life is only within a few hundred yards of water. I shouldn't think it has changed since the time of the Pharaohs. The men do nothing or ride on their little donkeys. The women work carrying everything on their heads and draped entirely in black - in mourning for their miserable life. The sun is scorching and the sand really burns one's bare skin, usually a bit of a breeze, pleasantly cool for comparison. The nights are cool and allow one to rest thoroughly. But it is sand and flies everywhere.

In his book *Sans Peur*, Alastair Borthwick describes the camp at El Tahag, reached by train,

> ...ambling through strange and exciting countryside, camels, canals, water buffaloes and similar novelties. No one liked Tahag. Tahag was a hell-hole. It was a bare, bleak, flat, gritty stretch of desert inhabited in times of peace

only by flies and ants... We were on the bare bones of the earth. We [5th Seaforth] lived there for the next ten days in great misery... Our faces peeled, our lips cracked and our bare knees itched... of all the plagues of Egypt, gyppy tummy was the worst.

Lt Leslie Meek, 51st Recce Regt:

We soon got used to the normal ME rations of bully beef six days a week and cans of meat and vegetable stew on Sundays. The occasional American type tinned bacon was good and fresh eggs were plentiful. Rice and locally grown sweet potatoes, fruit from the Delta and Palestine was plentiful and good. Australian, South African and locally brewed Stella beers were available. Free issue of seven cigarettes (Victory V, made, it was said, from Indian tree trunks) were very strong and took some getting used to.

The General meanwhile was meeting the 8th Army management:

Altogether my impression of HQ 8th Army was not one at that time to give great confidence. I stayed with Ramsden, GOC 8th Corps – unimpressed. Stanley Morshead, GOC 9th Australian Div had no regard for the British armour; he warned me not to let the Division be broken into the 'Jock' Columns [mixed arm raiding forces], as I would never collect them back. Short three days Cook's Tour and met Brian Robertson. Rear HQ 8th Army living on bully beef and Maconachie rations. Attended Corps Conference held by Ramsden, much belly-aching and friction.

Wimberley made a 300 mile drive into Palestine as HD might be sent there or to Syria, to train in desert conditions. On his return; "It was a curious life in Cairo, there was dancing every night in Shepherd's Hotel. A Court of Inquiry set up re the causes of disasters which led to recent retreat to Alamein." On 28th August he listened to the evidence given by all the senior officers of 8th Army. General Wimberley had been known by his battalion as 'Long Tam,' by the Division as 'Big Tam' but the Scottish newspapers now christened him 'Tartan Tam' for his noticeable support of all people and things Scottish!

The gunners of 128 Field Regt RA, "Exchanged greetings with Egyptians from local Arab villages, thus learning some Arab words. Probably 'Saeeda' or 'Saida' was the most common meaning 'Good Day', but the children shouted to us [Geoff Durand & Co] for 'Backsheesh' an Arabic word for 'Alms or Gifts.'" The majority of the Division had disembarked at Port Tewfik and Geneffa but was soon concentrated at El Quassassin camp. In fact there were 50 identical camps (blocks) each being a rectangle, 1000 yards by 500. Desert training started with warrant officers and NCOs from 50th Northumbrian Div and the RSM of 11th Hussars (amongst others) giving instruction on supply in the desert, use of sun compass in desert navigation to get the MT drivers used to desert driving and formations, digging into defensive positions, basic cooking on a Benghazi cooker (a tin half filled with sand and fuelled with petrol), the necessity to ration water (1½ gallons per man per day) and re-filtration to wash clothes. Hygiene was always a problem because flies swarmed everywhere and gyppy tummy (dysentery) was unfortunately widespread. The camp had a well stocked NAAFI Canteen and a camp cinema presented up to date films in the evening. Units were taught 'sunburn drill' a special parade in the afternoon, in effect toasting the body (shirts off) for five minutes a side, so that sunstroke or heat exhaustion was unheard of; soon the 8th Army suntan was acquired.

Important visitors arrived to inspect the HD; General Wavell just back from Russia, where he had met Stalin, came on 19th August and three days later the Prime Minister and CIGS, General Alanbrooke, visited and talked to many officers and men:

> He was in excellent spirits, inspected guard of 5th Camerons, laid on by Ronny Miers (he put his cigar he was smoking, behind his back!) I [the GOC] drove with WC and AB in open car amongst the troops, gave everywhere his famous V sign. He was wearing the most extraordinary boiler suit, topee and very dark glasses. 'Nap' Murray 153 Bde HQ, knowing the form, gave him a quick drink. He gave a first class 5 minute 'pep' talk to all the senior officers.

But Alanbrooke, CIGS, the professional soldier, noted:

> I had seen HD recently at home. Men now looking very fit after their sea journey but not yet tanned by the sun, all pink and white having not yet been absorbed by the desert. The officers were walking about with long Scottish sticks that did not blend with the flat sandy surroundings. The whole division had an appearance of rawness, but of great promise.

And Churchill wrote: "The 51st Highland Division was not yet regarded as 'battle worthy,' but these magnificent troops were now ordered to man the Nile front."

These visits were good for morale, and 8th Army morale was probably at an all time record low. The arrival of a little general with white knobbly knees from the UK was now significant:

> Monty arrived in Cairo on 12th August - at once he gave me [the GOC] five minutes of his time on how to train my Div for the Desert though at the time he can have hardly visited it under Active Service conditions. It was so like the man and as usual, the soundest commonsense.

"General Montgomery arrived in a sandstorm. I [Brigadier H Houldsworth] took him to 1st Black Watch, then the Argylls, then to 7th Black Watch. I said to the Army Commander, 'Of course, sir, you know this battalion comes from Fife?' He stopped dead and said 'Where's Fife?' That line of officers - what a gallant lot they were - stood gaping with their mouths open." General Montgomery: "You see, I have never been to Scotland."

General Alexander now gave out orders that General Wimberley, from 24th August, would take over operational command of all troops in Cairo, prepare a defence plan as Rommel was due - soon - to attack at El Alamein. The command was equivalent to an Army Corps of 60,000 troops. At the end of August the Division moved via Khatatba to Mena on the southern outskirts of Cairo within sight of the Great Pyramids, in order to defend the south-west and west approaches to the city. The new camp was in the desert and so training was stepped up. General Freyburg, GOC of the experienced New Zealand Division and 9th Australian Div sent some officers and NCOs on exchange over to help in the training; and several key HD staff officers swapped with those with desert experience. Douglas Spencer Nairn, the DAQMG was replaced by 'Geordie' Ross.

Divisional HQ was at Ghizira Island; and the Mena House hotel near the Pyramids was popular for its large outdoor swimming pool. The social life of Cairo - even more hectic with Rommel on the doorstep - centred on the famous Shepherd's Hotel and the Gezira Club.

General Wimberley believed that a well-turned-out, well-disciplined soldier was likely to make a good fighting soldier. In 1939 he said of his battalion, "I expected them to clean and polish till they got to Berlin." He now lobbied Monty: "I told him I intended now to put up our HD Div sign again on all the troops and on all the vehicles. He heartily agreed and it was not long before the custom extended to every formation in 8th Army." Pte Eric Atherton LAD: "As soon as we stopped anywhere our unit sign HD went on show and gave us the nickname, 'Highway Decorators.' I had the LAD recovery lorry and it usually fell to me to put out the sign."

Two brigades were responsible for the river Nile crossings. 1/7 Middlesex guarded five crossings along the El Mulut canal. 152 Bde was at the Delta Barrage, 153 Bde in the outer zone of the El Giza-Mena canal and 154 Bde formed the garrison of the crossing at the Delta Barrage. Flies, dirt and Egyptians all vying with each other as major annoyances. The 7th Black Watch were bivouacked in one of the Egyptian King's orange groves but cases of dysentery and fever appeared. Lt Roderick MacPherson 1/7 Middlesex had his platoon of medium machine-guns in the Pyramids themselves, found to be an excellent cool storage for beer. The art of 'dhobying', washing of clothes was learned by the gunners of 128 Field Regt by watching a nearby Indian regiment who spent hours thumping their clothes on a huge rock, stopping only to re-soap or re-soak the material. 'Dhobying' removed all traces of dirt or grease, after which the clothes were left to bleach in the sun. Shirts and shorts - once khaki - became almost white. In most camps Egyptian Dhobymen would, for a few Piastres, collect the dirty washing and return it a few hours later nicely cleaned and finished.

The Division were still guarding Cairo and the Delta when on

30/31st August General Montgomery gained his first (defensive) victory on the Alam El Halfa Ridge. By 7th September Rommel withdrew towards the Heimeimat Ridge having suffered 3000 casualties, losing 50 tanks and 55 guns.

8
"Going up the Blue... tinkers carts"

Leaving the relative civilisation of the Delta, the Division moved in early September towards the front line, into the desert regions. Alastair Borthwick, "the greater part of the desert was flat or gently rolling country composed of rock with only a thin layer of sand or dust on top of it. All desert tracks were bumpy, the sand hiding the rock ledges underneath." Movement of vehicles ground the sand to dust. "This dust was diabolical stuff, orange in colour. It settled on the skin, smooth as face-powder and before long, skin, hair and clothes were in colour and texture a uniform matt orange. Eyeshields of some kind were essential." And Geoff Durand, 128 Field Regt:

> We soon learned driving in convoy could produce mushrooming clouds of fine dust, a real hazard to drivers, and a 'dead give away' to the Luftwaffe. The first concentration area was near El Hamman, called 'H' Box which together with 'M' area became a desert training ground. Vehicles carried 'sand channels', lengths of perforated metal to dig under bogged down wheels to get traction.

Patches of deep sand were a continual hazard. 154 Bde on 8th September moved to 'F' Box at Alam El Khadim about 15 miles from El Alamein. The HD relieved 44th Home Counties Division in 'E' and 'F' boxes and took responsibility for the protection of the left flank and rear of 8th Army. Each box was a brigade area, wired, defended by extensive minefields, and was self supporting for seven days in food, water and ammunition.

Five full-scale night attack exercises were now carried out with infantry advancing behind an artillery barrage backed up by 1/7th Middlesex medium machine-guns. The objectives were to accustom infantry to the terrific din of artillery barrages; practise penetration through enemy minefields for a distance of five to six miles; practise advancing closely behind artillery barrages; and to consolidate by digging-in on the capture of the objective, (and thus be ready for the predictable enemy counter-attack at first light). The exercises were of course held at night in an area eleven miles to the south of 'E' and 'F' boxes, against dummy German positions. Sappers cleared minefields, taped and lit the gaps. Once the objectives were secured the tanks came through with the second waves of infantry. Montgomery favoured text book attacks with enormous artillery support. The three field gun regiments of HD, 126, 127 and 128 - always provided fast, furious and (usually) very accurate fire. Geoff Durant:

> We practised Regimental deployment of our guns and vehicles going into action, dug gunpits, command posts and various types of slit trenches. The signallers practised line laying, all procedures of passing artillery fire orders by telephone and wireless. The telephone exchanges were dug in. The surveyors calibrated directors and compasses by taking observations on the Pole Star in conjunction with the Polaris Charts. These calculations ensured that True North bearings and magnetic variation could be calculated more accurately than normally shown on our maps.

Durant found that most maps were inaccurate, showed few land features, not that there were many, other than altitude lines (heights above sea level): "Training in Desert Navigation was essential, using the sun by day and the stars by night to determine the Northerly direction. Many officers and NCO's carried a compass, most leading vehicles were fitted with a Sun compass." The GOC's insistence on inter-unit liaison now bore fruit. The 5th Black Watch knew by Christian name 'their' gunners of 304 Battery of 127 Field Regt. RA. Their FOO, Capt Ken Aitken was accepted as a member of Battalion HQ. Similarly with the sappers in 276 Field Coy RE, and machine gunners of 1/7th Middlesex. The GOC now noticed that Div HQ with its vehicles were scattered (correctly to minimise Luftwaffe strafing): "We started a custom that we kept up right across Africa. We mounted the Div HQ Piper in a lorry, drove around the area at 10mph, lustily playing the notes of Johnny Cope, etc."

Lt Col Jerry Shiel, CO 128 Fd Regt RA, later CRA 51st Div (Geoff Durand)

The War Office had decreed the use of a four gallon non-returnable petrol can, made of the thinnest of tin. The thrifty and practical Highlanders now used the discarded tin plate for flytraps, washbasins, cooking pots, Benghazi cookers, lampshades, seats (including latrine seats), revetting of trench walls, even cookhouses! But captured German petrol tins - Jerricans - were strong and substantial, could be refilled and re-used time and time again. Good cooks were in demand away from the regiment on battalion cooks trucks, for Recce groups or FOO/OPs. Meals were usually based on cooking bully beef in as many different ways as possible. Most vehicles started to look like tinker's carts with cooking tins dangling from the back.

"It usually fell to me to put out the HD sign," recalls Pte Eric Atherton of the LAD, "once near some trees for a 'hide-out,' Jim the Sgt told me to take a rest. 'I will put the sign out' he said. He walked away with it some 25 yards when he trod on an A/P mine and was killed instantly. Two other LAD members were injured." The LAD often slept in two-man bivouacs on the ground or over a small dug-out. Lice and scorpions were occasional hazards.

The HD was now affiliated to 9th Australian Division; the 7th Black Watch to the 15th Australian Bn, from Queensland. Half the Black Watch and all their officers, gained first-hand knowledge of fighting in the desert after being attacked for several days near Alamein Station. The Australian patrols went forward with the Jocks 'under instruction'. The 5th BW were linked with 28th Australian Bn who had fought in the siege of Tobruk alongside 2nd Black Watch. The 7th Argylls mentors were 17th Australian Bn whose dry humour was much appreciated, and 1/7th Middlesex were paired with 2/2nd Australian Machine-Gun Bn and carried out harassing shoots in the front line.

As Carrier Platoon Commander under Lt Col Horatius Murray [later to become a General], Captain Charles Barker 1st Gordons described his CO, known affectionately as 'Nap' because of his bald head and somewhat rotund appearance, which made him look like Napoleon. "From Quassassin Camp I went up to the front to learn desert warfare from the extremely tough 9th Australian Division. At my first meeting 'Hello, limey coming out on patrol tonight?' 'Of course, I replied, and I was in - to penetrate 'no mans land' to locate and retrieve a crashed Desert Airforce fighter with a Scammell recovery vehicle and tow it back. What a night that was."

> During pre-Alamein training Brigadier Houldsworth made it perfectly clear we did not go to ground while under small arms fire and certainly not under any form of fire when in attack... Further if we took prisoners we would have to feed and water them, therefore it was suggested we 'take no prisoners'. We had no intention of taking prisoners anyway. Discipline was very strict and rightly so. [Private Roy Green, 1st Black Watch].

General Horrocks was the new Corps Commander and on 15th September Monty held a conference with Horrocks, Leese, Morshead, Freyburg, Pienaar (SA) and Lumsden (Armoured Corps). General Wimberley took his trusted GSO1, Roy Urquhart with him:

> Alamein was to be a real 'set piece' attack of the WWI type with a barrage behind us and Red, Blue and Black lines in front of us, Australians on my right and NZ on the left. In the 'M' area a few miles inland from the boxes with the aid of our sappers we laid out an exact replica of the part of the enemy's defences, our job it was to attack. I took my troops, a Bde at a time, practised every Bn in the exact job I had decided it was to do in the initial attack... various dummy trenches to be taken were Camerons - Inverness; Argylls - Stirling; Black Watch - Killin, using maps and air photos. Div artillery fired the exact barrage, same rate, with some pauses for leapfrogging. Div Signals same outline plan reporting capture of objectives. Sappers cleared mines through dummy minefields. Biggest exercise night 2nd October with 153, 154 Bdes.

Monty was a firm believer in 'walking the course' and every division carried out these meticulous preparations for the huge task ahead. At a full scale conference on 6th October the Australian and NZ GOCs had differing views on the speed of troops advance and pauses or objectives, but eventually resolved. And on 17th October General Wimberley and all officers, lieutenant colonel and above, attended the final conference for the Battle of Alamein.

9

Preparing for the Battle of El Alamein: "a new philosophy"

Monty's plan was to use the infantry divisions to force gaps through the huge German minefields and Rommel's outer defences (Operation Lightfoot), through which the Armoured Divisions (in Operation Supercharge) would pour through and envelope the German and Italian defenders. 13 Corps plus a concentration of dummy tanks and vehicles would simulate strong attacks in the south, whilst Oliver Leese's 30 Corps would put in the main attack in the north against the enemy's main defences. Between the coastal road and the Qattara Depression the 8th Army and the Afrika Korps faced each other across the minefields and barbed wire. From north to south Rommel placed in front *164 Infantry, Trieste* and *90th Light Division* and behind them *15th Panzer, Littorio* and *Bologna* divisions; then *21st*

Panzer, *Arriete* and *Brescia* divisions, the *Fulgore* and *Pavia* divisions. In between the six Italian divisions were German infantry including the famous *90th Light Division*. Facing them, also north to south were, 9th Australian and 51st Highland to force the Northern Corridor through the defences, and 2nd New Zealand and 1st South African with 4th Indian Division in reserve. Then came 50th Northumbrian, 44th Home Counties divisions and the Free French.

General Oliver Leese described the HD GOC: "Douglas Wimberley - mad keen - goes into the most minute details about everything. His 'army' has a fine spirit and will I feel live up to their tremendous reputations of the last war. He is 6ft 3in, lean and cheerful, radiates sterling commonsense." They had known each other since 1922 and had been at Staff College together. Leese recalled that "the Commonwealth commanders tended to refer 'difficult' questions back to their Governments." Wimberley (jokingly): "Well, if that's the form and I get anything to do that I don't agree with, I shall complain to the Secretary of State for Scotland."

'Lang Tam' - the GOC Maj Gen Douglas Wimberley

Lt Col 'Wallaby' Bruton CRASC was responsible for building up HD's requirements before the battle - no less than 500 rounds per gun (96 25-pdrs to be 'fed') were needed. (Brigadier Elliott, the CRA was also loaned 78th Field Regt.) Bruton dumped the reserve stocks of gas capes and anti-gas equipment at Burg El Arab to free transport. Between 4th-20th October the RASC drivers, at night for security reasons, carried out the dumping programme, some of it well forward of the guns. They buried shells in the sand so that the guns could advance without waiting for replenishment from the rear. Before the battle the five divisional artillery units for nine days frequently moved between 'E' and 'F' boxes to maintain the deception that the Alam El Halfa area was being reinforced.

Lt Colonel Jerry Sheil, CO 128 Field was continually on the move studying the battlefield, attending battalion, brigade or divisional HQs. OPs were repositioned if more suitable positions became available. From the GOC downwards it was always acknowledged that the gunners' map reading and surveying standards were the highest in 8th Army. General Wimberley relied heavily on his CRA throughout Operation Lightfoot. Once Corps HQ insisted that the survey co-ordinates of 128 Field were inaccurate. After much checking it was clear that a mistake had been made by an adjacent division.

Each infantry battalion was to go into the attack without any transport except Bren carriers carrying ammo, including grenades, mortar bombs, supplies and water. Each man carried his personal weapon and equipment, small pack with cardigan/jersey and Tam O'Shanter or cap comforter, two grenades in .55 anti-tank ammo bandolier or spare respirator haversack (one .36 and one .69), 50 rounds of extra ammo in a bandolier, one day's rations and a full water bottle. All were equipped with a pick or shovel and an entrenching tool. Four sandbags were carried tied to the small pack which contained ground sheet, shaving kit and iron ration. White St Andrews crosses of scrim for identification were tied across the back of the small pack. No anti-tank rifles were to be taken. The attack formation consisted of two companies forward and two in reserve with battalion HQ led by a compass party in the centre of the square. Distance between individual soldiers was to be maintained at no less than five yards; very difficult because human nature prefers clusters which are easier targets for enemy fire. The speed of advance was 100 yards in two minutes up to the first enemy minefield, then 100 yards per three minutes.

Each battalion frontage would be about 600 yards and its depth about the same. The General's plan was:

> 152 Seaforth/Cameron Bde would be holding the line taken over from the Australians, 153 Black Watch/Gordons Bde on right and 154 Black Watch/Argylls would attack on the left but 2 Seaforth detailed as Corps

reserve. Given both a wide frontage of attack and a very deep one, I divided my frontage (2500 yards) into six lines, two right hand ones to 153 Bde, four left to 154 Bde as the enemy's defences were thicker on my right than on my left. Here our Armour planned to break through.

On the night of 22/23rd October the HD moved up along tracks (Sun, Moon, Star, Boat, Bottle and Hut) and by 2300hrs settled in and concealed themselves, spending the whole of the next day resting in the previously constructed slit trenches. The 5/7th Gordons reached their assembly area near the railway on the night of the 19th, and three nights later moved up to occupy the prepared slit trenches east of El Alamein station. Movement to and from latrines was strictly controlled. No cooking was possible and men ate their cold meals as they lay in their slits.

"Zero hour loomed nearer. Each foxhole held two men," Pte Roy Green, 1st Bn Black Watch shared his, "He was a good lad and only 20 like myself. After our dinner we were still hungry I said, 'Paddy, if we have to die lets go on a full stomach.' It was known to be wiser to have a last meal some five hours before action through experience of stomach wounds..."

Brigadier Graham had great difficulty finding 1st Gordons as their holes in the ground were so well camouflaged! Their Jocks regarded the RAF bombing up ahead as a free spectacle and just before the main attack had to be discouraged from sightseeing.

The divisional objectives were to secure 7000 yards of African desert, across and through minefields, barbed wire, enemy dugouts and slit trenches against well-armed German and Italian formations.

5th Seaforth had the difficult task of laying white tape along the 2500 yards of the HD start line and from there tape back nine separate routes so the other battalions could advance to the line. Sixty men on the night of 19/20th October finished the start line, with metal pickets every 50 yards. On the next night the nine routes had been plotted and laid - in all nine miles of tape. On the third night Lt Col Stirling guided the other battalion's representatives to mark their own boundaries and centre points.

The GOC's plan of attack from north to south was 1st Gordons and 5th Black Watch in right lane, then in left lane 5/7th Gordons, next 1st Black Watch, 7th Argylls, then the Recce Battalion with some tanks [50 RTR] and finally on the extreme left/south were 5th Camerons next to the NZ Division. They had first to take two objectives when 7th Black Watch would pass through. Leapfrogging by battalions could only take place on the two flanks. Six battalions of the HD would advance side by side into battle.

The first objective was Green Line, from right to left, Arbroath, Forfar, Cruden, Dollar, Mons Meg, Paisley, Drummuir, Inverness. Next

Red Line (in front of 5/7th Gordons) Turriff, Insch, Killin. Then the Black Line, Dufftown, Braemar, Strichen, Perth, Greenock, Blath and Dundee. Finally Blue Line, Aberdeen, Stirling, Nairn, Kirkcaldy on the final Corps objective. The two divisional Passwords were 'Uncle' for Day 1, 'Harper' for Day 2.

Highland Division commanders before Alamein

General Montgomery sent a personal message to his 8th Army: "We are ready now. The battle which is now about to begin will be one of the decisive battles of history. It will be the turning point of the war. The eyes of the whole world will be on us, watching anxiously which way the battle will swing. We can give them the answer at once. 'It will swing our way.' We have first class equipment, good tanks [although the Armoured Divisions would not agree], good anti-tank guns [6-pdrs had just arrived], plenty of artillery [over 1000 guns] and plenty of ammunition and we are backed up by the finest air striking force in the world. All that is necessary is that each one of us, every officer and man, should enter this battle with the determination to see it through - to fight and to kill - and finally to win..."

I can see him [Montgomery] at a senior officers of 30 Corps Conference, with his map on his battle van beside him and his fly whisk in his hand and he told us not only what his plan was, but exactly what was going to happen. He filled us with confidence and trust. He never failed to put his commanders right into the picture before every operation, and between every operation. He saw to it that every soldier knew not only what he was going to do but why he was going to do it. That seemed to be a new philosophy of war. A philosophy that wins battles. [Brigadier H Houldsworth, 154 Bde].

The key events of the first two days of the El Alamein battle are described from north to south as HD advanced west along six centre lines in parallel, 153 Bde on the right, 154 on the left (see Map).

The GOC moved his TAC HQ up to an old dugout built by the South Africans on the main coastal road to Derna, an elaborate concrete affair with electric light. There he was visited by Monty the day before the battle:

> To see if I was well and confident. I told him we would 'do our stuff.' I then issued my short battle message to the troops. 'Scotland for ever and Second to none.'

> One thousand guns were to start firing at 2140hrs. I watched my Jocks filing past in the moonlight. Platoon by platoon they filed past, heavily laden with pick and shovel, sandbags and grenades - the officer at the head, his piper by his side. There was nothing more I could do now to prepare for the battle. It was only possible to pray for their success, and that the HD would live up to its name and the names of those very famous regiments of which it was composed.

However the GOC meant business. Part of his Order for the Day read. "There will be no surrender for unwounded men. Any troops of the Highland Division cut off, will continue to fight." And so they did.

Order of Battle at Alamein

GOC	Major-General D N Wimberley (Camerons)
GSOI	Lt Col R Urquhart (HLI)
AA & QMG	Lt Col J A Colam (RA)

152 Highland Brigade
Brigadier G Murray (Seaforth)

| 2nd Seaforth | Lt Col K McKessack |
| 5th Seaforth | Lt Col J E Stirling |

153 Highland Brigade
Brigadier D A H Graham (Cameronians)

1st Gordons	Lt Col H Murray (Camerons)
5th Black Watch	Lt Col T G Rennie
5/7th Gordons	Lt Col H W B Saunders

154 Highland Brigade
Brigadier H W Houldsworth (Seaforth)

1st Black Watch	Lt Col W N Roper-Caldbeck
7th Black Watch	Lt Col J A Oliver
7th Argylls	Lt Col Lorne M Campbell
1/7th Middx Regt (Machine Gunners)	Lt Col J W A Stephenson
The Royal Artillery,	CRA Brigadier G M Elliott
126 Field Regiment RA	Lt Col H J A Thicknesse
127 Field Regiment RA	Lt Col H M Perry
128 Field Regiment RA	Lt Col W A Shiel
40 Light AA Regiment	Lt Col R A L Fraser-Mackenzie
61st Anti-Tank Regiment	Lt Col J H B Evatt
The Royal Engineers	CRE Lt Col H W Giblin
239 Field Park Coy RE	Captain R S Maitland
274 Field Coy RE	Major S B Russell
275 Field Coy RE	Major H L Lloyd
296 Field Coy RE	Major John Lamb
The Royal Corps of Signals	Lt Col C P S Denholm Young
The Royal Army Medical Corps	Colonel R W Galloway
174 Field Ambulance	Lt Col A M Campbell
175 Field Ambulance	Lt Col R M J Gordon
176 Field Ambulance	Lt Col C H Kerr
The Royal Army Service Corps	Lt Col H H Bruton
Recce Regiment	Lt Col E H Grant (A&SH)
Divisional Workshops REME	Lt Col G S McKellar
APM	Major A A Ferguson (Camerons)
RAOC	Lt Col G E G Malet
Senior Chaplain	Rev Jock Elder (Church of Scotland)

10

Operation Lightfoot
"bayonets gleamed in the moonlight"

Captain A Grant Murray 5th Seaforth, out with a patrol covering the start line: "Suddenly the whole horizon went pink and for a second or two there was still perfect silence and then the noise of the 8th

Army's guns hit us in a solid wall of sound that made the whole earth shake. Through the din we made out other sounds - the whine of shells overhead, the clatter of the machine-guns... And eventually the pipes. Then we saw a sight, that will live for ever in our memories - line upon line of steel helmeted figures with rifles at the high port, bayonets catching in the moonlight and over all the wailing of the pipes..." Lt Col Jerry Sheil, 128 Field Regt kept a diary:

> 23rd. Morning of battle. We are all ready and keen and very fit. This should be a good scrap. The FOO are Capt Beaton (307), Capt Connell (308), 2/Lt Horne (307), Lt Inglis (308). The brothers John and Jim Inglis (492) working with 5 Camerons. The barrage opened at 22.00 hrs and was a magnificent sight. The darkness of the night was stabbed by flashes as far as the eye could see and the roar of the guns and whine of shells overhead most impressive. It was not long before the first success signal came in. 5 Camerons had reached their first objective. So it went on through the night. Confused reports kept coming in. On the whole the information from our FOO was splendid.

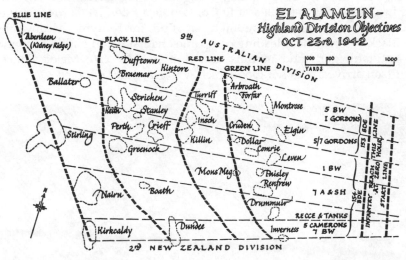

Sheil had devised a plan for the FOOs; a very strong line party laying cable on foot; one FOO with pack carried No. 11 set; and FOO following up in Bren and a strong intermediary station line and R/T combined. It would of course be a minor disaster if a FOO could not get through to his battery or regiment.

> After a long wait for news I [the GOC] got the code word 'Inverness', the first of many to come in that night, but it did my heart good. Ian Davy with his Camerons had taken their first objective on the way to the Red line. Hour by hour the code words came in and by dawn it was clear to me that we had eaten deeply into the enemy's position and casualties might well

have been worse [over 2100 during the battle]. The Green line, the Red line and the Black line. Only the final objective of the Blue line was in doubt. Later news came in that 7 BW on the left, next the NZs were over the top of the Miteriya ridge and at Kirkcaldy on the Blue line. In the centre Nairn and Stirling were still in enemy hands. On the extreme right 1st Gordons were on the feature Aberdeen.

The General was disappointed that the Bays and 10th Hussars of the supporting Armoured brigade had failed to take their Kidney feature objective - apparently due to poor map reading. Wimberley was blown up when his jeep went over a mine and was dazed and deaf for a time. His LO Wallace drove him back to main Div HQ.

Piper Duncan McIntyre piped Lt Col Rennie's 5th Black Watch into battle playing the Regimental March, 'Hielan Laddie.' He was wounded twice and died still playing. Montrose was secured by 'A' and 'B' Coys led by Capt Augur East the Navigation Officer, eyes on compass, advancing at 50 yards to the minute. 'C' followed up towards Arbroath, 'D' on Forfar. By midnight 'A' had reached the final objective on the Red line. Lt Dovey gathered together the survivors of 'A' Coy and Lt Denton RE was killed at Lt Col Rennie's side. 1st Gordons came through from Montrose at midnight en route for Kintyre. Meanwhile 5th Black Watch whose leading companies had suffered badly, brought up anti-tank guns and mortars and dug in. The 2i/c Major Chuck Thomson arrived with hot food which was gratefully received.

5th Seaforth attack at Alamein

The 1st Gordons soon lost their CO, Lt Col 'Nap' Murray who was wounded. Capt Keogh's tape laying party reached the Red, then the Black line and 'C' Coy advanced on Kintore losing many casualties with two officers wounded. 'D' Coy on board 50 RTR tanks ran into an unreported minefield and five Valentines were blown up. By 1000hrs on the 24th, Braemar had been taken by 'A' and 'C' Coys but Capt Skivington leading a bayonet charge, was mortally wounded. Only 22 survivors of 'C' Coy and 40 of 'A' Coy reached their objectives, a truly brave performance. Major Hay was now acting CO until he too was wounded. Later two platoons of 'D' Coy almost reached Aberdeen (Kidney ridge) which was finally taken on Tuesday morning by 'B' Coy with a battery of the new 6-pdr anti-tank guns in support. Major Fausset Farquhar took command as 1st Gordons dug-in until being relieved on the night of 1st November. During Operation Lightfoot Lt Ewen Frazer of 'A' Coy was awarded the DSO for conspicuous bravery.

5/7th Gordons were led by Lt Col Saunders up 'Sun' track and quickly took Elgin and Cruden but with some casualties to spandaus, artillery and mortar fire. The sappers in front did stalwart work, and on the Gordons went, taking Insch, Turriff and the Red line. Lt Felix Barker's account:

> The whole thing was rather fantastic. It was like no battle the men had ever heard of, or could have imagined, in the wildest flight of imagination. Magazines were filled because it seemed out of the question to go into a major attack without rounds in the rifles, but many a man never fired a shot all that terrible night. Bayonets gleamed in the moonlight, fixed as a token gesture, to give confidence. A few men started at the high port with text book punctilio but most had slung their rifles before long. It was a moonlight walk to places called 'First' and 'Second Objective' with death in every form lying between the walkers and their destination. It was an endless journey - five miles or ten? All the way the steady, remorseless taking of position after position stumbling into enemy machine-gun and mortar pits, passing over the bodies of Germans and Italians lying dead in their holes.

'A' and 'B' Coys quickly dug in and 'C' and 'D' pressed on to reach Strichern and Keith, but 'D' vanished into the smoke and fury and were not seen again. The next day their dead including Capt Sharp and Lt Jackson were found in an enemy minefield.

"Mostly in pairs," wrote Lt Felix Barker, "the men dug the slit trenches, like foxes they had holes. Wearily and gratefully they fell into them. As the sun dried the heavy dew which followed the night, numbers were counted. Here eight signallers had been killed out of a single section; over there one company [D] could muster only 24 out of the 100 who had started the night before. A great many had not completed that moonlight walk."

Captain David Johnstone, Navigating Officer, led 1st Bn Black Watch forward commanded by Lt Col Roper-Coldbeck. They reached the Green line on time via Leven, Comrie and Dollar. Officers (including Lt Michael Allen) as well as men used the bayonet. On the way to Red line, when Killin was taken, Pte G McCulloch bravely ran forward and took a machine-gun post. Private Roy Green, 'A' Coy, gives his account of the battle:

> There were 33 of us in the Platoon. We lost many men through 'S' mines as well as shell and mortar fire, everything seemed so unreal and of course we took no prisoners. 'B' and 'C' Coys were up in front in the first stage and very lucky as most of all the enemy had pulled back from the hellish barrage. In the second stage we came up against a mixture of both Germans and Italians. The screams and shouts and yells were almost alarming and no stopping for the poor wounded. After more killing we arrived at the final objective with only two L/Corporals and ten privates left in our platoon, Richardson and Brown. There was only one officer left in the company out of four.

The survivors of 'A' Coy, including Green, were ordered to contact 'D' Coy on their right: "After a few hundred yards we came across the enemy - Italians - who immediately gave themselves up. I saw one duck back inside his foxhole whereupon I killed him with a hand grenade."

The 7th Argylls under Lt Col Lorne Campbell, were supported by 50 RTR. 'C' Coy (Major Macdougall) had the objectives Paisley and Mons Meg, then on to the Red line to capture Greenock. 'D' Coy (Capt Buchanan) on the left had the objectives of Renfrew, Halkirk and finally Greenock. Paisley was captured to the strains of 'Monymusk' on the pipes, and Mons Meg and Halkirk reached by 2300hrs, but A/P mines and booby traps caused many casualties. At midnight Red line was reached about 500 yards from Greenock. The advance was resumed at 0100hrs and many casualties incurred before Greenock was taken at bayonet point. The Italians appeared to surrender and as the Highlanders lowered their rifles threw grenades. The Argylls consolidated on Greenock, but as 'A' Coy and 50 RTR tanks had not appeared delayed the attack on Stirling.

> On the second night the Argylls had the job of capturing 'Nairn'. As assistant IO, I laid the starting line and stood beside the CO, Lt Col Lorne Campbell watching two companies advance in the moonlight with nothing but a compass bearing to guide them. A little later we received a message that they needed anti-tank protection. [2/Lt Angus Stewart]

So 2/Lt Stewart was sent up with a section of carrier-towed anti-tank guns to Nairn - and got lost, ran into a minefield losing two carriers and guns. So Stewart made a second and a third attempt, the last with a radio to establish contact but obstructed by mines: "In bitter frustration we had to turn back. But the next morning a squadron of tanks made contact with our companies on Nairn."

The Recce Regt had found that their Humber LRCs were unsuitable for desert conditions and for this battle were reformed into a composite squadron and an infantry squadron. On the evening of 23rd October 11 and 17 Assault Tps covered RE's gapping enemy minefields. Lt Jocker commanding the sapper party, dismantled mines until he was wounded. Capt RR Park of 51 Recce rescued several wounded sappers and later re-appeared with 30 Italian prisoners. The composite Sqn supported 50 RTR in their attack on Nairn. German 88mm anti-tank guns knocked-out four Recce carriers in seconds and three RTR tanks.

51st Recce Regt only had seven serviceable vehicles at the end of Operation Lightfoot out of the original fleet of 70. They had 17 men killed and many wounded including Doctor George Jolly who was wounded in a Stuka bombing raid. Lt Bobbie Gall, 'C' Sqn, had his carrier knocked-out, was wounded, transferred to another which was also knocked-out. With all his carriers disabled he continued the attack with his men riding on tanks. Lt Leslie Meek:

> Once the shells started falling there were times when it seemed they would never stop. Men suffered the most appalling injuries. They would be lying on the ground, crying out for help, covered by a mixture of blood and sand - hardly recognisable as human beings. It was night-time and with the sand being churned up by the shelling it resembled an impenetrable fog. Vehicles were burning fiercely, many with the crews trapped in them. The battle had to go on, despite the carnage and the stretcher-bearers were being killed too. One could only utter a few words of comfort that 'somebody will be along shortly.' This was real warfare - no holds barred. It was man against man and deadly machine against machine.

5th Camerons were split for the start of the battle to carry out two separate tasks. 'A' and 'C' Coys provided eight covering parties to protect sappers making vehicle gaps through the enemy minefield after the capture of the first objective. On the extreme left of the divisional front 'B' and 'C' Coys under Major IAG Davy were to lead (under command of 154 Bde) and subsequently 7th Black Watch would pass through them. Pipers led playing the 'Inverness Gathering' and despite heavy casualties Inverness (Green line) was captured with 50 POW taken. Lts Fawcitt and MacIver and CSM MacPherson were killed, Major Davy badly wounded, so too were Capt CA Cameron, Lts Inch and Henderson, the Padre Capt Reid and the RMO Capt Milnes. Two MCs and two MMs were awarded for their action. When 7th Black Watch came through they had two key tasks, the capture of the north-west end of the Miteiriya ridge and Point 30, known as 'The Ben.' The crest of the ridge ran between Black and Blue lines. Red line was reached but then heavy and accurate shelling continued throughout the

23rd. The battalion compass party lost six consecutive Navigating Officers, and many ORs. Passing through one minefield booby traps and AP mines caused heavy casualties. On reaching Black line 'B' Coy was down to a platoon in strength, and 'D' down to two platoons. Captain CF Cathcart's force struggled through a minefield and wire and heavy fighting took place on the far side of the ridge before the Black Watch reached Blue line. The Bn support group with anti-tank guns, mortars and carriers got well forward through the RE minefield gapping parties. At least two unexpected, unmapped minefields were encountered and aerial bombs linked by trip mines. During the El Alamein battle, the battalion had 78 KIA including six officers and two WOs, with 183 wounded, including 13 officers - most of the losses incurred on the first day of battle.

Lt Col Sheil's diary (128 Field Regt) continues on the second day:

24th. The fog of war is with us, in truth. Nobody knows just where leading infantry are. 7 Black Watch on left claim to have reached their objective: so do NZ on their left. Nothing known of Recce, who should be on right of 7 Black Watch. 7 Argylls have got to 'Strichen' or near there. 1 Black Watch claim to be in the same area. 1 and 5/7 Gordons on right seem to have made less progress... There has been very hard fighting with heavy casualties. Roughly speaking we have got forward five to six thousand yards a fine performance. Quite a lot of prisoners have come in. They are a dishevelled lot - mixed Boche and Italians. We are to attack again tonight.

The gunner field regiments had done well. For the opening barrage across the front 20 field regiments and three medium had fired 550 rounds per gun in a 5¾ hour period. One unit fired 670 rpg. The gun barrels became so hot that they were rested ten minutes every hour and cooled with water. Capt Jim Inglis was killed supporting 5th Camerons' attack on Inverness and his brother Capt John Inglis was wounded supporting 7th Black Watch. He attended their Bn HQ 'O' Group in a quarry behind the start line and noticed their Pipers dressed in Royal Stewart tartan kilts "bright red and very distinctive; when dawn broke the track of the advance showed scattered bodies of the dead and wounded. Two Pipers were lying there with the other bodies."

At dawn on the 24th the 1/7th Middlesex machine-gun platoons carrying guns and ammo made their way forward through the gaps in the minefields. Their TAC HQ could see the golden rain rockets burst startlingly in the air to show that Green and Red line objectives had been taken. 'C' Coy 1/7th Middlesex with 153 Bde on the right had made good progress but 154 Bde with 'B' Coy had a harder nut to crack and neither 7th Argyll nor 7th Black Watch had been able to reach their final objectives on the crest of Miteirya Ridge, so the machine-gun platoons dug in on the reverse slope, only No. 12 platoon had a direct shoot. Pte Jeff Hayward:

My Pltn (12) with 5/7 Gordons, was behind the two leading infantry Coys. We were to carry our Vickers guns, tripods and ammo plus 48 hours rations. I was No 3 and had four belts of ammo (1000 rounds), rifle and shovel. The barrage opened and away we went! The night quickly became obscured by sand, smoke and cordite. We were on a compass bearing and could only follow the man in front. As we took casualties their loads were distributed amongst the rest of us. The platoon sgt at the rear carried an amazing eight belts of ammo. That night we covered about five miles towards our objective. The Gordons had run into an uncharted minefield and we had to dig in. Several positions in front were manned mainly by Italian infantry. We gave the Jocks supporting fire as they went in with the bayonet.

General Montgomery unleashed 8th Armoured Brigade on the 24th but 88mm anti-tank guns on the crest and dug-in enemy tanks on the forward slopes of a further ridge picked off the Valentines and Crusaders with heavy losses. "Behind us elements of the Armoured [Bde] were halted unable to cross the minefield. German tanks were on their side of the wire and we [Jeff Hayward, 1/7th Middlesex] spent a very unpleasant few hours as both sides slugged it out, a non-stop stream of the A/P passing about six feet above us." Tanks of 2nd Armoured Bde passed between the two Gordon battalions and vicious but unsatisfactory tank battles raged almost continuously.

Pte Roy Green, 1st Black Watch:

On the 24th five stragglers returned to us [A Coy] and also the Middlesex heavy machine gunners whose presence was more than welcome. It was like a butcher's shop on the way up to us they said. Meanwhile we had a 'holding' position while other infantry tried to press ahead. We just had to suffer constant shelling and mortaring and watch numerous Sherman tanks brew up with their crews having no chance to escape. On the second day [25th] in broad daylight Brigadier Harry Houldsworth came to our positions wearing the kilt and Glengarry. It gave us tremendous courage to see that. The amazing thing about the 51st was that while we knew we may fail as individuals (get killed), we did not at any time think the battle would not be won by us. Defeat was just not on the agenda. Our officer Lt Cathro came back and complimented us for our action during the initial attack. Alamein was First World War tactics with Second World War weapons, creeping barrages, walking through minefields ahead of armour, each man five yards apart to save casualties.

5/7th Gordons passed an uneventful 24th, consolidated at Insch and Turriff and in late afternoon grabbed Strichen. The next day two counter-attacks with tanks came in on Braemar but anti-tank guns and Shermans beat them off. All day on the 24th, 7th Argylls positions were subjected to heavy shelling and their Pipe Major Maclachlan was killed by snipers. At 1600 2nd Seaforth put in a gallant but unsuccessful attack (from Corps Reserve) on Stirling and forced a bridgehead through a minefield. In 36 hours they suffered 100 casualties.

On the night of the 24th, 7th Argylls made a silent attack from Greenock towards Nairn and the Blue line. On their start line they were heavily shelled and machine-gunned. Capt Ian Cameron:

> This Sunday night battle, enemy machine-guns kept chattering viciously during the attack, very soon casualties began to mount up. 'A' and 'D' companies had no officers left and were commanded by sergeants. The battlefield was bathed in brilliant moonlight, sections of the enemy were seen moving about. Eventually they began to retreat, and our troops chased after them causing some difficulty in control. The way the men went in at the point of the bayonet was magnificent. After Nairn was captured the companies dug in on the reverse slope. Throughout this attack the courage and determination of the men were splendid. Major Hugh Foster, FOO 126 Field Regt RA brought down defensive fire all round the position saving the force from being over-run.

When visiting 1st Black Watch on the 24th, the GOC's jeep struck a mine killing the driver and orderly and blowing General Wimberley twenty yards away. The following day Monty visited the heavily-bandaged GOC for a conference but made no comment. Later Monty said that if he had commiserated Wimberley would only have felt worse! Lt Col Jerry Sheil's diary indicated the progress of the battle:

> 25th October: It wasn't possible to attack last night: situation too confused. The armour moved up this morning but has been unable to progress. There is clearly a further enemy minefield and we haven't really got 'Aberdeen' 'Stirling' and 'Nairn'. There is to be another attack tonight.

> 26th October: The situation is now clearer. Our attack last night gained ground but the enemy still hold the high ground on Aberdeen, Stirling and Nairn. Our armour is milling about in front but when they move forward to attack are quickly knocked out by cleverly concealed 88mm guns. There are now two OPs below 'Nairn' and 'Stirling' (307 and 308) and Major Field has a good OP on the 'Ben'. It is an old Boche OP complete with maps.

It was vital that Stirling should be taken as its ridge dominated the whole divisional front. Brigadier 'Noisy' Graham now ordered 5th Black Watch to make a 'silent' attack two hours after a three hour artillery barrage. By midnight on 25th Stirling had been found abandoned, apart from dead and dying Germans and several guns. Twenty anti-tank guns and a squadron of 50 RTR arrived ready to deal with counter-attacks. Early on the 26th three fine Black Watch officers were casualties within an hour. By midnight 1/7th Middlesex had suffered 66 casualties. A Stuka had bombed 'B' Coy HQ, and the Luftwaffe was very active and 40 LAA put up protective fire across the divisional front with some success.

By the night of the 26th October the Division had reached all its objectives - an advance of six miles - for a loss of over 2100 casualties. The sappers laid new defensive minefields and the forward infantry put up wire. 1/7th Middlesex now carried out direct harassing shoots on all known enemy positions. Corporal Sam Stealth, already wounded three times with 12 Platoon went back to Coy HQ and with Major Meak brought up ammo, food and water. Wounded again, he was awarded the DCM.

On the night of the 27th, 5th Seaforth moved up to Sniper Valley near Tel el Eisa to relieve an Australian battalion, remaining there to the 30th. Almost every hour brought casualties by snipers and despite mortar bombs fired, "a careless movement still was answered by the snip of an automatic rifle fitted with telescopic sights. Nerves became frayed and even at night one became fearful to move." So wrote Lt Alastair Borthwick. The 7th Black Watch received 100 reinforcements on the night of 27/28th but patrols sent out on 27th and 29th had their commanders killed or wounded. On 31st October they were relieved by a South African battalion. 7th Argylls were subjected every day to heavy and constant shelling and dive-bombing. On the 30th they too were relieved by an SA battalion and marched back ten miles. Capt Ian Cameron:

> Back through battlefields [which] all around bore evidence of the terrible struggle - enemy guns and vehicles lay scattered, the twisted pieces of metal smoking and burning furiously. The night was brilliantly lit by moonlight. We marched on, most of us unshaven for days, we could smell the stench of the dead.

The Argylls were then sent immediately back into the line 'in the centre of a minefield.' On the 27th the RAF shot down two Stukas, 1st Armoured Division tanks had a clash with the enemy in front, a major force of reinforcements arrived for 5th Black Watch and General Wimberley visited next day. Lt John McGregor: "Word went round that 'Tartan Tam' was visiting and that did wonders for morale. He explained that 9th Australian Division were attacking that night near the coastal road to drive a hole through for the armoured divisions to pour through."

Lt Col Jerry Sheil's diary continues:

> 27th October: A very good day 'Nairn' and 'Stirling' surrender 'Copper' goes forward and interrogates about 400 [POW] coming in off Nairn. They fought well up to the very last and took a heavy hammering. We get up to 'Nairn' in the afternoon and break up a tank counter-attack by Regimental concentration. Very unhealthy on 'Nairn'. Major Owen has got an OP forward on 'Sterling' in close touch with 5 Black Watch (Colonel Rennie). Lt Allan, survey officer has done splendid work carrying his survey forward to new gun areas.
>
> 28th October: The signallers are having a difficult task to maintain lines

owing to shell fire and the depredations of our own armour. I make a point of getting into Div HQ most evenings to give my impressions of the day.

For the next five days the Division was in a defensive role. 1st Black Watch guarded Stanley, Strichen, Keith and Ballater. 7th Black Watch were next door to 21st New Zealand Bn and their 'local' passwords were of course 'Kiwi' and 'Jock' in case of an unplanned confrontation. When 5th Black Watch finally captured 'Stirling' their CO Lt Col Thomas Rennie, later to command HD, was awarded the DSO. He had escaped in 1940 from St Valéry, now he was wounded by a shell splinter in the neck. During eleven days of continuous action the battalion had lost 250 casualties including 68 KIA. 7th Black Watch also suffered heavily with 165 casualties including 78 KIA. "As the full stories of friends killed and wounded began to come in and the figures to mount up, the fresh courageous impulse of the first night began to sag. Then they had known nothing of the meaning of fear and had never seen death. Now overnight they were veterans." Thus wrote Lt Felix Barker, 5/7th Gordons; "The battalion was to continue to fight magnificently but it could never hope to know again the careless heroism of that first night."

Lt Col Sheil's diary continues:

> 30th October: 152 Bde are now withdrawn and we [128 Field] are supporting 154 Bde and 5 Black Watch. Food up from NAAFI - a welcome surprise and good work on the part of the Padre (Capt Leach).

> 31st October: Our Air Force have been magnificent. All day long the big bombers are going over in huge formations. Enemy fighters are rare over our lines. The Stukas too seem to have given it up as a bad job.

At the end of the battle General Wimberley wrote:

> I congratulated myself I had as my three Brigade Commanders [Murray, Graham and Houldsworth], three real fighting solders. All had been in the 1914-18 war as Infantry Soldiers and all 'knew the form' of taking their walking sticks, or Cromachs and going unmoved by shellfire among the Jocks on a daily visit that did so much to help morale in long-drawn out battles. Monty came and saw me on several occasions, putting his head out of the top of the tank in which he travelled.

The GOC had half a dozen young liaison officers from the Lowland Regts sent out as reinforcements, "I sent them up every night to live with the most exposed battalions. By personal visits, by telephone, by buried cable, by wireless I had a clear picture of all that was happening on my Div Front."

Corporal Geordie Reay was a gunner in a 3 RTR Crusader tank during Alamein:

> We were supporting the Highland Division and they were advancing with fixed bayonets across desert as flat as a table. As I watched them I thought, 'They're the only real soldiers in the British Army.' Men were dropping

right, left and centre - their mates were dropping right beside them but they just carried on. They'd been told to stop for nobody. I turned to Major Crisp and said. 'Isn't this a bloody disgrace, sir?' 'It's against human nature.' It was a terrible sight. They couldn't have done it without strict discipline."

The battle of El Alamein raged up and down the line - hammer and tongs until Monty believed that his breakthrough was imminent.

11

Operation Supercharge
The Second Battle of Alamein

General Montgomery judged that the 'wearing down' in terrible attritional fighting of the Afrika Korps was completed by the end of October. The 7th Armoured Division had threatened a breakout in the south and on 29th October after bitter fighting 9th Australian Div had advanced in the north across the coastal road. The salient they created forced the Afrika Korps reserve including *21st Panzer* and *90th Light* divisions to try to contain it. The Australians held firm on the 30th and 31st despite ferocious counter-attacks. Operation Supercharge was to be in two parts. A night attack by 51st Highland and the 2nd New Zealand divisions would by advancing 4000 yards on a 4000 yard frontage put intolerable pressure on the defenders. A gap would be created through which the British armour (1st Armoured and the NZ tank brigades) would maraud like pirates. The dangerous salient was called Thomson's Post or simply The Thumb. 152 Brigade (and 151 Bde of 50th Northumbrian Div) were placed under command of Lt General Freyberg. Behind a murderous barrage of 15,000 rounds fired over 4½ hours at 0100 on 2nd November, 152 Bde set off, 5th Camerons on the left, 5th Seaforth on the right, each with a 1000 yard frontage. 2nd Seaforth would follow through and mop up along the ridge known as El Wiska.

"The night of 1/2nd November was the first time, not for a few, but for all of us," wrote Alastair Borthwick, 5th Seaforth,

we were to fight more skilful actions and achieve more for less cost. We were to learn guile. But never again were we to go in as we did that night with so much verve. Of course it was a wasteful action. It had to be. We were raw troops with more spirit than sense and we chose a bad night to grow up. There was nothing wrong with the plan; men just threw their lives away. We were to advance 2000 yards, pause for half an hour, then advance another two thousand yards and dig in. Then the armour would come through. The attack was successful. The armour did get through and the Afrika Korps broke and ran.

Lt Col Stirling was invalided out with a septic arm and Major Walford took command. "The battle had almost started before he reached us. Billy MacKintosh and Jack Davidson were the only ones with a firm hold on the plan." At the startline, "the men knelt 10 yards apart along the white tape, black silhouettes against the sand. Officers and NCO's moved whispering last instructions... don't bunch... keep close up to the barrage... don't lose sight of your neighbours." Borthwick described the barrage:

> When some hundreds of guns are firing at once, the high shrill sound grows until the whole sky is screaming. When the first shells land the earth shakes, clouds of dust and smoke arise and the immense crash drowns the approach of the shells which follow. The uproar swells and fades and swells again, deafeningly numbing the brain. Through it comes the enemy's reply, the crump of mortars, ripping through everything the crack of bredas, the vicious pup-turr, pup-turr of the German Spandau machine-gun.

Sgt Carnduff, 14 Platoon: "After [knocking out a tank] we carried on again, saw people. There was Col Miers of the Camerons. He didn't know where half of his companies were, never mind ours. He said to dig in with him until we knew the form." When 'C' Company who had started a hundred strong reached their objective, five out of seventeen survivors were strays from Bn HQ. 'B' Coy was down to half strength. At 0430hrs on their final objective digging-in was impossible, the ground was like iron. Lt Robertson, the only surviving officer of 'C' Coy:

> At dawn our tanks came up and began fighting and firing while what seemed like every tank and anti-tank gun in the Afrika Korps fired back... I saw 30 of our own tanks brewed up in that small area and as many Boche ones were blazing and smoking a thousand yards away on the Tel el Aqqaqir Ridge.

5th Camerons went in behind the murderous barrage and achieved at a very high cost their objectives amidst the enemy armour. Four officers were killed and nine wounded. Of the ten officer reinforcements which arrived during the battle of 26/27th October all but one had become casualties by 3rd November. Lt Fraser Burrows wrote of his first action:

> The creeping barrage is sufficient to destroy anything in its path. A few shell-shocked Italians emerged out of the smoke and dust. I was convinced we would take our objective without any difficulty. I was not afraid until I was hit twice within a few moments by a couple of stray shells.

Lt Col Miers was awarded the DSO, the first in HD in North Africa,

Major Noble the MC, CSM Ahern who commanded 'D' Coy when all the officers became casualties, and L/Corp Mightens, the MM for destroying an enemy tank and its crew. At 0535hrs HQ 152 Bde predicted that casualties would not exceed 40 per Bn.

At dusk 2nd Seaforth and 50 RTR made a further advance and helped mop up. The GOC wrote:

> My own 152 Bde on left, dead flat ground, no features. George Murray [the Brigadier] did splendidly, 5th Seaforth first attack lost 12 officers, 165 men but reached their objectives, then dug in, the midst of an armoured battle. At night the tanks retired, so the Jocks dug in deeper.

By 0600 the Brigade had achieved its objectives. The enemy counter-attacked early afternoon on the 2nd and a few hours later 152 Bde made a further advance of 1500 yards without loss, taking 100 Italian POW. General Freyburg wrote to the GOC on the 3rd: "After a very short but very distinguished attachment to our Divison your 152 Bde returned to your command last night... will you give Murray our congratulations on the most successful attack on Skinflint."

The Padres and Medical Officers always had a very high standard of efficiency and bravery, Lt MacRae and Sgt Mackay (5th Seaforth). Capt Donald MacRae (2nd Seaforth) amongst others performed miracles. Farquhar MacRae the 5th Seaforth MO worked out in the open, even performing amputations under fire.

The success of Supercharge now rested on the capture of Point 44, Tel el Aqqaqir in the El Higeif area which would allow the armour a complete and final breakthrough. 5/7th Gordons were placed under command of Brigadier Houldsworth's 152 Bde for a night attack on 3rd November. 7th Argylls marched five miles cross-country to their start line, which was occupied already by 5th Camerons! The bearing of 293° for the advance had to be changed to 280°. In a dense smokescreen the forward Argyll companies lost 31 casualties mainly to HD guns. However by 0645 on the 4th an enemy Div HQ crammed full of valuable documents and equipment was captured, plus large quantities of Chianti and champagne, Iron crosses and Afrika Korps badges. On the 5th the Argylls captured 2200 POW but during the eleven day battle of El Alamein they lost 72 killed and 203 wounded. 5/7th Gordons under Lt Col Saunders attacked south-west across the key Sidi Abd el Rahman track. 8 RTR tanks were late on the start line so 'B' and 'C' Coys scrambled onto the leading tanks and set off behind a smokescreen. The joint attack, tanks and infantry, were shelled by 88mm guns which knocked-out seventeen tanks and killed fourteen Gordons, including two CSMs, and wounded 46 others. Lt Felix Barker: "The huge covering barrage was cancelled as unnecessary. The preliminary screen was of tanks, smokescreen and low flying fighters. It was impossible [for the battalion] to go far over such flat country under the fire they met." At darkness 5/7th Gordons reorganised and dug in on the Sidi Abd el Rahman track south of Tel el Aqqaqir. During the night patrols found that the enemy had departed. At first light armour reached the Daba track meeting no resistance. The next day the Luftwaffe bombed the Gordons inflicting another seven casualties.

General Oliver Leese had ordered the final attacks in Supercharge. General Wimberley insisted on a huge barrage in support: "Monty was very pleased with the result of my two attacks." But Leese wrote in his memoirs, "Wimberley saw those tanks coming out of action, covered with the dead bodies of his Highlanders [Gordons]. It was an unpleasant sight and bad for any troops morale." He telephoned General Leese and told him "Surely its not necessary to continue like this?" By the end of Supercharge, HD with 2827 casualties and the Australians with over 2000 casualties had suffered much more than any of the other eight divisions fighting alongside them. The GOC's journal continues

> The news was coming in fast that the enemy were in full retreat and our morale was accordingly high. It seemed that the long weary battle was over at last and we had won a great victory. All over the countryside near my battle HQ, huge bodies of tired dispirited POW were filing past to the rear. We ordered the Recce Regt through the 'G' in Gap to advance on Fuka. In that long 11 days of dog-fighting there were so many attacks, and reliefs of bns and switches of command, one's brain was going all out, day after day. As soon as one attack was over, one forgot it all, preparing for the next. I certainly had two magnificent commanders to work under in Oliver Leese and Monty. I must have seen M every day - arriving in his tank at my HQ. As the battle went on he seemed to me more and more to breathe a spirit of determination that win he would. When he did not himself visit me, he would send his ADC, Poston whom I much liked.

Wimberley had little opinion of the armoured leaders, Lumsden, Gatehouse, Fisher, Kenchington nor even Briggs, GOC 1st Armoured Div. But then their tanks were inferior, and the German 88mm anti-tank guns lethal.

When the battle was over, congratulations poured in from all over Scotland. The Lord High Provost of Edinburgh, the Clyde Shipyard workers, the workers at Leith, the Burgh of Aberlour, Council of Inverness, Lochiel, the Lord Lieutenant of the County (from Fort William), General Andrew Thorne, GOC Scottish Command and many others. The GOC was awarded an immediate award of the DSO and wrote "My cup of pride was very full." But he mourned the many good friends lost in the battle. Fraser MacKenzie (CO 40 LAA), Hamish Macdonald (5th Camerons), Greenhill Gardyne (Gordons), W I Mackintosh (Seaforth), JHB Evatt (61st Anti-Tank Reg) and others. Wimberley himself was 'walking wounded;' "I was bandaged on both knees, one wrist, my arm and both ankles, plus desert sores and abrasions treated with gentian violet painted on."

Lightfoot and Supercharge were over; it was a stunning victory and did wonders not only for the morale of the 8th Army (despite the heavy losses) but for the people of Great Britain who for so long had prayed, and hoped , for a victory. Church bells rang through the land.

12
Pursuit: "Sand treacherous as treacle"

After the great battle Monty addressed 30 Corps officers: "I well remember that night on 23rd October when the HD went into battle with its bagpipes for the first time. I don't suppose anyone will forget that night. I know that the HD was anxious to do its stuff well, to wipe out and avenge the debt passed on to them by that other HD that fought at St Valéry. There is no doubt that the HD did its first battle right well. I had to leave it behind in the pursuit battle but so long as I command this Army I shall never leave it behind again."

Lt Neil McCallum, a reinforcement, was turned down by 2nd Seaforth because he was not wearing their Gaelic motto in his cap badge but on 6th November joined 5/7th Gordons. One soldier told him his impression of the Alamein battle: "Everyone was shouting, screaming, swearing, shouting for their father, shouting for their mother. I didn't know whether to look at the ground or the sky. Spider mines on the ground, flashes in the sky, shells were coming all ways."

Severe rainstorms hindered the pursuit. Most of the 8th Army tanks were bogged down but Rommel's forces withdrew skilfully to the west along the coastal road. HD had now started to have a regular armoured partner. 23rd Armoured Brigade was commanded by a Welshman, Brigadier 'Ricky' Richards: "The GOC tried to pinch some of my signallers because they were Jocks. Not only were they useful, not only to keep Bde HQ efficient, but also as interpreters. At El Alamein my wireless operator would turn round to me and ask what 'twa' meant. I put my foot down when Douglas Wimberley tried to snick *my* Jocks."

For nearly two weeks the sorely battered HD was out of the line, absorbing reinforcements, collecting prisoners, clearing up the battlefield detritus of enemy and 8th Army wrecked equipment. Troops drove captured German and Italian vehicles of weird provenance. And of course the retreating Afrika Korps had a fine selection of 8th Army transport vehicles to help them on their way. Private Roy Cooke, 'I' Section, 5th Seaforth: "Along the famous desert highway, the Via Balba, in 3-tonner trucks crammed with Rommel's men who had surrendered. They all wore the Afrika Korps long-peaked caps and tropical uniforms with lace-up boots."

The 'Highway Decorators' had by now acquired a reputation for smartness. "We again began to 'Spit and Polish' in which I so firmly believe. My smart kilted Gordon sentry outside my caravan and my Div HQ flag fluttering in the breeze. The first test," wrote the General in his journal, "of a first class fighting formation was to smarten up directly after battle." Major Angus Ferguson, CMP ensured the HD axis was always marked by HD signs made of tinplate and painted appropriately.

The Corps Commander, Lt General Oliver Leese visited HD and wrote. "I left my staff car, walked over the sand to a Black Watch Jock on solitary guard. 'Good morning, I am Leese, yours Corps Commander.' The Jock looked at me and said. 'Aye, weel, I'm Montgomery,' Later the guard commander assured me that his sentry's name really was [Private] Montgomery!" Leese wrote in his memoirs. "HD is a remarkable division. Rather like the Brigade of Guards in their knowledge of each other, but more inbred."

Shortage of transport and petrol meant that the HD was now far behind the front line concentrated north and south of the railway line at El Daba and Sidi Haneish. On 7th November the 7th Argylls were at Ras El Kanaysis when a captured German corporal, from 32 Luftwaffe was driven into their camp. When told of the American and British landings in North Africa the young Nazi responded, "The longer you keep us prisoners in Egypt, the sooner we shall be free. We have the whole of Europe. Heil Hitler!" A spirited reply but dubious logic. Eighteen year old Signaller George Wagstaffe joined 127 Field Regt RA just after El Alamein: "I was dropped off at dead of night and pulled into a dug out by a Jock who was manning a telephone exchange. An irate infantry major was speaking to the CO of 126. 'Look here Sandy, one of your bloody guns is firing short. Its putting the fear of God into my chaps.' The CO apologised and said. 'I'll get Wagstaffe to calibrate the guns in the morning.' Well I was the only Wagstaffe I'd heard of until then! Fortunately Major Wagstaffe RA was the W referred to!"

The 5th Black Watch, still 250 under strength, held a Memorial Service on Sunday, 8th and Lt Col Rennie read out the names of the 68 who had been killed in action. The Pipers played the old lament 'Flowers o'the Forest.' Captain Stephen their MO found an enormous dump of medical stores at El Daba in a field guarded by Brigadier Graham's 153 Bde. They were all neatly packed, ready for loading so RAP and ADS stocked up with bandages, lint, cotton wool and other medical supplies.

Tobruk was taken on 13th, the Martuba airfields two days later and

Benghazi on the 20th. IID's move westwards started on 19th when 153 Bde left for Tobruk and the remainder on 21st and 24th.

On arrival at Agadabia many vehicles were bogged down in very soft desert sand. Alastair Borthwick, 5th Seaforths:

> Each truck carried two sand channels and many shovels. Each driver, if he knew his job, kept his eyes skinned for the best going. Smooth yellow sand, attractive to the uninitiated, was deadly. Pebbly going was usually good but sometimes was a deceptive crust with soft sand underneath. In some places the desert was smooth and firm as a racetrack for miles on end and in every direction. On hard surfaces speeds of 18mph were possible. In other places it was treacherous as treacle.

"We march. The enemy is retreating in transport. We follow on foot," recalled Lt Neil McCallum 5/7th Gordons:

> March through the blistering day, hard sand, soft sand, hot sand, shuffling through the sand hour after hour. This army of men goes on stumbling, sweating, pursuing an invisible enemy across the leagues of African desert. We swarm over space like insects crawling across a field. At ten minutes to every hour a whistle blows. Rest for each company. Flop in the sand. Smoke but do not drink. Lie on the sand and ease your body... A shabby gritty landscape. The sweat oozes and trickles all day... The thud of feet on the sand ninety four times every minute, fifty minutes an hour, hour after hour, day after day. And every night, dig. The shovel has saved more lives than the rifle. Dig in case the bombs drop. Dig for discipline. Dig to save your skins. Dig through sand, if necessary through rock. Dig for bloody victory.

The Recce Regt Composite Sqn carried out reconnaissance on the coast road to Fuka, taking 500 POW. But on 14th the blow fell. Colonel Grant came back from GHQ in Cairo with the news that the regiment was to become a motorised infantry battalion and would move back to the Delta to reorganise. (On 14th January they became 14th Bn Highland Light Infantry and their place as divisional recce taken by 2nd Derbyshire Yeomanry).

154 Bde crossed Halfaya (hell fire) Pass on 20th November entering Libya and reached Tobruk the next day, and harboured near El Adem. Training continued until 4th December but the moves west continued via Bir Hacheim, Antelat to Adjedabya and on to relieve 152 Bde astride the main road opposite Mersa Brega.

Alastair Borthwick's 5th Seaforth set off on the 21st followed the coast road to Acroma, almost 300 miles of travel. "Its slender black ribbon unwinding across the miles of sand and rock was a sight which cheered both the Germans and ourselves. It was the one living stream in a dead ocean. A sight-seeing tour with the blue Mediterranean on our right hand, the haze of the desert on our left and all around us the litter left in the wake of the retreating Axis army," Borthwick described, "the art of desert navigation (Ralph Bagnold's 'Libyan Sands'), and the principle of the Bagnold or Cole sun-compass, ie a sun-dial in reverse. A six-inch metal plate with a needle rising vertically from the centre of it and the hours of the day marked round the edge. It was set for the bearing the convoy wished to follow. After some adjustment drive in a direction such that the shadow of the needle fell across the correct line... Desert navigation was fun." Major George Green, the Seaforth Navigating Officer had a little seat built high behind the driver's cab. The cab roof acted as a desk on which was the sun-compass, ordinary compass in hand. In his pocket were pencils, a protractor, enormous notebook and a wad of squared paper. He was surrounded by binoculars, map boards, water bottles and other vital equipment. Behind him were 150 battalion vehicles. Acting as advance guard, Major Green led over a thousand vehicles. Ahead lay 200 miles of desert.

5th Black Watch set off in 'Desert Formation' on 25th November to cover the 400 mile journey to Adjedabya, passed due south to Bir Hacheim where General Leclerc's French Legion had put up such a gallant fight. In the notorious 'Knightsbridge' area two days later they saw some of the 100 British tanks wrecked and burnt out by the dug-in German tanks and 88mm guns. On 30th November, St Andrew's Day, Monty came to visit, brief and encourage his Highlanders.

13

El Agheila

"Mines and booby traps - a nightmare day"

Although the Afrika Korps had lost 30,000 captured at El Alamein (mostly Italians), they were still a formidable fighting force. The indomitable trio, *15* and *21* Panzer and the now famous *90th Light Division*, battered and bruised, fought skilful delaying actions all the way to the west.

Pte Roy Cooke 5th Seaforth:

Now on past the famous white mosque at Sidi Abd el Rahman which was reported to be Rommel's HQ during the battle of El Alamein, and onto Fuka with masses of smashed Luftwaffe fighter planes on the airfield. We bypassed Mersa Matruh and all along the highway were many burnt out Italian trucks, both Army and Italian Air Force, also some Italian tanks which were sometimes referred to as 'mobile coffins' as they were pretty well useless. We finally halted at Mersa Brega as Rommel had decided to make a stand at El Agheila.

In most wars the Army lives off the land they pass through. In the case of the desert this was understandably rather difficult. "There were other Divisions in the Army who actually referred to the Highland Division as a 'circus'," recalls Major Alan Daglish:

> In North Africa we had a quantity of livestock with us. We had highly trained animals - a sheep and a box of hens, so well trained that at a ten-minute halt they could be seen to dismount from the vehicles, relieve themselves and remount without further trouble. Actually they were probably the only living creatures to read the march tables. As a Brigade Major it seemed to me that the best disciplined and smartest animals were those that wore the Red Hackle.

"After making our tea we dried the used tea leaves in the sun, sprinkled some fresh tea on top and traded with the Arabs for eggs and dates. One of our [5th Seaforth] drivers Willie Thain acquired a broody hen and some eggs, put them under the hen in his vehicle toolbox. Everytime the convoy stopped Willie let his brood out. Many a driver swore at Willie as he tried to catch his chicks when the convoy was ready to move," James Younie recalled; "however, they made a tasty meal."

1st Black Watch's first capture on the breakout was of a huge bakery with bread in all stages of production and the second was a store of enemy boots (brown). Thousands of pairs were worn until Tripoli and Monty's parades. "The move up the desert was one of constant movement in 3-ton trucks for days, punctuated by an odd day of strenuous marching through the sand. One day I [Pte Roy Green 1st Black Watch] carried the Boyes Anti-tank rifle which weighs 41-lbs all day without relief. Some more casualties always occurred. The true 'glad', 'sad' feeling always overtook us. The immediate re-action, 'I am glad it is him and not me.' But at the same time 'I am damn sorry it was him.'" Roy Green, originally a sniper, was transferred to the signals; "Captain Wallace told me due to many casualties I was to join his squad of signallers, as laying telephone lines to all Companies often under fire was hazardous. First to locate the break, then to effect the repair with shaking hands and thumping heart - who isn't afraid in times like that? The German cable was very much better than ours and we took every opportunity to acquire the 'booty'. The 18 set wireless units were mostly useless. It took so much time to tune all sets in and a few shells would knock many of them haywire."

The enemy now held the Agheila line from Mersa Brega in the north to Suera in the south with a large marshy area in the centre, difficult for vehicles and tanks. Montgomery's plan was for HD to attack Rommel's defensive line astride the coast road whilst the NZ Division made a deep left flanking movement in the south. 152 Bde would make the main attack, with 153 Bde to follow through when required. For six days HD trained and waited whilst forward airfields were prepared after the 400 mile advance. On 13th December 8th Armoured Bde trundled into the desert to outflank the enemy at Giofer.

The GOC frequently praised his faithful gunner regiments. He always reckoned that they always knew exactly where they were even in the featureless desert. Geoffrey Durand, an OP Ack with 128 Field Regt RA:

> Very inaccurate maps were supplied to us, so our CO (Jerry Sheil) decided to make a map of his own. A full ground survey of OPs allowed registration of many land features (around Mersa Brega). From observed shooting and the CO's knowledge of field work, we (128 Field Regt) produced an exceptionally concise map of the battle area. General Wimberley was so impressed, he had it reproduced and released to all his Bn COs. The only map which showed in true detail where we were and gave accurate locations of enemy positions."

The GOC noted in his journal:

> 11th Dec, signs were the enemy were thinning their front, getting ready to retire, firing off surplus ammo. They were very windy on our front sending up coloured lights and fire drumfire burst of shells. The village of Mersa Brega thickly covered with mines known to the Jocks as 'Jumpin' Jacks'. 13th Dec. 7th Black Watch had a most efficient night advance and by daylight were behind the village. Both BW Bns were involved in the envelopment of the village and suffered casualties from mines."

7th Argylls who entered Mersa Brega lost twenty men to 'S' mines and 5/7th Gordons fifteen to a counter-attack.

> 14th was a nightmare day due to mines and booby traps left behind. I saw every 100 yards or so wounded men, mostly sappers. On the verges a

mixture of Teller mines and AP mines, thickly strewn, all the side tracks mined. Plenty of tempting souvenirs, Italian sun helmets, German steel helmets, bottles of wine, ration boxes, all booby-trapped. Some of our own corpses, men lost on patrol were all booby trapped when later burial parties went out to locate and bury them. The Italians were streets ahead of us at mine laying.

90th Light Division had masterminded a skilful defence but had vanished during the night.

Monty now told the GOC that he must send one of his Brigadiers - 'a first-class man' - back to the UK to run the new School of Infantry at Barnard Castle: "Either George Murray or Harry Houldsworth. Douglas Graham is a magnificent leader but does not seem to be a good lecturer. Harry seemed more tired than George. I knew he would lecture very well indeed. Harry was dead straight and brave and honourable." Thomas Rennie, CO 5th Black Watch, awarded the DSO for Alamein and recovered from his recent wound was appointed to command 154 Bde, Major 'Chick' Thomson took command of 5th BW. When General Wimberley inspected the El Agheila defences he told the 5/7 Gordons: "If they had only stayed and fought it would have cost us alone 600 lives to have broken through. Thank God," he said as he looked across the flat waste land of the desert desolate in the pouring rain, "they didn't. I wouldn't like to have left my Jocks behind in a graveyard such as this."

Soon 7th Armoured Div came through and took up the pursuit and HD came into Corps Reserve around El Agheila. So training again particularly for young 'leaders' and specialists. Exercises were carried out at night in co-operation with tanks to practise assault against prepared positions protected by minefields.

Inter-unit football matches were played and welcome honours and awards arrived for El Alamein. 1st Gordons received an MC, a DCM and two MMs; 5/7th Gordons three MCs and three MMs, 5th Black Watch two MCs and an MM.

Reinforcements poured in and a number of lightly wounded veterans of El Alamein returned from hospital. 'B' Coy, 5th Black Watch was reformed under Major Blair Imrie. Church Parade on 20th December was cold and wet and most battalions wore battledress again. The Black Watch produced a sophisticated pantomime 'The Agheila Angels' with orchestra (drums, bugle, violin, accordion and trumpet).

7th Argylls (and others) suffered from a violent sandstorm in December. Capt Ian Cameron: "Far away in the desert could be seen a wall of sandy dust about a hundred feet high coming towards us. It struck us with terrific force and the fine sand got into everything, including the hair, eyes, ears and throat. It turned day into night whilst it lasted, afterwards came torrential rain (15th) - a truly unpleasant experience."

To the west of Mersa Brega 1/7 Middlesex trained by the sea. Their successful Christmas Day was spent in swimming, football and rifle shooting. On the menu was roast turkey, pork, Christmas pudding and a small ration of beer. A large consignment of Scotch whisky suddenly arrived at 7th Bn Black Watch and 'toddy' parties were held. Their training included snipers courses, wire cutting practice, field firing, mortar and anti-tank gun practice and of course route marches. And loads of mail enhanced morale. Monty sent a Christmas message to all ranks of 8th Army ending 'Good luck to you'. And in the words of Tiny Tim, in Dickens' Christmas Carol, 'God Bless us all, each one of us.' The RASC had to drive back either to a desert airstrip or to 'Marble Arch' to collect the Christmas goodies, Monty had ordered for his 8th Army.

Alistair Borthwick: "The Bn [5th Seaforth] lived on the edge of the sand dunes and slept to the roar of the waves. On Christmas Day the CO, Lt Col Stirling, the Adjutant and RSM were piped into each company area where with a glass of whisky he proposed the company's health. His speech inevitably became longer with each Coy he visited... At four o'clock the pipes and drums beat Retreat on the edge of the marshy flat. The sky was the colour of lead."

The Seaforth, Argylls and others spent some time at Ras El Aali unloading ships at the pier and roadmaking.

Whilst out of the line HD suffered no less than 89 casualties to mines including the CO of 2nd Seaforths, Lt Col Kennie Mackessach and an RE officer, Lt Pearson, demonstrating a new type of mine. New strict orders were issued that if an unfortunate soldier was blown up by a mine, he could not be rescued until a path had been cleared and swept to where he lay.

The triple festivals of Christmas, Hogmanay and Red Hackle day were spent relatively at peace with the world. "Christmas Day," noted the GOC, "was, lazy, late reveille, bread for breakfast, beer for all at lunch, a 'Treasure Hunt' for all at Div HQ and an open air church service. A nice mongrel dog called Daba was adopted, petted by all. Last day of the year Oliver Leese with bottle of Drambuie had a great guest night. We danced reels after dinner to a Gordon piper of the Defence Platoon, midnight rum punch, 'Auld Lang Syne'. Hard work dancing reels in soft sand." Later, "excellent show by Balmorals our concert party in the open desert." The pipers were still going strong at four in the morning.

14

Advance to Contact
Buerat, Homs and the coastal road

Gordon Young, *Daily Express* reporter wrote: "The New Year opened with the two armies facing each other in the region of Beurat across a no man's land between a ravine called Wadi Kebir on one side and Wadi Zem-Zem on the other. Back in Cairo people were spending the New Year celebrating this long trail of victory. Desert tanned troops snatching brief leaves bought fly-whisks from street hawkers and queued up all day long outside the cinemas. The German main positions stretched in a rough triangle from above Buerat on the coast, inland to Gheddahia and then south to Fortino. The Wadi Zem-Zem was stony and impassable in many places with high cliffs: small wadis in front, artillery on the ridges, heavily mined with barbed wire fences. It was an excellent defensive line." The enemy forces from north to south were the Italian divisions *Trieste, Pistoia, Ramcke, Spezia, 164 Division, 88 Force* and the German *90th Light.*

The GOC had built a good team around him. He thought his GSO1 Roy Urquhart (later to command at Arnhem): "First class, a better commander than staff officer; popular, firm and thorough, very long suffering with me." Of his CRA Brigadier George Elliott, "Was first class, I always found that good artillery officers were the best at topography. In Jerry Shiel and Tony Thicknesse I was fortunate in having two really first class regular gunner Lieut Colonels (I was very sad that both were to be killed before the end of the war)." Thomas Rennie had been blown up on a mine and Roper Caldbeck took over temporary command of 154 Bde. "I decided to make 'Jumbo' Stirling of 5th Seaforth, Brigadier of 154 Bde, HQ as a forceful and energetic CO. He was not a success. Jack Walford, new CO 5th Seaforth became a legendary figure by great bravery and leadership."

The King sent congratulations to General Wimberley on his award of the DSO. There was a great deal of publicity for him as GOC HD in the Scottish papers, as the only Scottish division then fighting. 15th Scottish and 52nd Lowland were still stationed in the UK.

On 2nd January HD carried out a brigade exercise gapping minefields watched by Oliver Leese and Monty. "The latter in tremendous form. I liked having him with us." Noted the GOC, who bet Monty "we would be in Tripolitania by the end of the year." Benghazi was not yet open as a port and supplies were limited. Three days later 7th Argylls resumed the hunt and moved in three stages 150 miles west to Wadi El Chebir, 15 miles east of Buerat to act as a firm base for 154 Bde. The ground was so hard there that the sappers used air compressors to dig in the anti-tank guns. The rest of HD moved on 9th January to a staging area in Nofilia.

The next day Monty held a big conference at 30 Corps HQ and explained his plans for the taking of Tripoli. A big storm at Benghazi had interfered with supplies for 50 Div. The GOC was told.

> We were not expected to be the first into Tripoli: a methodical advance along the main road close to the sea, clear the axis for supplies to get forward by road to Tripoli, when it was captured. First, a straight forward attack on Buerat with 7th Armoured Div; New Zealanders did their usual left hook via the desert, under Oliver Leese, whilst HD directly under Monty with 4th Armoured Bde in reserve. Not enough ammo available so one Bn attack on Buerat on narrow and deep front, the enemy having a strong minefield in front. The advance and attack on Beurat was carefully planned with a detailed sand table and four phases Silk, Satin, Cotton and Rags. It all went like clockwork.

On the 12th Monty sent 8th Army a message: "Tripoli is the only town in the Italian Empire overseas still remaining in their possession. Therefore we will take it from them." By the 14th, HD were at the Wadi Chfef, 3000 yards from the enemy lines. At 2330 hrs the next day 1st Gordons punched a hole in the enemy defences behind a barrage, supported by 40 RTR, a dozen Scorpion flail tanks, sappers with Bangalore torpedoes and played forward by their pipers. 5/7th Gordons were to follow through and if necessary Douglas Graham's 153 Bde would attack Buerat on three successive nights. 152 Bde would then pass through to capture Misurata and finally Jumbo Stirling's 154 Bde would lead right up to Tripoli.

Despite four Scorpions being blown up clearing the 500 yard depth minefield, and two more to an anti-tank gun, by 0240 the centre was gapped, and with the loss of 31 casualties, the Gordons pressed through but found the enemy had quit Buerat.

Norman Smart, *Daily Express* journalist watched the HD attack on Beurat:

> Shadowy figures which were infantry rose up from the desert and begun stumbling forward over the rocky ground under the protection of that steel curtain flung by our gunners from far back. With them went sappers prodding the ground with bayonets feeling for the metallic contact which means the edge of a minefield. Through the night air, pallidly but insistently came the sound of the bagpipes, fighting for a place in that tremendous noise of battle. It came from the pipers going forward with each company.

The GOC sent a message, "Slainte Bydand" (Here's to the Cock of the North) to 'Hammy' Farquhar, CO 1st Gordons and to 'Chick' Thomson, CO 5th Black Watch for their battalions' performance. In one rearguard action was Jeff Haward, 12 Pltn, 1/7th Middlesex:

Tanks and trucks ahead were knocked out and burning with many casualties to the infantry. The elevation was too high for our Vickers guns to engage the enemy. An order came to withdraw, down the road a car roared towards us. Out jumped 'Big Tam' the GOC. 'Where do you think you are going?' We explained the situation, the following conversation took place. BT. 'Where do you live?' Me. 'Finchley, Sir.' BT. 'Do you want to go back there?' Me. 'Oh yes, Sir.' BT. 'Then turn round, get those hills to Tripoli, then keep on until you reach Berlin and then you can go home to Finchley.' Me. 'Yes, Sir.' BT. 'Then get going.' Lt Wigan [later Major, MC] climbed to the top of the nearest hill some distance ahead with a slope about 45°. He came tumbling down. We were behind the enemy rearguard. We then manhandled our four Vickers and ammo to the top of the hill.

12 Platoon then successfully engaged Italian infantry with big Lancia trucks and shot up troops of *90th Light Div*. The CO of the Die Hards, Lt Col JWA Stephenson arrived, congratulated 12 platoon and handed out a packet of ten cigarettes to the 26 members of the Die Hard platoon!

Despite Monty's indication that there was no particular urgency for HD, he now ordered, "advance will be pressed on night and day with utmost vigour." Lt Col Ronny Miers, CO 5th Camerons in the lead was wounded in the face. He was the first DSO gazetted to HD for the Alamein battle. On the 17th Oliver Leese' conference stated that the enemy was not expected to make a stand until the Homs line. There was some opposition at Taourga where 90 Italians were made POW and five guns captured. But Monty had to change his plans. The left hook inland by the New Zealanders and Desert Rats was held up. So HD and the advance along the coastal road, backed by 22nd Armoured Bde now had top priority. Monty made it clear that Tripoli, 200 miles ahead must be reached by the tenth day of attack to receive new supplies there, or face the grim possibility of retreat. So the new orders came to drive all night and reach Misurata by daylight. Jumbo Stirling's 154 Bde in the lead making straight for Zliten cutting off Misurata for George Murray's 152 Bde to capture.

Capt Paddy Nairn 5th Seaforth: "There was no real fighting not even by the advance guard. There were many alarms and excursions, often a fog of dust and sand." Next morning Monday, 18th January: "The gladdening sun arose and shed its glow on the Promised Land, the bogeys and anxieties of the night [march during darkness] disappeared like bad dreams. Before our eyes lay fields of tall green asphodel, trim white villas, high water towers, small green trees: scarcely two miles away stood Misurata, gleaming white, romantic and seductive through the black olive trees. But 'Bash on' and another 14 miles to Garibaldi."

2nd Seaforths entered Misurata on the 18th then 7th Black Watch led and covered 12 miles in two hours. Major DFO Russell wrote:

> During the morning the white walls and towers of Crisbi and Gioda could be seen shining in the sunlight some five miles to our right. Late in the afternoon after topping some small hills we looked down on the cultivated strip of coast land near Garibaldi, an escarpment of small hills, fertile cultivated plains closely covered with vines and olive groves, dotted with Italian settlements. And a background of shining white sand hills with palm trees silhouetted against a particularly blue sea and sky, a vivid contrast to the brown and amber colours of the desert.

At Zliten deep irrigation channels, low mud walls, clumps of palm trees reduced the speed of advance. It was slow tiring work having to lift jeeps over the walls. Another Monty conference eight miles south of Zliten. As a result 154 Bde were urged on towards Homs. The GOC joined Simon Ramsay's 'C' Coy, 7th Black Watch in the vanguard with 1st Black Watch on the left trying to move over Jebel country on the left. Nine road demolitions were encountered between Zliten and Homs.

Garibaldi was an Italian farming community numbering about one thousand residents. The holy town of Zliten with its innumerable white tombs of dead Arabs was set in fertile countryside of palms and olive groves. When HD reached Homs, a small town by the sea, it was a wreck with looted and smashed houses, flats, shops and offices.

The local Senussi were 'employed' to fill in the craters, make diversions across wadi beds and indicate where mines were buried. On the GOC's jeep mudguards were an Arab and a stray Italian POW encouraged by the General's revolver, as they reached Leptia Magna at 1700 hrs on 19th. As dusk fell Homs 23 miles from Zliten was found unoccupied by 7th Black Watch. As a result of the new orders for HD to press on regardless towards Tripoli, no one had told Rear Corps HQ and Jack Colam's (AQMG) indents for petrol had been cut with supplies allocated to the two 'inland' divisions. Lt Col Young: "It was evident to CRASC Lt Col Bruton that there was insufficient petrol to make Tripoli, so he went to the DDST at Corps HQ, Brigadier Pat Essie. Fuel was then allocated to HD but it was beyond the range of the RASC Columns vehicles with the fuel that was left. Fuel was siphoned out of vehicle tanks and one lorry towed two others to reach the fuel dump. In the event there was still insufficient fuel to carry the infantry into Tripoli, so they were carried on tanks and carriers." Captain Bobbie Gray found two damaged German half-tracks. After a quick repair, one of them towed seventeen 3-tonners from Homs to Tripoli. Resourceful fellows, the RASC!

The shortage of petrol grounded 126 Field Regt and 152 Bde were left at Misurata for two days to refit. And 153 Bde were ordered to follow as fast as possible for the same reason. Two pursuit forces were formed at Homs, known as Hammer Force and Thurso Force. Both bumped the enemy rearguard on the 20th.

15

'Edinburgh Castle'
Corradini and the capture of Tripoli

Four miles west of Homs, patrols of 7th Black Watch, on the 20th discovered that a rocky feature, nicknamed 'Edinburgh Castle' dominated the main coastal road. Until it was taken or outflanked further advance was impossible. Moreover an anti-tank ditch ran inland from the sea for several miles. The big, deep Wadi Zenadi also ran in front of 'Edinburgh Castle' into further steep hills. The defenders as usual were the indomitable *90th Light Division*. 1st Black Watch put in a frontal attack on 'Edinburgh Castle' which failed and the battalion was pinned down by heavy and accurate fire. From Homs 7th Argylls with 40 RTR tanks tried to turn the immediate right flank of the castle, and swing south-west through Beni Hassam towards the main road which passed through the rocky crags around Edinburgh Castle. Tanks and transport could not get through the soft sand and across the anti-tank ditch. So the GOC ordered a right flanking movement and the Argylls marched about sixteen miles through loose sand dunes and later rough bumpy ground. Within sight of the main road they saw twenty enemy vehicles and guns about 3000 yards ahead. Lacking artillery, mortar and tank support the Argylls planned to attack the column at night. But the enemy had gone and a clash with 1st Black Watch (who had lost 100 casualties including 51 missing) was narrowly avoided. The castle was found empty the next morning. With no bulldozers available the 20 foot deep, 20 foot wide anti-tank ditch took a lot of filling. Manual labour included the GOC which had an electrifying effect!

In a 15-cwt truck was the 'Media', Norman Smith, *Daily Express*, Aubrey Hammond, Allied Newspapers, Henry Gorrell, United Press. As the huge anti-tank ditch was finally filled traffic began to move forward. The GOC refused to let the journalists truck through: "You take that truck and park it over there until I tell you to move. I've got guns and ammo to get through here as quickly as possible. You can't write about the war until we've won it." Half an hour later General Wimberley suddenly appeared. "Now you can go forward, but mind you don't block the road. Good luck!"

Brigadier 'Ricky' Richards now commanded Hammerforce consisting of 23rd Armoured Bde, a company of Middlesex, anti-tank guns and a battery of 25-pdrs. Their hot pursuit along the main road was a 'cavalry' charge of eleven miles through unoccupied entrenchments and low hills until they met a tough rearguard a few miles short of Corradini. Hammerforce was quickly reinforced by the dead-tired 1st Bn Black Watch in MT arriving from Edinburgh Castle. The GOC ordered George Murray to come forward to Richard's HQ.

The problem was that Monty had sent Major General Bobby Erskine, his acting Chief of Staff along to the HD area to see what progress was being made. Wimberley had no time for Erskine "a poor commander subsequently sacked in Normandy," who promptly returned to his master with an adverse report (before the Castle fortress was captured and the right flank advance started). Monty then sent Wimberley 'an Imperial rocket' received after dark on the 28th.

"We must throw our usual thoroughness and caution to the winds, attack the instant we could with 5th Seaforth into the battle (near Corradini). Our maps were bad. I could clearly see two hills close behind the enemy's position, pointed to them, told Murray they were his objective - the El Nab feature. Radio communications very bad. I got through to Jumbo Stirling at last in clear, in Hindustani, told him what our line of attack was to be. I gambled *90th Light* would be too busy!"

5th Seaforth on the march

So the second Battle of the Hills (or Pimples!) started on the 21st. "At the assembly area we met the CO [Lt Col Walford]," wrote Capt JAF Watt 'B' Coy 5th Seaforth, "we were to attack two sharp conical hills [El Nab] we could see faintly outlined against the sky two or three thousand yards away." On both sides of the main road some three miles short of Corradini they were natural defensive points. The Brigade IO, John Thornton, warned the Seaforth that the maps were unreliable. So with medium guns pounding away and 40 RTR tanks in support the Seaforths set off before dawn. The broken ground and wadis held up the tanks and also 'A' Coy, as mortar bombs and spandaus opened up. CSM Durrand, the Adjutant and Battalion HQ followed the line of the road, to take 'a wee hill' a hundred yards ahead. "We spread out again, fifty yards from the top every bloody thing in creation opened up on us. Point blank it was. There were three machine guns dug in on top of the hill and the Boche were heaving tattie-mashers at us too. There was a sniper out on the right. It was still dark and he was shooting at the noise. We got down. The first burst had killed six or seven and wounded two or three." Later, "If we lifted our heads the machine-guns in front got us," recalls CSM Durrand, "and if we lay still where we were the sniper got us. We could hear a terrific racket coming from 'B' Coy over the hill." Jimmy Watt's 'B' Coy was counter-attacked by infantry and a half-tracked troop carrier. CSM Elder was killed, Lt Dimack shot and in very close fighting both sides lost heavily. But the sniper dominated the HQ Coy "only 200 yards away he got Sgt McKirby through the head, wounded Mr Nairne and Mr Ross the Signals Officer, one or two others got it too. He was just picking us off." On the way back to the wadi, the sniper and the machine-guns tore the Seaforth to pieces. During this savage action 5th Seaforth suffered 81 casualties, many killed outright by deadly sniper fire. They were saved by the success of the right flanking mvement by 2nd Seaforth and 7th Black Watch. From Wadi Zambra the going was impossible and all MT was abandoned. The native guides and maps were unreliable but the two battalions struggled through the night and by 0420hrs were in the vicinity of Wadi Genima. They had been on the move for thirteen hours and were ordered to put in an attack at 0600hrs on the El Nab feature from the coastal side. Ahead of them 7th Black Watch saw a convoy of vehicles streaming towards Tripoli from Homs (and Edinburgh Castle). They opened fire but stopped when they realised they were British transport.

They were captured British vehicles! The Germans quickly recovered from their surprise turned every weapon they had on 7th Black Watch and launched an overwhelming counter-attack. 'A' Coy were caught on a forward slope and suffered heavy casualties. Supporting tanks could not get across the wadi. Another fake enemy column appeared with a tank and several anti-tank guns towed by British 'quads'. 'A' Coy now lost a number of prisoners. Major Steven, OC 'B' Coy, was killed by a mortar bomb, Major Ramsay and Capt Keltie of 'C' Coy were captured. The situation was now critical as ammo was in short supply, when heavy machine-gun fire opened up from the high ground on the left. Major Monk of the Die Hards won an MC for the brilliant work of 1/7th Middlesex which saved 7th Black Watch from probable destruction. Behind a smoke screen *90th Light* defenders withdrew. 7th Black Watch suffered 97 casualties including 40 missing and 2nd Seaforth, who attacked two miles east to cut the main road and force the enemy to retreat, also had heavy losses. The skilful *90th Light Division* had deployed heavy 210mm guns, many 88mm anti-tank guns, a dozen dual-purpose 20mm guns and many mortars in their defensive action.

The petrol crisis was now even worse. 7th Black Watch, 1/7th Middlesex and several field artillery batteries had no fuel; 5th Black Watch, 5th Seaforth, no TCVs and 5/7th Gordons only eight TCVs. The GOC divided his scattered division into seven groups according to their localities, reconstituted Richard's Hammerforce and gave strict orders to Andrew Fergusson's Military Police that traffic could only be forward (except for ambulances). Trucks out of petrol must be towed. Lifts must be scrounged: if no lifts, march but no stopping until Tripoli was reached. Despite the 'Imperial Rocket,' Monty came up to see the GOC "before we got the road open, seemed pleased and quite impressed, after seeing all the battle debris littering the Corradini battlefield. New orders - press on to Castelverde 16 miles way. Clear the road for 23 A/Bde to move directly on Tripoli." The exhausted Black Watch resting after filling in a crater were exhorted by the GOC 'Lorry-hop to Tripoli.'

The efficient CRE, Lt Col Sugden and the sappers worked non stop through the night of 21st to clear the demolitions. 1st Gordons, 1st Black Watch, 7th Argylls were used in turn filling in craters, making diversions and pushing vehicles and guns through and over the wadi beds.

By 2200hrs Hammerforce was on its way and Castelverde was entered unopposed at dawn. There were still more mines and two blown bridges over anti-tank ditches but by 0530hrs on 23rd January 40 RTR and 1st Gordons riding on tanks entered the main square of Tripoli. It had been a magnificent effort.

> Tremendous spirit of the Jocks, dead tired as they were. Those with petrol [wrote the GOC] pulled one or more vehicles behind them. Others swarmed over the tanks. It was clear that every man there was determined now to get to Tripoli by hook or by crook.

And they did.

Captain AL Aitkenhead, 128 Field Regt RA was woken upon the night of 22nd January to command an escort for General Wimberley to catch up with Hammerforce and enter Tripoli:

> Soon a convoy of two OP vehicles, white Scout cars with their usual crews, followed by the General in a jeep and a third Scout car moved off at a steady pace. It was quite eerie. It was a pitch dark night. The road was completely empty and not a sound to be heard.

Just before dawn the convoy proceeded into the City.

> We found our forces in the city centre in a jubilant mood. We left the General with the Gordons in the main square and found a corner in which to 'brew up', surprised at our good fortune to be sharing this historic moment. [Capt Aitkenhead]

The New Zealanders had expected to be first into Tripoli but it was probably a dead heat. The city in the early hours was dead, the occupants too frightened, hiding in their shuttered houses. The GOC ordered the pipers of the Gordons to play in the main square, the 'March Past' of all the Highland regiments. Monty and Oliver Leese entered Tripoli during the 23rd before noon for a ceremony as the local Mayor handed over the city to the 8th Army. The GOC 'rescued' some paint from the Italian hospital and large HD signs were erected the same day. Douglas Graham, the town Commandant, with HQ was in the citadel by the sea. The Gordons, Argylls and others worked in three shifts around the clock in the docks unloading huge cargoes of food and ammunition. Guards had to be provided on nine gates in the town wall, (Benito, Azizia, Taguira etc.) and key factories (Fiat, Lancia) railway station, wireless station, water-pumping station, hospitals and also guarded from looting! But new boots, tinned fruit, chocolate and cigarettes appeared in quantity from the dock areas! Lt Col Fausset-Farquhar, CO 1st Gordons:

> Last night we went to watch some of our men unloading stores in Tripoli harbour. Tank landing craft had been moved up to an improvised quay. The outline of the sturdy little ship stood out sharply against the tropical stars, the whole operation taking place beneath the towering walls of the old fort which governs Tripoli harbour. In the bowels of the LCT men, naked to the waist, their backs glistening with sweat, hoisted steel boxes filled with heavy shells on to roller runways. Gangs of men sent the boxes hurtling down the runways in a clattering rhythm to the waiting lorries. When the cargo was discharged the men went back to their billets singing as they marched through the silent streets of Tripoli.

And Norman Smart, *Daily Express* journalist:

> A piper marching up and down the Piazza Castello filling the morning air with the music of Scotland. Italians came on to their balconies above the square to take a peep at their conquerors. The Italian police with their polished boots, Sam Browne belts and revolvers who clicked out salutes to

British officers. British tank men brewing up their strong sweet tea in the middle of the square with water fetched from the fountain. The happy fighting men who whistled and sang in their success as they shaved and washed by their tanks.

And Field Marshal Alan Brooke wrote in his diary:

February 5th. PM and I stopped in Monty's camp. It was most interesting seeing Tripoli for the first time. The streets and house tops were lined with sentries who held back the local inhabitants. When we arrived on the main square and seafront we found there the bulk of the 51st HD formed up. The last time we had seen them was near Ismalia just after their arrival in the Middle East. They were pink and white - now they were bronzed warriors of many battles and of a victorious advance. I have seldom seen a finer body of men or one that looked prouder of being soldiers.

Sapper Bill Hughes and his friend Ron were posted to 275 Field Coy RE. When they reached Tripoli they were ordered to repaint tin hats and vehicles and blanco their webbing for the victory parade:

We sat stiffly to attention, rifles between our knees, in battle order and sat looking straight ahead as Winston Churchill took the salute. Four days later we were ordered into battle and doing everything possible to dirty the new paint and white webbing!

The Miramare Cinema was commandeered for the Balmoral Concert Party under Sgt Felix Barker and on the 28th played before Monty, Oliver Leese and an audience of 1800 and played again on 31st. NAAFI arrived but so did 'spit and polish'. Each battalion produced a quota of Highlanders (except for the Die Hards) for the grand Victory Parade, all equipment scrubbed a snowy white, plenty of boot polish, paint and HD signs. A hundred pipers followed behind General Wimberley, a composite RA formation, RE Coy, Middlesex, Div signals and a composite HD brigade (Black Watch, Seaforth, Gordons, Camerons and Argylls) under Brigadier George Murray. The rest of 8th Army wondered how the Highland kilts had arrived so promptly! Each Bren gun carrier had a Highland battle honour painted on it (Balaclava, Waterloo, Assaye or Territorial districts such as Buchan or Badenoch). The GOC's was 'Beaumont-Hamel - 1915.'

I have never felt prouder in all my life. As the Pipes and Drums played our famous Highland Regiments past in turn to the strains of 'Highland Laddie', Pilbroch O'dhomnuill-Dugh, the 'Cock of the North' and the 'Campbells are coming.' My heart was very full and there were tears in my eyes. However I [the GOC] was certainly in good company that day. I noticed the same in Alan Brooke's and as for Winston, the tears were running down his cheeks.

We drove slowly round the lines and then came back with the men cheering the PM all the way [Alan Brooke diary]. We then took up a position on a prepared stand and the whole division marched past with a bagpipe band playing. It was quite one of the most impressive sights I have ever seen. The whole division was most beautifully turned out and might have been in barracks for the last three months instead of having marched some 1200 miles and fought many battles. This had been a memorable day and one I shall never forget but what stands out clearest was the march past of the 51st Division. As I stood by Winston watching the division march past with the wild music of the pipes in my ears, I felt a lump rise in my throat and a tear down my face. I looked round at Winston and saw several tears on his face. For the first time I was beginning to live through the thrill of those first successes that were now rendering ultimate victory possible. The depth of those feelings can only be gauged in relation to the utter darkness of those early days of calamity when no single ray of hope could pierce the depth of gloom.

Black Watch, Tripoli Victory Parade

The next day the New Zealanders had their parade outside Tripoli and HD lent them their Massed Pipes and Drums.

On his return home Churchill told the House of Commons: "I have never in my life seen troops march with the style or air of the Desert Army. Talk about spit and polish the Highland and New Zealand Divisions paraded after their immense ordeal as if they had come out of Wellington barracks."

The Black Watch beat 128 Field Regt RA 1-0 in the Divisional Football Championship. Sightseeing in Tripoli was allowed for the majority of the division bivouacked outside, although shops and market stalls sold poor quality goods. But fresh fruit and vegetables were now available. Lt Neil McCallum 5/7th Gordons described the local wine, "sour, purple of exceeding coarseness, harsh on the palate, stained the teeth and lips," and the city, "mixed architecture - Moorish,

Turkish, Arab and Fascist, in a melange as striking as a Hollywood set, a lavish stage prop, slightly the worse for wear." He described Monty's big conference on 9th February: "We gathered in the Miramare Cinema. The auditorium was crowded and on the stage was a notice 'No Smoking'. The stage was brilliantly lit from the sides and above. In this setting he stood dapper, neat and alone. His cockiness, his unbounded confidence have long ago become a byword. All this is part of his success as a general. 'Rommel has the jitters' he said." Later Monty wrote a forward to a pamphlet about the HD. "The Division is splendidly led and fought magnificently. It is now a veteran division skilled in battle and with a morale that is right on the top line."

Many short refresher courses were set up as reinforcements came in. A divisional piping competition was held and set-piece battle demonstrations held for all the top brass to see; at which US General Patton was not impressed! A divisional battle school trained or retrained the young leaders at company and platoon level. On 11th February the GOC took all his senior officers back to Homs to view the savage battlegrounds of the Battle of the Hills.

> Looking back on it all, I think my getting of the HD to Tripoli in a week was probably the best bit of soldiering I ever accomplished in all my 30 odd years of soldiering. 250 miles at an average speed of 35 miles per day. One sharp little battle at Corradini and several advance guard actions. We captured 250 POW, caused a lot of casualties, crossed six A/Tank ditches, took 10 guns but lost 350 battle casualties. We filled in over 100 road craters and made ten deviations around blown road bridges. I had really accomplished quite a feat of arms.

So wrote the GOC. Yes, he had indeed.

Well might Churchill tell the HD: "You have altered the face of the war in a most remarkable way. The fame of the Desert Army has spread throughout the world. When a man is asked after the war, what he did, it will be sufficient to say, 'I marched and fought with the Desert Army.'"

16

The Battle of Medenine: "a cheerless spot"

Rommel and Von Arnim decided to hold the 8th Army in the east and defeat the inexperienced British 1st Army and the Americans in the north-west. Montgomery was now ordered to take as much pressure as possible from the 'green' troops in Southern Tunisia, just as the US II corps was driven back in disorder to Tebessa. West of Tripoli the *90th Light* and *164 Infantry* divisions fought with their usual skill, but on 15th February, 7th Armoured Div - the Desert Rats - cleared 15 *Panzer* out of Ben Gardane and to the outskirts of Medenine.

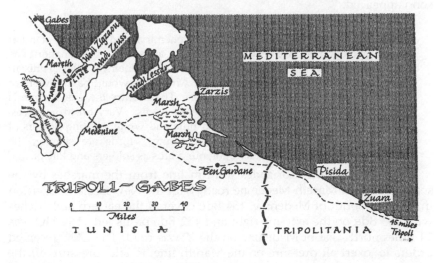

Medenine, Mareth Line

So from the relative fleshpots of Tripoli, HD on 12th February set off to war again, marching twelve miles a day as TCVs and petrol were still in short supply. In pouring rain 5/7th Gordons crossed the Tunisian border with their pipers playing 'Cock o' the North' in front of the newsreel cameramen of the Army Film and Photographic unit. The first time there was no film in the cameras! Lt Felix Barker:

> Ten kilometres beyond Pisida we relieved the Queens Brigade. It was a cheerless spot, that narrow strip of hard desert sandwiched between the sea and the salt marshes, grimly reminiscent of all the horrors of Libya. Alarming stories of a fabulously strong defensive line - 'the Maginot of North Africa' were beginning to circulate. Mareth, or some such name" and later, "Two mines that morning were to strike the Bn perhaps the most serious blow of the campaign. Five officers [Lt Col Saunders, Capt Herbert (Middlesex) and Major Barlow (FOO), Lts Rhodes, McAndrew] and three ORs were wounded and Major Cochrane killed. It was a nightmare of mines.

From one crater the RE removed sixteen S-mines and on the road to Ben Gardane the sappers lost 13 men of whom six were killed. Lt Col Jock Sorel-Cameron now took command of 5/7 Gordons.

On 17th Oliver Leese the Corps Commander held a conference and 50 RTR came under command of HD with orders to concentrate east of Medenine. The CRE Lt Col Sugden perhaps unwittingly reconnoitred the outskirts of the Mareth line alone in a solitary jeep. The next day the remainder of 153 Bde appeared at Ben Gardane with 5/7th Gordons in Zarzis, a pleasant area where Arab vendors of eggs and chickens soon appeared.

Lt Neil McCallum's, 5/7th Gordons diary:

> 24th Feb. It is common knowledge that the enemy intend to make a stand at Mareth. Montgomery, we hear is pleased. Our attitude is of resignation. The easy chasing mile after mile could not last. The enemy's other Tunisian campaign against the First Army and the Americans would be a travesty of all strategy unless a stand were made here. The country towards Mareth is undulating. Sandy ridges and bush covered wadis. Very green in places. The scrub is full of flowers, yellow and blue and white, exciting flowers of pure colour. The air is suffused with spring. Birds are singing, the refreshing magic of spring underlining our status as soldiers and killers.

By 26/27th all three brigades were in line from the marshes by the sea to the main Mareth-Medenine road, with the New Zealand Division in position south of Medenine. 154 Bde covered the eastern approaches with 153 Bde on the extreme right and 152 Bde on its left. Div HQ was 14 miles north-east of Medenine on the Zarzis road. The GOC received orders to 'exert all pressure on the Mareth line, to take pressure off the Americans where situation is grave.' HD now had a firm base along the Wadi Zessar from where a panorama of the Mareth line six miles away could be seen. Three more wadis ahead meandered into the sea, the Melah, Zeuss and the Zigzau, which the enemy had made into a substantial anti-tank ditch running south-west to the Matmata hills. The 5th Camerons and REs spent two days making a causeway over the Wadi Zessar, known as Cameron causeway.

The sappers had a dangerous and unpleasant role both in laying 'friendly' minefields and in clearing 'hostile' minefields.

> With the enemy defending the Mareth line very strongly we layed down a minefield to protect the infantry in the line. As there was a range of fairly high sandhills in front of the German line we were able to complete this in daylight. I [Sapper Bill Hughes, 275 Field Coy RE] was in a party laying our stretch and with mortar shells coming over we weren't messing about. My pal Ron and I got the job of laying the trip wire against the enemy, who were firing the 10 barrelled mortar, nicknamed 'Moaning Minnie.' Our lorry came back again with 500 mines on board. Without any warning at all with a tremendous explosion the lorry blew up with 500 mines on it. We dived to the ground pulling our tin hats over the backs of our necks and the air was full of shrapnel, picks, shovels, coils of barbed wire. We cautiously went round the sandhill between us and the lorry to be met with the most horrible sight; dead and dying all over the place, arms, legs, heads scattered around There was a huge crater where the lorry had stood... When we went out we were a party of 24, when we went back we were down to eight. In camp we who had survived were given a meal and sent straight out again laying mines so that our nerves didn't crack. Extremely sad and

trying days.

When General Wimberley visited 1st Black Watch the order was given for all ranks to leave cover and to stand to attention, which they did. Pte Roy Green just relieved from 12 hours on duty at the telephone exchange lay at the bottom of his slit trench under a blanket. "There was an almighty bang and smoke and dust. A single (?88mm) shell landed about eight feet in front. No less than three men lay dead and five more wounded as they stood to attention. The jeep with the General disappeared quickly."

General Wimberley drove 140 miles to see the Corps Commander, who recorded: "Douglas W. Has just been in - very well. He was like a terrier, surrounded with Tommy guns and petrol cans and straining at the leash."

It was now known that several Axis divisions had been moved from the American front to help defend their Mareth position and when the GOC visited 7th Argylls on 1st March he warned them of an enemy attack 'in about three days time.' The divisional front was an extended 22,000 yards with four major strong points selected with extensive minefields and wire in front. The Die Hards were active every night with harassing shoots and on 3rd March No 12 platoon claimed 60 victims. On the 2nd and 3rd two half-hearted night attacks were made on 153 Bde on the right flank losing 120 casualties in the process. As insurance Oliver Leese ordered up 201 Guards Bde from Tripoli 150 miles away. He visited General Wimberley and asked him: "Are you happy in your disposition to meet a really heavy armoured attack on Wadi Zessar?" The GOC asked for more anti-tank guns, within 24 hours a whole regiment of anti-tank guns appeared. "What a wonderful little commander I was serving under, in Monty." Monty sent a personal message, "The enemy is now advancing to attack us. This is because he is caught like a rat in a trap and he is hitting out in every direction, trying to gain time to stave off the day of final defeat in North Africa."

In the one day battle that followed on 6th March, 126 Field Regt (and the other field regiments) fired 6750 rounds on no less than 42 regimental targets plus battery and troop targets. Most of these shells landed amongst the unfortunate *90th Light* and some on *126 Spezia Division*.

No attacks came in on the 4th or 5th but the Battle of Medenine started in the morning of the 6th with a determined attack by three Panzer divisions which fell mainly on the Queen's Brigade of the Desert Rats on the left flank. 153 Bde were never engaged but 154 Bde on the left suffered a 'minor' attack. 7th Black Watch had previously withdrawn from Wadis Hachana and Moussa to a stronger position astride the Wadi Zessar. Two companies of infantry were seen off comfortably by Bren guns and Lt Tobbut, the gunner FOO. But heavier attacks came in on 1st Black Watch and 7th Argylls on the left and on the right. Mortar and artillery fire dealt with the former, from *126 Spezia* and *90th Light* divisions. No. 7 Platoon of the Die Hards had a good shoot against 200 enemy infantry, but they infiltrated into the Wadi Hachana, then the Wadi Moussa. This went on all day and at 1600hrs a more forceful attack came in backed by Stuka dive bombing. It was fast and furious whilst it lasted. The Argylls lost 30 casualties but a counter-attack was completely successful against *90th Light* who left 7.5cm, spandau and Breda guns behind as they retreated. Other booty appeared, 'lots of abandoned US cigs, chocs captured by Afrika Korps and recaptured by 8th Army.'

Rommel lost 52 tanks mainly to the infantry anti-tank guns of the Queens and 201 Guards brigades and corps DF artillery concentrations. But 'cornered rats' can be dangerous. The main battle of Mareth which followed was a brutal, slogging match, at one stage very finely balanced.

17
The Battle of Mareth
"confusion reigned everywhere"

The Afrika Korps after their expensive sortie withdrew to the Mareth line defences. On the 7th the GOC talked to Major General 'Crasher' Nichols, GOC of 50th Northumbrian Division who were to make the main attack on Mareth. Two days later Monty held a big conference to discuss his plans. "On the 5th March Rommel addressed his troops in the mountains overlooking our positions and said that if he did not take Medenine by the 6th March and force 8th Army to withdraw, the days of the Axis forces in North Africa were numbered. The next day he attacked the 8th Army... Forward to Tunis. Drive the enemy into the sea." Since the breakout with Supercharge, HD casualties had been 385. They were now ordered to make ground in the north opposite the forts of Ksibia (Point 42) and Zarat (Point 39) north of the Wadi Zeuss and establish a firm base for 50th Division to make the main assault over the formidable anti-tank ditch. If all went well 4th Indian Div and 'Ricky' Richards 23rd Armoured Bde would be pushed through. 201 Guards Bde were to attack the 'Horseshoe' hills feature in the south-west of the Mareth defences. 7th Armoured and the NZ Division would make a long detour south-west then north to try to outflank the Mareth line, via the Matmata hills in the Gabes gap.

From their arrival in front of the Mareth line on 23rd February most units were under daily enemy shelling, frequent air attacks and some ground attacks for 34 days.

Assuming all went according to plan, HD would follow after the 4th Indian penetration and with 'Mace Force' combined infantry/armour push north towards Tunis. Before the attack General Wimberley noted:

> Now in earlier battles it was generally the practice for the leading waves of attacking infantry in the moonlight to walk straight through the minefields and take in their stride the casualties involved when mines blew up under their feet. Behind them came the sappers who then made gaps through which the supporting guns and tanks could follow. We had by now decided this was a foolish way to attack a heavily mined position. It was better to make a narrow gap under cover of a protective barrage, using Sappers and Scorpions [flail tanks] protected by infantry. Through this gap the infantry could walk without encountering heavy casualties from AP mines and then the gap could be widened, behind them for vehicles, anti-tank guns to follow.

The Division had been relatively inactive for over two weeks. The Die Hards and the three field regiments RA carried out harassing tasks. The infantry battalions in the line sent out patrols practically every night. Amenities had caught up. A NAAFI canteen arrived, a mobile cinema showed Dorothy Lamour nightly in 'The Fleet's In' and one 'coup' was 138 eggs for half a pound of tea. Every night formations of 18 American Mitchell bombers flew westwards - once a bomb load was dropped on the Black Watch causing 13 casualties. On 15th March the GOC briefed all HD officers down to company commanders on the forthcoming battle, including details of the ill-fated Wadi Zigzaou anti-tank ditch with its six foot vertical wall.

On the night of 16/17th Brigadier Graham's 153 Bde attacked at 2330hrs, as did 69 Bde of 50 Div and 201 Guards Bde in three 'probing' moves forward but the latter lost many casualties to mines.

Major Lamb of 276 Field Coy RE reported a gap of 810 yards in the minefields ahead which 5/7th Gordons tackled. They had had two rehearsals beforehand, one by day, one by night. The Scorpions negotiated an Italian bridge, swept 300 yards through a minefield and the leader broke down. The second Scorpion also broke down, the third succeeded. So 'B' Coy walked at 0300 on to their objective. Capt Napier and 'C' Coy had a more difficult time. Their first Scorpion crossed, the second stuck and held up the third. Spandaus made life very unpleasant. Capt Douglas and three ORs were wounded by a mine. At 0500 the CO and Capt Dey were knocked out by the same mine, so Major Hay (1st Gordons) took over command. Dawn found both companies in the minefield, three hours behind schedule but by 0900 were on the two hills they had to take. There they spotted 30 Italian soldiers emerging sleepily from their slit trenches before rifle and Brengun fire rudely disturbed them. The whole sector of 153 Bde was under heavy shellfire on 18th and 19th. On the 20th the Northumbrian Division attacked and soon captured five strongpoints, but infantry and tanks of 21st Panzer Div counter-attacked strongly, recovered three of the strongpoints and knocked out most of the Valentines of 50th RTR. Casualties in 50th Div were extremely heavy and the situation was precarious, as they could not get their anti-tank guns across the wadi, nor of course could tank support get over.

5th Seaforth in anti-tank ditch, Wadi Zigzaoug

The GOC was ordered to help and two battalions of 152 Bde were sent up to hold a sector of the Zigzaoug anti-tank defence ditch. 5th Camerons and 5th Seaforth were the unfortunate battalions selected. It was a very confusing situation. 5th Camerons were first ordered to send up one company to come under command of 5th Seaforths, then two companies, and finally the whole battalion. Brigadier Murray briefed the Camerons who with a troop of anti-tank guns and a platoon of Die Hards were to move through the 5th Seaforths minefield; turn right, occupy the 1000 yard vacant space in the vast anti-tank ditch; then send forward two companies 500 yards to scupper the enemy posts interfering with 50 Div's crossing. The Adjutant, Capt Pringle-Pattison led 'B' and 'C' Coys forward and immediately discovered that the vacant space in the anti-tank ditch was only 500 yards in length. The enemy fired starshells and the Camerons were pinned down and the entrance to the Seaforth minefield was shelled.

So 'A' Coy were ordered back just as enemy defensive fire fell on the
two companies in the ditch, and the Divisional artillery fell short,
landing on the Camerons. Packed like sardines heavy casualties were
inevitable. By dawn every radio set in the battalion had been put out
of action. Shelling continued for nearly 20 hours and the Camerons had
121 casualties including eight officers and nothing to show for it. The
5th Seaforth had relieved 7th Green Howards in the ditch 24 hours
earlier and were just to the left of the Cameron's sector. Alastair
Borthwick:

> Except for an occasional dog-leg it ran straight throughout its length. The
> wall nearest was vertical, about six feet deep, capped by a parapet of
> varying height and thickness. It could only be defended by men lying on
> top of the wall, under the parapet with nothing but empty air to protect
> them from shells and bombs bursting behind them. The ground was like
> iron. Individual slits did not exist. The ditch was one big slit and the
> whole battalion was in it.

The Indian Division should have been guarding the left flank, but
weren't. The Seaforth watched 50th Div with supporting Valentines
attack on the Ouerzi and Ksiba defences. But later, the shelling
increased "small and then bigger and bigger parties of khaki clad
figures came filtering back over the slopes on our right. Clearly all was
not well with 50th Div." Corporal Parkinson, 'D' Coy had two shells
land within a few feet of him as he lay on the parapet:

> I landed on top of CSM Aitken and Mr Gammie. I was dazed and startled
> by the suddenness of it all... blood stank in my nostrils. I grabbed the CSM
> by the tunic and shook him but his head dropped to one side... he must
> have died instantaneously. Confusion resigned everywhere. I sat where I
> was, and wept. Lt Gammie tried to speak but in two minutes he was dead.
> Two of the stretcher-bearers were killed outright also. The third was badly
> hit. L/Sgt Bert Brookes and Pat Davidson were hit in the lung by shrapnel;
> Capt Robertson wounded in the legs. Of the 16 men in Coy HQ only three
> escaped injury. My blanket was used to cover the dead.

During the night, 5th Camerons were seen in their attack. "When we
saw our guns change from HE to smoke we knew they were in trouble.
When daylight [on the 23rd] came we could see their wounded and
dead lying out on the bare bullet-swept plain and there was nothing we
could do for them."

The Seaforth had nearly a hundred casualties and the two HD
battalions were taken out of the appalling Wadi Zigzaou by 0300 hrs on
24th March under cover of a smokescreen.

The HD had been ordered to simulate an attack on the Mareth line to
prevent the enemy thinning their line and sending reinforcements not
only to limit the American advance, but also to block Monty's famous
left hook which in the event decided the Mareth battle. So 152 and 154

Bdes were ordered to send out strong fighting patrols. 5th Black Watch put in a two company attack on 'Carrier Hill' backed by a Corps barrage, starting at 2100hrs on 24th. Unfortunately many of the shells dropped on the start line and 'A' Coy lost 60 casualties to 'friendly fire'. Major Guthrie was badly wounded, Capt Higgins and many others killed or wounded. The Corps Commander sent them a special message of sympathy. "It speaks worlds for their discipline and esprit de corps that the battalion reached their objectives and captured 30 (Italian) POW after being shelled heavily by our own guns on the start line." And the GOC: "It was certainly a fine performance by 'Chick' Thomson's men." 7th Argylls sent out a strong fighting patrol to mortar the Fort Ksiba Ouest on the night of 25th but in mine clearance operations lost 14 men. Both Gordons battalions were active on the 26th and 27th, drawing machine-gun fire and mortar fire. Early on the 28th patrols from several battalions reported that the enemy had withdrawn. Indeed on the night of 25/26th one patrol of 152 Bde had penetrated a mile beyond the Wadi Zigzaou.

The left hook had drawn *15 Panzer Div* from the Mareth defences. 7th Armoured, the New Zealanders and 8th Armoured Bde broke through on the afternoon of 26th and fanned out towards El Hamma and Gabes.

The Battle for Mareth was over - a classic rather brutal Monty victory as 50 Div (and to a lesser extent HD) tried to battle their way forward against a professional defence. And then the long but dramatic and highly successful 'Mareth left hook.' The GOC praised his three Brigade Majors - James Scott Noble, Bill Bradford and Harry Cumming-Bell, three key staff appointments in HD.

Lt Felix Barker 5/7th Gordons: "The actual attack [Mareth] when it came was regarded by most of the battalion as 'the next worst thing to Alamein.'" And Alastair Borthwick, 5th Seaforth: "We left eleven dead in the ditch and carried out the wounded... the anti-tank ditch will never be forgotten so long as there is a man alive who lay in it."

18

The Battle of Wadi Akarit
"infantry had a gruelling time"

The three brigades crossed the Wadi Zigzaou but were held up by minefields on the far side. The GOC noted: "Much struck by strength of the Mareth defences, plenty of concrete, complete communication trenches, the forward saps reminded me of 1914-18 war. In the anti-tank ditch, the debris of war, still unburied dead of my

Seaforth and Camerons still lying where they had fallen." The advance to Gabes was a race and the Bren carriers of 5th Camerons led 152 Bde and Mace Force in as the New Zealanders arrived from the west at 1305 hours on the 29th. HD was given 48 hours to rest and reorganise around Gabes, with 153 Bde six miles east at Wadi Mersitt.

General Montgomery intended to take the port of Sfax before 15th April. But 20 miles beyond Gabes was a natural 'bottleneck' defensive position. From the coast north-west to an area of lakes and marshes runs for 12 miles the formidable Wadi Akarit dominated by the steep Roumana hills. Monty planned a major assault again with 201 Guards Bde under command of HD on the coast road to Sfax then 50th and 4th Indian Divisions inland. There were the usual minefields, an anti-tank ditch, the Wadi Akarit itself, and behind it and to the left, the mile long Roumana ridge rising sharply to 1600 feet.

The whole approaches were under enemy observation. The GOC and General 'Gertie' Tucker, GOC 4th Indian Div were both unhappy with the initial plan of attack. General Oliver Leese visited his divisional commanders practically every day and a new plan was made. On the extreme left 4th Indian would make a silent night attack deep into the hills to seize Djebel Tebaga Fatnassa. On HD immediate left 50th Div's task was to make a bridgehead over the Wadi and anti-tank ditch west of Roumana for the New Zealanders and armour to penetrate the defences. The HD were to take and hold the ridge, make a second bridgehead over the anti-tank ditch and Wadi Akarit east of Roumana and the Guards would protect the right flank.

The two Gordons battalions were sent forward to contact some 2000 yards from the Wadi Akarit with 1st on the right, 5/7th on left. Lt Felix Barker, 5/7th Gordons:

There was an awful feeling of endlessness about the campaign in North Africa. Each battle seemed as if it would be the last and then wasn't. Everything would be concentrated against an enemy defensive position, but no sooner was it taken than another, Hydra-like, took its place a little further on.

On 30th March battledress was withdrawn and khaki drill issued and on the Scottish Festival of 'Hunt t'Gowk' on 1st April, 5th Black Watch exercised with 50 RTR's Valentines and had time for bathing parties. The next day the 7th Argylls harbour party leaving the Oasis de Usseps failed to take the correct turning off the main road, drove into the enemy lines and had 22 men captured. When the GOC held a sand table conference on the 4th to explain to a hundred officers (down to company commanders) his plan of attack, it was rudely interrupted not only by long-range shelling but by Jerry fighter planes strafing Div HQ.

"It was a complex plan, about the most difficult job we had ever had," noted the GOC. The infantry Bns were still short of men after recent casualties. When Lt Fraser Burrows returned to 5th Camerons from hospital in time for the attack on Wadi Akarit, he found "for the first time we had to deal with some Jocks who went missing but turned up next morning alive and well with the excuse 'we got lost.'" Nearly everyone suffered from 'desert wounds' and minor ill-health.

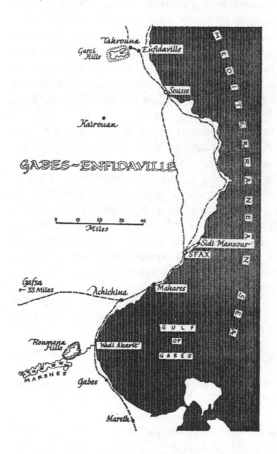

"The appalling conditions of the desert were not entirely over, desert sores," wrote Captain Ian Cameron, 7th Argylls, "had been a source of great discomfort. Such illnesses as jaundice, sandfly fever and dysentery were quite common. Flies were the root of all trouble. If one settled for a second on the smallest scratch a desert septic sore soon formed. Food contaminated by flies caused dysentery."

152 Bde was ordered to capture Djebel Roumana (with from left to right 5th Camerons, 5th Seaforth, 2nd Seaforth) and keep touch with 50th Div on immediate left. 154 Bde would punch a hole in the defences on the coastal plain. 7th Argylls would make a vehicle gap through minefields then over the anti-tank ditch with 7th Black Watch coming through: then turn left-handed behind another artillery barrage, move westwards, rolling up the defences until they had linked up with 2nd Seaforth on Point 112 on Roumana. 'Ricky' Richards 23rd A/Bde would tow sixteen vital 6-pdr anti-tank guns behind their Valentines as the usual lorries were easily knocked-out by shellfire. Six Scorpion flail tanks were also available. The Die Hards had a platoon of machine-gun

with each of the attacking battalions. The General ordered all attacking Jocks to carry the St Andrews cross of Scotland on their backs, white 4" x 2" rifle cleaning flannel. Unfortunately there was a shortage of shells for the field regiments which limited concentrations and barrages.

On the night of the 5th the attacking battalions moved to their assembly positions. Each man dug his own slit trench in which he lay for several hours rest, then ate his meal as he rested. The starting lines of white tape were silently laid out by compass bearing, pegged in their place as HD had done so many times on the long route from Alamein. Monty sent Wimberley a message: "Good luck to you tonight. If you get your objectives the break out should be a certainty."

Wimberley's small TAC HQ was far forward and through field glasses could see the whole divisional front and for 24 hours controlled the battle. The Chief of Signals Lt Col James Cochrane had laid out telephone wire to 153 Bde HQ, to GSO1 at Main Div HQ, to the CRA and to 'Ricky' Richards 23 A/Bde.

Sapper Gordon Mackay, 275 Field Coy RE:

> As Engineers our task was to make a crossing point over the anti-tank ditch which stretched the whole length of the front at the approach to a valley at the very western end of a rocky range of hills (Roumana Ridge) which ran from the coast. The defending troops, Italian and German could observe any movement. An apron of barbed wire had been laid over a thickly sown minefield. Behind this lay the anti-tank ditch. 15 Sappers took three hours standing on the parapets working frantically shovelling the stony soil into the ditch. The Seaforth infantry clambered over the rocky slopes towards their objectives under constant machine-gun fire, rifle fire and mortaring. When the Nebelwerfer 'Moaning Minnie' mortars were fired at a very high trajectory, as we heard the barrel organ beginning to play we quickly jumped back into the ditch to await the terrifying sound and multi explosions. At 0730 the first tank crossed but 88's had now targeted this narrow entrance to the minefield and the ditch beyond. Our officer, Lt Tom Duncan was wounded by a piece of shrapnel, hurriedly evacuated by the Seaforth stretcher bearers.

5th Seaforth crossed their tape at 0330 hrs, 'C' and 'A' leading on a compass bearing of 318 degrees. The long grass was wet with dew, and the initial 2000 yards was at the rate of 100 yards in four minutes. "No one spoke and probably few of us were even thinking much. Before a battle there might be heart searching and worry, but apathy was apt to take over once the start line was crossed leaving only a tightness in the pit of the stomach and a blank mind. One just plodded on," wrote Alastair Borthwick. 5th Seaforth reached the foot of Point 198, the highest part of the ridge with the barrage climbing the rocks ahead. Behind were 2nd Seaforth who were to swing right-handed and go for the east end of the ridge to link up with the 154 Bde attack. Men scrambled up the rocky heights and by 0545hrs the Seaforth were on the crest of Roumana and 2nd Seaforth had secured a hill much further to the right. So far so good.

5th Camerons on the extreme left advanced at 0330hrs over the open plain, 100 yards in two minutes, a rate too slow which caused bunching. 'D' Coy on the left, 'A' on the right with the objective of scaling Roumana and consolidating in the wadis north of it. 'C' was in reserve and 'B' plus sappers were to move to the gap between Roumana and the foothills of Tebaga Fatnassa, seize it, clear it of mines and make a tank crossing over the anti-tank ditch there. Soon 400 Italians were made POW, the leading Coys swarmed over the Djebel whilst 'B' cleared their 'gap' and consolidated on the left hand bump of Roumana.

The huge barrage started at 0415, which partly disguised the noise of the Scorpion flail tanks and eight Valentine tanks towing 241 Anti-Tank Bty 6-pdr guns. Despite intense shelling the minefield gapping and anti-tank ditch bridging were completed by midday. Captain Ian Cameron, the Navigating Officer, 7th Argylls, led 'B' Coy on the right, 'A' on the left at 0515 hrs, across 600 yards of open ground, through the minefield using Scorpion made gaps. With the help of captured Italian POW 'C' Coy climbed the ten foot high anti-tank ditch. 'A' captured the ditch and two posts beyond it, and 'B' a long sand hill. At 0800 7th Black Watch came through.

From his eyrie the GOC noted, "0550 5 Camerons/5 Seaforth seized top of Roumana. 0630 2 Seaforth attacking well along the tops towards Pt 112 behind barrage. Best of all George Murray's 152 Bde made vehicle gap through minefield, anti-tank ditch on left boundary, cleared for tanks and anti-tank guns being towed. Excellent news. Lorne Campbell's Argylls over both Wadi and anti-tank ditch, reached their bridgehead objective. 0800 153 Bde have taken 2000 POW mainly Italians, going splendidly my spirits rose accordingly. But 50 Div on immediate left failed to cross anti-tank ditch."

Lt Col Thicknesse, CO 126 Field Regt RA:

> Thousands of Italians attempted to surrender while the struggle was going on between British and German troops. An extraordinary spectacle like a bewildered football crowd that has strayed on to the field in the middle of a match. Many very gallant things were done on that day and there were heavy casualties. It is probably true to say that the 8th Army reached the top of its curve at that time. 126 Field Regt fired 7000 rounds mainly on DF tasks and calls from FOOs. One FOOs carrier went up on a minefield one man killed, the others badly shaken. He then carried a wireless set on his back, shortly afterwards took command of the infantry company he was supporting and led them on to their objective.

Captain Bishop 297 Bty was wounded four times during the day as FOO in the 7th Black Watch bridgehead and was cited by his CO for the DSO.

The GOC's diary continues: "Rory Horne's 2 Seaforth reached Point 112 but lost it to German counter-attack, heavy fighting, bursting mortar bombs, losing ground" Both the leading 2nd Seaforth company commanders were wounded so the Adjutant Capt Mellandy took over. Lt Col Horne led three desperate attacks on the ridge. Major Gilmore led the other two companies but try as they might, 2nd Seaforth could not recapture Pt 112.

"0900 50 Div still failed to take first main objective. Argyll gap only 8-10 feet wide. 0930 'Jumbo' Stirling got final objective against end of Roumana. Unless 2 Seaforth retake Pt 112, 7th Black Watch will be in nasty situation."

The German *90th Light* had placed their vulnerable Italian allies in the front line whilst they prepared a savage counter-attack to drive HD down from the heights back into the plains. This fell on the six battalions during the day.

The 7th Black Watch were tasked with passing through 7th Argylls and to continue the attack north-west on the far side of the ditch until contact was made with 2nd Seaforth. Although the barrage of smoke shells fell on their forming-up area across the anti-tank ditch, quite soon 1000 Italian POW were put in the bag. But heavy artillery, mortar and machine-gun fire decimated the right forward company, all officers and most NCOs being knocked-out. Major Hopwood the 2 i/c took command and led it forward again. At 0930 the battalion was on its final objective. Many enemy trenches provided good cover. Supporting tanks got across the ditch below but due to heavy anti-tank fire could not get forward to support. But early in the afternoon tanks and infantry of *90th Light Division* over-ran the front two 7th Black Watch companies. A 1st Black Watch company was sent up as reinforcement.

"The Argylls were under severe attack. Six tanks made an effort to assist them but all were gutted by the 88s. At about 4pm we set off to reinforce the crumbling line - it was a nightmare. The Germans threw everything at us and we suffered casualties but we made it eventually." Pte Roy Green saw a three foot sand bank and moved close to it. He was ordered to move past it to the right. He ignored the order. His friend Corporal Richardson took his place and was immediately wounded, later died, from an 88mm shell. But the battle on the Roumana ridge raged all day and at 2330 hrs the Brigadier advised 7th Black Watch to withdraw 1000 yards and establish closer contact with 7th Argylls.

Major Jack Davidson, OC 'D' Coy 5th Seaforth was their lynch-pin in the battle to hold Point 198 on which the success of the whole battle largely depended. They started with a strength of 40 and after surprising a hundred pyjama-clad Italians reached the top of Roumana only 20 strong. At 0545 they dug-in amongst the rocks and an hour later an avalanche of mortar bombs fell on them. For eight hours they played a vicious game of hide and seek until Capt George Willock from Battalion HQ appeared with a Bren. Despite showers of stick grenades they hung on grimly until 5th Black Watch arrived at 1800 hrs to take over. It was touch and go. Major Davidson was awarded the DSO for this gallant action, but 5th Seaforth lost 128 casualties that day including ten officers.

Pte Geoff Jones, I Section 5th Seaforth:

> The best part of *126th Regt* of the *Spezia Div* were prisoners before they knew what had happened. When the German crack division, *90th Light* launched the counter-attack it looked as if they were going to succeed. It was a battle of machine-gun, mortars and rifles at close range. Things were looking really bad when across the plain behind us came the Black Watch in open formation to give us a hand. The battle raged all day, our artillery laying terrific rolling barrages across the enemy lines. Six Junkers 88's came over to try to give us a hammering but they were all smashed to bits in mid air by the finest piece of Ack-Ack shooting I've ever seen.

At 0530 the next morning the IO and his section climbed Roumana, "Dead Germans lying everywhere, minus heads, limbs, most of them 17 or 18."

By the morning of the 7th, the 7th Black Watch had suffered 191 casualties including 11 officers (and 73 missing) but they had captured 46 guns, 14 mortars and 70 machine guns, nearly all Italian. The four rifle companies could only muster 135 between them and the total battalion strength was down to 412.

The Argylls also had a very difficult day. At about 1300hrs, 18 RAF bombers dropped their bombs on 'A' Coy. Intense shelling and mortaring of the key minefield gap caused many casualties and ambulances were hit deliberately by AP shells. The first counter-attack came in at 1600 hrs with eight enemy tanks and infantry, but the divisional artillery broke them up. Two hours later a two battalion attack with tanks came in, forced 'A' Coy back 300 yards and also forced 7th Black Watch to withdraw. Major MacDougall rallied 'C' Coy HQ (CSM, batman, clerk, runner and wireless operator) and they charged as he shouted "No surrender 'C' Coy!" and took 12 POW!

The Argylls held out, having suffered 11 officer casualties, 150 ORs. Lt Col Lorne Campbell (pictured right) who already had two DSOs was awarded the Victoria Cross for his bravery and skilful command despite being wounded in the neck by a mortar bomb. The Argylls took 700 POW; and 21 guns, 10 mortars and 33 machine-guns were part of their 'booty.'

When 5th Black Watch came to the rescue from their position as Divisional reserve, Lt Col Thomson realised that General Wimberley was in a considerable 'flap' about the outcome of the battle for the Ridge. By the end of the day they too had suffered 76 casualties including six officers, with 'B' and 'C' companies losing many men. Lt Melville stormed to the top of the ridge beside the Seaforth, under shell, mortar, rifle and grenade fire and later died of his wounds.

On the far left the forward companies of 5th Camerons fought with gallantry against the *90th Light* in the wadis. 'D' Coy were reduced to 20 men under Lt Ainslie and so too was 'A' under Lt Stewart. When the latter was wounded, Ainslie took command of a combined 'D' and 'A' with a total strength of 20. CSM Macrae led three bayonet charges, personally killing nine of the enemy. By nightfall the Djebel was firmly held but the Camerons had lost eight officers and nearly 100 ORs. Ainslie was awarded the MC, as was Lt Stewart also, on his return from POW camp at the end of the war.

The GOC at the height of the battle asked Julian Gascoigne, Brigadier of 201 Guards Brigade on the far right to simulate an attack to draw off

enemy troops opposite the Argylls, Seaforth and Black Watch. Oliver Leese had told the GOC that Point 112 must be held by first light. It was.

HQ 152 Bde reported at 0245 on the 7th that the enemy were withdrawing, and by 0500 the GOC was trying to construct a Divisional Advance Guard to follow up.

Wimberley praised his CRA whose three field regiments gave magnificent defensive fire when the heavy counter-attacks were coming in. The Die Hards suffered too, 'D' Coy lost 38 and Lt Cross won the MC helping 5th Seaforth. The GOC noted that it was fortunate that HD faced the Italians in the dawn battle and not the Germans. "It was a different story when *90th Light* and *15th Panzer* counter-attacked." He sent a message to his Jocks: "Thanks one and all for the gallantry, uncomplaining cheerfulness, endurance and skill that Scotland's troops have once again shown the British Army that they are still 'second to none.'"

The battle of Wadi Akarit raged for 24 hours non-stop and battle honours went to the Black Watch, Seaforth, Camerons and Argylls. Later on at the end of the North African campaign in a Divisional Piping competition, the best tune selected was 'Wadi Akarit.' In Monty's memoirs he wrote: "My troops fought magnificently particularly 51 and 4 Indian Divs who hung on to the key localities they had taken." The Divisional Intelligence summary No 135 stated: "There is no doubt that the day marked the fiercest fighting that the Divison had experienced in this campaign... Our infantry had a gruelling time and several units suffered very heavy casualties..."

19
A Last Lap: "hopes were high"

The two Gordon battalions had but minor roles in the Wadi Akarit battle and so with 'Ricky' Richards 23 A/Bde now led the advance. Oliver Leese had ordered HD, with 201 Guards Bde to follow-up, advance and capture Sfax. 'Spear' Force included 5th Black Watch, RA, RE, followed by the rest of 153 Bde under Douglas Graham. 'Ricky' commanded in daylight, HD took over at night covering the tanks. "We regarded Ricky as one of our Brigadiers," noted the GOC.

Lt John McGregor briefs 'B' Coy, 5th Black Watch at Gabes, April 1943

It was a slow advance, narrow tortuous roads, mined and defended. Corps ordered at 6pm on 6th: "Not to worry about pressing on!" 152 Bde was left behind without MT. 5th Camerons had a drill parade on 8th and the Pipes and Drums played 'Retreat.' 'Spear' Force halted at Cekhira for the night but at Burj el Achichina, 30 miles from Akarit met heavy gunfire and 88mm anti-tank support. Inland were 7th Armoured Div and New Zealanders. At Mahares an action took place against *90th Light*, ten miles short of Sfax which the Gordons entered after dawn, unopposed on 10th. Once this big town had a population of 50,000 with a large French colony, but the port had been heavily bombed on the 8/9th. Moreover the Afrika Korps had looted the town. 5/7th Gordons were quartered in the military barracks, 1st Gordons in the public gardens.

128 Field Regt RA, Mareth-Gabes (Geoff Durand)

On the 11th Monty visited Sfax, now garrisoned by 153 Bde. 7th Black Watch formed the Guard of Honour (with borrowed kilts) and the pipes and drums welcomed the Army Commander. At a large formal lunch with the local Beys, Arabs and French, speeches were made (in French) about Les Ecossais and the 'Old Alliance.' Football matches were played, 5/7th Gordons produced stevedore parties to unload supplies on the 13th. Sfax was so unhealthy that HD moved out a few miles into olive groves. A Divisional school imparted battle wisdom to the many reinforcements who now arrived.

Inter-unit Highland games were played. There were concert parties. The mobile cinema showed the film, 'Desert Victory.' Many Jocks thought and said it was a feeble effort. There was a dance in the Salle des Fetes with pretty, but well chaperoned French ladies. General Wimberley was keen to top-up his depleted infantry battalions with Scottish reinforcements and asked Monty if he could tour the reinforcement camps (RHUs) and line of communications troops "and appeal for all Scots asking them to apply to join us." Monty agreed, so the GOC on 15-19th motored back hundreds of miles to Tripoli to 'top-up' HD. Monty also told Wimberley that HD were leaving Oliver Leese's 30 Corps to join Horrocks' 10 Corps and that 51st Div must undertake no offensive role, suffer no casualties - with a view to the next major offensive. His latest personal message to 8th Army: "Drive northwards on Sfax, Sousse and finally Tunis... the triumphant cry now is 'Forward to Tunis' 'Drive the enemy into the sea!' General Oliver Leese to HD: "Your attack [on the Akarit position] will be an outstanding epic in the annals of the Highland Brigade... You have fought unceasingly in 30th Corps since your first attack on 23rd October at Alamein."

Brigadier Kippenburger, a NZ Brigade CO was a great friend of HD. He asked Brigadier George Murray, "Did HD take their pipers into battle, as he had noticed them at Akarit?" George Murray, "Yes," but added gloomily, "those pipers get hit everytime and the pipes cost £80 per set." Fortunately the Highland Society of Edinburgh then sent out a free set of six sets of pipes.

For ten days HD spent an unpleasant time absorbing punishment under constant shelling, mortaring and sniping among the mass of steep hills, needing mules to bring up supplies. Sgt Spence, 5th Black Watch, a very big man, was made i/c battalion mules. One day the CO saw him limping and asked the reason. "One of those f—ing mules kicked me, Sir." "So what did you do, Sgt Spence?" "I kicked the b—r back, Sir." Patrols were sent out every night to harass and annoy, but no planned actions since the Division's role was only to simulate aggression, allowing the New Zealanders to push up the main coast road. Geoff Durand, OP-Ack with 128 Field Reg RA: "On 22nd April our guns fired over 1000 rounds in counter-battery fire. Pack mules had to be used to reach the FOOs on Takrouna.

The GOC flew to Cairo on 28th for a big conference and stayed at Shepherd's Hotel. He met many convalescent HD officers of the

Camerons (Jock Sorel-Cameron, Ian Grant, Francis Head, Alastair Noble, Ian Davey, Thomas Rennie, Saunders of the Gordons and others). He tried to rescue the Recce Regt reformed as 14 Bn HLI. Their CO 'Sandy' Monro persuaded the authorities to break up the unit and return several hundred men back to HD. In his absence Brigadier George Murray acted as GOC, 'Nap' Murray as GSO1.

Tunis and Bizerta surrendered on 7th May and HD was relieved by the Free French. Capt A East, 5th Black Watch asked them if the Foreign Legion was as cosmopolitan as its legend indicated. "All our NCOs are German", was the answer, "The Germans make the best NCOs in the world." Sousse was captured on 12th, Enfidaville and Takrouna on the 20th. 153 Bde moved up the next day along the Sfax-Sousse road, turning west into the Garcia hills, west of Enfidaville relieving parts of the 4th Indian Division.

5/7th Gordons had, as Felix Barker noted:

> Growing sense of excitement as news arrived that the 'war' was nearly over. The 8th Army was at the gates of Tunis, the Americans at Bizerta. With this news in mind the battalion withstood its last bitter days at Enfidaville in extraordinary good humour. They had been done out of a promised 48 hour rest. One company was heavily mortared and men killed and two officers wounded. Battalion HQ was shelled: a small patrol was captured. But hopes were high.

> Enfidaville, a somewhat evil place, a ridge of hills captured by 4th Indian Div. There were only 18 men left in the company we relieved and the stench of dead bodies was about the worse we had come across. Cover from shelling and mortaring was sparse, only shallow 'sangars' made of stone. The high velocity German 88mm gun gave no warning at all, just a bump and then an almighty explosion. We marvelled at the Indians being able to take such high ground. The end came quickly and we moved on to Djidjelli.

Pte Roy Green, 1st Black Watch was given 24 hours leave to Bougie. There he met brother Jim (Hampshires, 1st Army) and brother Bill (RN Corvette) - three brothers briefly re-united.

HD moved to a rest area near Monaster and sent a detachment plus their massed pipes and drums to the great victory parade in Tunis. After the long march of 1850 miles, HD had suffered no less than 5400 casualties (7th Black Watch 644, 5th Camerons 564, 7th Argylls 556, 5th Black Watch 510, 2nd Seaforth 483, 5th Seaforth 472, 5/7th Gordons 393, 1st Gordons 344, 1st Black Watch 299, the gunners lost 354 and the sappers 294).

The Division had come to rest - for the time being. They had added battle honours of El Alamein, Mareth and Akarit to their many other laurels.

General Alexander cabled Winston Churchill: "It is my duty to report

that the Tunisian campaign is over. We are masters of North Africa."
And the GOC was in Cairo at 30 Corps HQ planning in great secrecy
the next major campaign for 8th Army.

20
Algeria: Preparing for 'Husky' - the Promised Land?

General Wimberley had been told that HD would move 500 miles
west into Algeria for combined training exercises with the Royal
Navy around Bougie and Djidjelli. In his congratulatory message on
14th May to his 8th Army, Monty gave nothing away of his future
plans: "All those well known enemy Divisions that we have fought and
driven before us over hundreds of miles of African soil from Alamein
to Tunis, have now surrendered... the campaign has ended in a major
disaster for the enemy. And what of the future?" The 8th Army were
asked/ordered "to see the thing through to the end," whatever that
might mean! But most of the Desert veterans thought such a long
move to the west must be the first step towards shipment home. Felix
Barker, 5/7th Gordons:

> Lush valleys and fields of corn, ripe for a magnificent harvest. Trees - great
> elms, oaks and poplars, not gawky palms provided shade to lazy well fed
> cattle. Willows wept over glistening streams. The journey into Algeria was
> like leaving Egypt for the Promised Land... On 25th May the Battalion
> heard for the first time, mention of boat training for combined operations.
> This was grimly obvious to all the officers and the more realistic other
> ranks, but the men as a whole simply could not bring themselves to face the
> facts. They simply could not believe that after coming all through the desert,
> always in the thick of the fighting, and now weary and well below strength,
> they could possibly be asked to go straight into the invasion of Europe.
> Many still thought it was bluff right up to the minute of the invasion
> itself...

Greece was a possibility, Crete, Sardinia, Corsica or Sicily perhaps,
even the toe of Italy or the south coast of France?

The 48 hour convoy was through beautiful countryside... through
the sacred but squalid Kairouan over the mountains through Kasserine
and Tebessa where the Americans and First Army had fought and
suffered.

To the Black Watch camped in a vast forest amongst beautiful shady
cork trees outside Djidjelli it was a veritable paradise, although the

Boche made almost nightly bombing raids. And a section of the 1st Bn were all killed or wounded by one large bomb which left a crater 40 feet in diameter.

Div HQ was at Phare Alia, five miles out of Djidjelli and on the 16th the GOC gave a talk to all officers. It was to be a curious mixture of amphibious training, loading tables, beach landings and exercises carried out in progressive stages with 'Beach Brick' parties with the Royal Marines. Then there was hill climbing and sea bathing to keep fit plus water polo. Will Fyffe the comedian and ENSA parties entertained, as of course did the Balmorals Divisional Concert Party. A rest camp was opened in Constantine and Jocks also went on sight-seeing expeditions. A pipe tune contest produced 30 entries and was judged by the APM Angus Ferguson (Military Police have no favourites), Ian Cameron 7th Argylls and Peter Norwell, RASC. L/Corp Macdonald, a Seaforth, won with his tune 'The Wadi Akarit.' The local coarse, tangy red wine was sold to the Jocks by their RI for five pence a pint. Alastair Borthwick: "One pint and Africa was wonderful, two pints and Africa ceased to exist. My batman once drank three but that is another story!" The ration was a pint per Jock - in theory.

Djidjelli harbour swarmed with craft of all sizes and shapes known by strange acronyms: LCI (Loading Craft Infantry), LST (Landing Ship Tanks), LCA (Landing Craft Assault), LSI (Landing Ship Infantry), LCM (Landing Craft Motors). And a mountain school taught an unfortunate minority how to climb ropes up cliffs. Great emphasis was laid on physical fitness with individual hill climbs and company marches. On 31st May Generals Alanbrooke and Alexander visited HD. And so did Sir James Grigg, Sir Archie Sinclair and Oliver Leese. When HM the King visited Algiers on 24th June, Lt Col James Oliver was OC the Guard of Honour with an HD detachment of 250 veterans. Wimberley was the guest of honour at lunch (his wife knitted HM a pair of Cameron khaki stockings).

Decorations were announced. The Die Hards CO, Lt Col JWA Stephenson was awarded the DSO. Their platoons had always been in the thick of the fighting with 263 casualties during the campaign. 5th Bn Black Watch received six MCs, Sgt Jennings the DCM, plus six MMs and a DSO for Lt Col 'Chick' Thomson. Many pale-skinned reinforcements brought the battalion strength up to 38 officers and 782 ORs.

5th Camerons were brought up to strength by a large draft from the old Recce Regt (14 HLI) due to the GOCs efforts. Capt Ian Cameron, returned from hospital in Cairo, described the 7th Argylls routine: "Landing craft and assault craft of various sizes and designs were at our disposal for this [amphibious] training, which was usually carried out at night. Generally we would march down to the docks at Djidjelli in the evening about 6pm and embark on landing craft which would then put to sea and land us in the dark on some part of the coast. Very often the landing was a wet one wading ashore chest deep in warm water. During the day we attended lectures on combined operations, practised a drill embarking and disembarking with landing craft."

There were a number of changes of 'management'. The 50 year old veteran Brigadier George Murray who had commanded 152 Bde for over two years left to command 56 London Div. He was succeeded by Brigadier Gordon MacMillan.   Brigadier H Murray (wounded at Alamein) took over from Brigadier Graham at 153 Bde and Brigadier Thomas Rennie (recovered from his last wounds) relieved Brigadier 'Jumbo' Stirling at 154 Bde. The GSO1 Roy Urquhart was promoted to command 231 Bde and was succeeded by Lt Col Dunlop. Lt Col Lorne Campbell VC was promoted to command 13 Bde and was succeeded by Lt Col Mathieson.   Lt Col Blair took over from Lt Col Roper Caldbeck at 1st Bn Black Watch and Lt Col Sorel-Cameron relieved Lt Col R Miers at 5th Camerons.

The GSO III produced air recce photos of the actual beaches where HD would be landing in Sicily (GOC's eyes only) and showed women bathing with bathing caps, "unlikely to be mines or underwater obstacles."   Greek interpreters were attached to HD as part of the deception plan.

On 24th June the Algerian 'holiday' was over and the long trek east to the ports of Sousse and Sfax began.   At the beginning of July HD entered the assembly areas where men, carriers, anti-tank guns, tanks, mountain guns were loaded all in their proper sequence. All vehicles had been messily waterproofed.   Brigadier H Murray delivered a lecture to 153 Bde, informative but without any clue as to the destination.

1/7th Middlesex now acquired a 3" heavy mortar platoon (from 2/7th Middlesex) to strengthen their medium machine-gun role. And 128 Field Regt solved their problem.   RHQ had acquired a pet German dachshund, who 'knew' when incoming fire was arriving by diving into a slit trench well before the arrival of the incoming 'hard'. Lt Col Sheil ordered it to be shot as it could not be taken with the regiment on its nautical ventures. Fortunately the RN took the little beast on!

Alastair Borthwick, 5th Seaforth:

> Paddy Nairne explained the ground once more.   Here was the tunny factory, and here the jetty where the gunpost was. This was Green Beach and this was Amber beach... this patch was the Assembly area, 5th Seaforth here, 2nd Seaforth here and the Camerons here... in the end we could see the ground with our eyes shut and dreamed about it at night," and, "on 5th July 1943 we marched down to Sousse docks and embarked. There were

few regrets about leaving Africa.

The first stop - rather surprisingly - was Malta. HD disembarked at Valetta on 6th and marched off to three separate camps and bathed and planned until re-embarkation on the night of 9th. Monty visited his Highlanders on the island and talked to every unit from his staff car. Local leave was granted and the Maltese proved very hospitable. The George Cross islanders realised their long drawn agony of constant bombardment was almost at an end. And the numerous canteens were well stocked with beer, wine and spirits.

The GOC, who sailed towards Sicily in a direct course sent a message. "Now we are called upon once more to enter Europe. As the time approaches to go forward into battle never must we forget that we of this division helped by our English comrades, are ever the proud bearers of that ancient motto (Scotland for ever) and in bearing it we carry with us Scotland's renown, Scotland's fair name and Scotland's prayers."

21

Operation Husky
Battles of Vizzini and Francofonte

The invasion of Sicily was on a huge scale. 13 Corps were to land south of Syracuse and 30 Corps under Lt Gen Oliver Leese were to come in with HD astride Cape Passero, the south-east tip of the island, with 1st Canadian Division, arriving directly from the UK, on the immediate left and 231st (Malta) Brigade on the right. General Patton's US 7th Army would land in the western sector of the island and all forces would converge on the north-east corner at Messina. HD would assault with 154 Bde on the right and capture the fishing village of Portopalo and the high ground behind it. 153 Bde on the left would then land at Cape Passero. The key objective initially was Rada di Portopalo (Amber Beach) where supplies would eventually be landed. 154 Bde with 1st Gordons would form the initial bridgehead through which 5th Black Watch and 5/7th Gordons would pass. The bulk of 152/153 Bdes in bigger LSIs and LSTs would transfer into smaller LCI, LCTs and land on 'Green Beach' at Pachino, and three battalions would land on 'Red Beach' and meet at a ridge (Goal) three miles inland. The enemy were known to have two German Panzer divisions (including the *Herman Goering*) in the centre of the island poised to counter-attack the invaders. The coastal regions were defended by six to eight low grade Italian Division (including the *Napoli*). Nevertheless the American landings to the west were heavily opposed.

5th Seaforth land in Sicily

Pipe Major Anderson played 1st Gordons out of Valetta harbour on the 9th as the *Royal Scotsman, Royal Ulsterman* and *Queen Emma* with assault landing craft slung outboard joined the huge invasion fleet. The sea on arrival off the Sicilian coast was so rough that the Navy asked the GOC to cancel the Red Beach landing and concentrate on Green Beach. Oliver Leese concurred with General Wimberley not to change the original plan. At 0345 on 10th July 1st Gordons had a 'wet' landing on Green Beach, captured Portopalo and Cape Passero island without difficulty and tanks were ashore by dawn.

On Red Beach 7th Argylls now under Lt Col Mathieson were on the left, landing unopposed but a 'Red Devil' grenade exploded in 'D' Coy's landing craft wounding 15 men. 'C' Coy took 50 frightened Italians captive and the battalion linked up a mile inland with 7th Black Watch who were landed by the Navy on the wrong beaches. The Die Hards as usual had companies supporting all the lead battalions and supported 5th Camerons in an attack five miles south-east of Rosolini. The Canadians and 231 (Malta) Bde had entered Pachino, and on the 12th, Rosolini.

A strike force 'Harpoon' consisted mainly of 'Ricky' Richards 23 A/Bde, plus Middlesex, RA and RE rapidly took Palozzolo, Busceni and by darkness on the 11th was within three miles of Vizzini - an advance of 20 miles.

The next day 1st Black Watch were heavily shelled in the Bucheri Hills by the Canadian artillery. The Die Hards had a good shoot at dusk on the 14th against enemy vehicles streaming down the Vizzini-Francofonte road. The 5/7th Gordons had lost their CO Lt Col Hay who was shot by his IO's accidentally dropped pistol. Short of transport, Major Napier (acting CO) had been told to 'find' personal transport urgently. Bicycles, handcarts and a fleet of 150 mules were collected, the latter admired by the Corps Commander, Oliver Leese. General Montgomery accompanied by Lord Louis Mountbatten (Chief of Combined Operations) had been seen on the beaches on D+1 in a borrowed Dukw.

Vizzini, perched on a 2000 ft hilltop was strongly held by the *Herman Goering* division. The main attack by the Maltese Bde had failed. The American 45th Division was on the western front and 153 Bde and 23 A/Bde then became involved. 14th July was one of the hottest day's in the whole of the Sicilian campaign. The GOC sent 5th Black Watch in from the south and 'D' Coy moved up the steep slope into the streets under heavy fire. Lt Stiff was killed, Captain Murray and Campbell Adamson wounded amongst the heavy casualties. 'A' Coy followed up into the town centre held up by heavy Spandau fire. Despite firing their 2" mortars almost vertically and an American patrol shooting off their bazookas, the German defenders fought on. By nightfall 5th Black Watch had secured the western side of the town. 127 Field Regt fired a barrage to support 1st Gordons who were tackling Vizzini from the eastern flank, as they scrambled up terraced hillsides among almond trees and vines exposed to Spandau fire. At dusk 'C' Coy were in the 'cathedral' area and 'A' Coy at the cemetery on the right. Lt Col Fausset-Farquhar at 0100 pushed 1st Gordons further into the town under a heavy 'friendly' artillery concentration, which unfortunately caused 1st Black Watch 30 casualties. There was little fighting; Capt MacMillan's anti-tank platoon captured 500 Italians under a railway bridge and better still, several hundred *Herman Goering* defenders surrendered. The battalion then had breakfast in the town's main piazza. 5/7th Gordons followed 152 Bde making for Francofonte, and cleared Ferla and Cassaro taking 140 POW from the *Napoli* division. The Italian CO wept at the shame of surrender, smiled at the prospect of being out of the war. Near Ramaca 'B' and 'C' Coys took prisoner 30 *Hermans* and 20 *Napolis*. Lt Felix Barker: "south-west of Scordia lying in a valley was Milettelo, strongly held." A combined attack with tanks succeeded. "The fighting was heavy, but by nightfall the town was in our hands, and in a state of mad confusion and wild rejoicing as the Gordons marched in. Plundering was going on in shops in all the streets. Delirious citizens carried away trophies from an abandoned

German quarter-master's stores."

Near Ramaca the HD column was attacked by the Luftwaffe. Brigadier H Murray and the GOC, "were browsing on a map when down the road came eight Messerschmitts. Horrible! I took a full length dive into the ditch, all the breath was knocked out of my body. I had been joined by the Divisional Commander. I said to the GOC [whose policy was that infantry should shoot back at attacking aircraft], "What about filling the air with lead?" He said, "What goes for a general and a brigadier doesn't go for the Cameron Highlanders." [i.e. infantry].

The second battle of the campaign took place on 13th at Francofonte, a hill-village seven miles north of Buccheri. The *2nd Bn German Parachute Regt* had recently flown in from the south of France. For 36 hours they gave 5th and 2nd Seaforth a torrid time, admirably described in Alastair Borthwick's *Sans Peur*. Concealed in numerous and dense olive groves which lined the twisting road into the village, the 300 paratroopers set a trap for the Seaforth:

EASTERN SICILY JULY/AUG 1943

At 1400 the leading carrier was knocked out by a gun in the orange grove. The column stopped, piled up in a long line - we began to clamber from our vehicles and the Boche in the cemetery opened up. It was a thoroughly unpleasant situation. We crouched in ditches, or behind trucks or wherever we could find cover. At least a dozen Spandaus were sniping down at us from the olive trees.

"The leading carrier [5th Seaforth] with Sgt Cecil Ross (from Elgin) was knocked out by an SP 88mm, and the crew killed."

I [James Younie] was ordered to drive the 'C' Coy jeep back down the convoy to bring all the Coy COs to the head of the convoy to consult with Colonel Walford." Younie brought the four company COs up to the head of the column. "Immediately a hail of bullets bounced off the bonnet of the jeep from Jerry paratroopers high up on our left in the village cemetery." Younie jumped up and leapt over Capt Rutherford and out! "The German machine-gunner raised his sights to get me. His next burst hit the bank on the far side of the road. All four officers got out but as Capt Agnew calmly walked away he was killed." Under fire Younie rescued his jeep. "Half an hour later with a tank spraying at random over our heads four of us tried to spot the machine gunners. They fired a burst along the top of the wall and killed or wounded a man on either side of me. The fight by this time had moved to the village. I was left to count my lucky stars." Alastair Borthwick: "Later it was a game of hide and seek among the olive trees and we could make no headway against it. The attack bogged down." In a day of bitter and confused fighting 5th Seaforth had four officers killed (Capt George Willock, Lt Borwick, Capt Agnew, Lt Baillie) another four wounded, and 22 men KIA and 57 wounded. Supporting tanks were knocked-out by sticky bombs. Pte Crowhurst 1/7th Middlesex won the DCM for taking out Spandau teams. 5th Seaforth pulled back to allow the divisional artillery to pound Francofonte. But when 2 Seaforth attacked at 1700 they suffered the same fate but eventually took the village.

5th Camerons attacked Francofonte from the west. A 'premature' shell from a battalion mortar wounded the CO, the MO and the 128 Field Regt FOO. 'A' Coy lost two officers and Sgt MacLean 'C' Coy was awarded the DCM leading a bayonet charge which took an enemy post with two 75mm anti-tank guns and a 20mm parachutist gun. The Brigade attack on Francofonte had proved once again that professional German troops well dug-in, well armed but without much air or artillery support would not only accept enormous punishment but also deal it out as well.

On the 15th the Camerons led into Scordia which had housed an Italian gunnery school. Padre Smith organised the POW cage with much zest in which 970 Italians and their major-general were now housed.

The next day in a heat haze 128 Field Regt bombarded 30 enemy tanks near a blown bridge over the river Gornalunga. They were in fact rather large but inoffensive haystacks.

By nightfall on the 14th, 154 Bde was on the left flank, Harpoon Force in the centre, 152 Bde on the right and 153 Bde were holding Vizzini, Mineo, Militello and Scordia.

"In each town we have come to, the Sicilian populace has cheered and clapped wildly in an exuberance of emotions sometimes less than an hour after the Germans have left them," wrote Lt Neil McCallum, 5/7th Gordons, "They show no sullen acceptance of defeat, no hostility.

They are happy at having lost the war. 'Viva gli Inglesi' and scrub out casually the slogans on the walls of houses praising Il Duce."

The 5/7th Gordons held a limited bridgehead over the river Gornalunga at Fapotto and were counter-attacked on the 16th. Near Palagonia a squadron of Messerschmitts raked a long HD column of transport with cannon and machine-gun fire. On the 16th 1st Gordons accepted the surrender of Palagonia from the Mayor (plus 70 Italian POW) and camped in orange groves. Ramaca was occupied by 154 Bde on the same day, beyond lay the open undulating Catania plain. Harpoon Force was now renamed Arrow Force and its new objective was the capture of Stimpata bridge. On the night of the 17th, 153 and 154 Bdes advanced with platoons of Die Hards, with battalions leapfrogging through the one ahead. The three almost parallel rivers Monaci, Dittaino, Simeto, tributaries of the river Gornalunga, aided the defenders and bridgeheads had to be established over each.

22

A Bloody nose on the Catania Plain
Sferro and Gerbini

By Saturday 17th July HD had spent a week fighting several small battles (not small for the battalions concerned) and had advanced some 75 miles. From the hills north of Palagonia the vast plain of Catania could be seen with noticeably little cover for infantry. The GOC now decided on a two brigade advance, 153 Bde on the left and 154 Bde on the right. Ahead were the *Herman Goering Division* who had already proved themselves at Vizzini and Francofonte.

Three rivers lay ahead, the Monaci feeding into the Gornalunga and several miles north the Dittaino running parallel to the railway line. Two key small towns obviously well-defended were Gerbini and to the north-west, Sferro.

A night attack led by 1st Gordons crossed the Monaci stream, found the Gornalunga river bed dry and by 2100 by the light of burning haystacks were dug in on their objectives. 5/7th Gordons advance went like clockwork and Brigadier Murray was delighted that his command had advanced 18,000 yards leap-frogging in the dark without artillery support. On the left flank 1st Black Watch led towards Gerbini across the river Dittaino but met very stiff opposition and had to consolidate around an anti-tank ditch. The three hour delay meant that the bridgehead over the river Simeto was held by 7th Argylls sandwiched in between 1st and 7th Black Watch. On the 19th the *Herman Goering*

Division could see that HD were on their doorstep and heavy shelling resulted.

128 Field Regt RA crossing River Simeto (Geoff Durand)

Battle for Sferro

5th Black Watch were dug in around the Wadi and the bridge with mortars, anti-tank guns, Die Hard medium machine-guns and the guns of 127 Field Regt to give them protection in their vulnerable bridgehead. The 19th was a bitterly hot day and the German defenders of Sferro thundered down heavy artillery, mortar and tank fire onto the Black Watch. Battalion HQ received a direct hit killing RSM Boath and Signal Sgt Watson. There were many casualties (about 60) but the divisional artillery DF targets deterred the threatened counter-attacks. Brigadier Murray decided to attack and capture the village of Sferro to relieve pressure on the Black Watch with attacks by both Gordon battalions. A heavy barrage came down at 2330 hrs. 5/7th Gordons had put a company on top of Mount Turcisi which was an excellent OP.

Felix Barker 5/7th Gordons:

> Sferro. Just a handful of houses. It was a little village of negligible importance, for years a lazy insignificant place housing a few poor peasants. Yet here destiny had decided that an important and bitter battle should be fought out. The enemy had seen that the land rose quite steeply behind, provided excellent cover and concealment for its 170mm guns. For the battle

of Sferro - the bridge, railway and the village - the battalion was split up.

'D' Coy went up to the Wadi and dug in by the bridge and came under command of the Black Watch. 'C' Coy went out on the left flank with an RTR tank squadron.

1st Gordons in their transport passed by Point 199 and half way down the forward slope the six companies (including 'A' and 'B' of 5/7th Gordons) advanced on foot. All agreed that the enemy's defensive fire was the fiercest bombardment they had ever endured. Soon the railway was reached, across many sidings packed with goods wagons some loaded with tar, now a molten mass. The main road was reached and 1st Gordon Bn HQ was established in the station yard. The two 5/7th Gordon companies on the right had forced their way into the village. In the street-fighting the wireless sets were all knocked-out and runners from 1st Gordons failed to get through. At day break on the 20th German armoured cars and an 88mm shot up 5/7th Gordons.

The Gordons stayed in the Sferro village and bridgehead until relieved by 5th Camerons on the night of the 24th. The missing 'A' and 'B' Coys 5/7th Gordons were not lost, merely strayed! Felix Barker: "Somewhere out there in front, in a pitch darkness fitfully lit by the golden rain of tracer and the flames of a railway truck blazing down the line, the companies were lost." They were holding the further edge of Sferro astride the Paterno road, with casualties of about 30 including three officers and CSM Bell. Capt J Ritchie drove a loaded ammo truck across the river bridge under heavy fire into the burning village of Sferro and a 3-ton lorry laden with water jerricans got through to the 1st Gordons.

Both Gordon battalions stayed in the Sferro village and bridgehead in great heat, persistent flies and intermittent shelling. Cheeky enemy raiding parties were active every night. Pte Hyland, 1st Gordons disguised himself as a corn stook and lay out all day 1200 yards in front observing and reporting back. The 1st Gordons described their ten day stay in the bridgehead 'one of the least pleasant billets.' During the 19th, 5th Black Watch guarding their Wadi were shelled all day, losing 14 KIA and about 40 wounded.

The left flank of the HD bridgehead was now open and border patrols by truck, carrier and on foot pushed up the Catenanuova road and found no enemy.

Gerbini Battle

The *Herman Goering* defenders had been eventually driven out of Sferro but they were just as resolute in guarding Gerbini, six miles south-east of Sferro with its barracks, railway station and airfield. 154 Bde were tasked with the capture of the town, 1st Black Watch leading followed by 7th Black Watch and 7th Argylls. The capture of the main road over the Simeto river was also a vital objective.

Major DFO Russell, 7th Black Watch:

> The battle of Gerbini 18-25th July proved to be an extremely unpleasant affair and although a tactical failure was undoubtedly a strategical success in that it very much accelerated the German withdrawal to the north... and... The country was very close being mostly hills to the north and flat open country to the south intersected by high canal banks and low hedges round each of the fields. The enemy familiar with this country infiltrated our positions with infantry SP guns and tanks.

On the 20th, the attack by 1st Black Watch on the town met with very strong resistance and they were pinned down at an anti-tank ditch, half a mile beyond the crossroads; they found that the barracks on the ridge ahead was strongly held. 'B' Sqn 46 RTR supported 154 Bde and late afternoon linked with 7th Black Watch to support their attack on the aerodrome. They too that evening met very stiff opposition. Then it was the turn of the 7th Argylls to attack Gerbini along the line of the railway rather than up the road, backed by a barrage fired by two field, two medium regiments RA and supported by two Sqns of 46 RTR. In the 20 foot deep anti-tank ditch, their start line, the Argylls found many dead Germans. 'C' Coy on the right soon lost all their officers, 'A' Coy were counter-attacked several times, and were surrounded by a German battalion with tanks on the morning of 21st and forced to surrender. 'D' Coy were involved in hand to hand fighting on the aerodrome. 'B' Coy came across an enemy company holding a pill box. Captain Ian Cameron, who was wounded in the action wrote:

> Bedlam was let loose. The battle had been fast and furious. At first light the tempo slackened. 46 RTR leaguered in the woods engaged enemy tanks. Later in the morning the battle flared up again. Two companies of Black Watch were sent up as reinforcements. Successive counter-attacks steadily reduced the strength of the Bn. With only four officers left and the Bn almost surrounded and attacked by enemy tanks after ours had been withdrawn ['B' Sqn alone had 27 casualties, lost five tanks] the Bn was ordered back to the line of the anti-tank ditch.

No fewer than 18 officers and 160 ORs were killed or wounded including 98 missing. The CO, Lt Col Mathieson was killed by an 88mm shell. Major Macdougall died of wounds in enemy hands. Four officers of 'A' Coy were captured. This was the last major action fought by the Argylls in the Sicilian campaign. Lt Col A Dunlop, Divisional GSO1 took over command and reinforcements soon arrived. By 31st July they were sent to Mont Franchetta as brigade reserve battalion.

1st Black Watch finally reached the barracks, found abandoned. Their CO Lt Col Blair was badly wounded and a savage counter-attack forced them back to the anti-tank ditch. 2nd Seaforth eventually suffered 80 casualties around the Gerbini airfields.

General Montgomery now shifted the axis of 30 Corps further west, withdrew the shattered Argylls and 1st Black Watch behind the Dittaino river leaving 7th Black Watch to hold the bridgehead. 5th Camerons were brought up to fill in the gap between 1st and 7th Black Watch, and later acted as rearguard when 154 Bde withdrew. The German defenders then withdrew from Gerbini equally devastated by the battle but returned later.

The GOC said at the time: "Emboldened by the speed at which we had gone forward we were now too hasty and took rather 'a bloody nose'." Lulled by relatively easy actions against the low-grade Italian coastal troops it was always a shock when the advance guards bumped the highly professional German rearguards deployed with SPs, tanks and 88mm guns.

Monty wrote to the GOC on the 21st:

> I have decided to make the right flank of the Army front a defensive front and to pull in to the best positions - ready for offensive action at a suitable moment later on. In ten days we have captured practically the whole of Sicily and the enemy is now hemmed in at the north-east corner - rather like the Cape Bon peninsular. Please tell all your soldiers that I think they have done magnificently. They have marched and fought over a very long distance in great heat, well up to the best standards of the Highland Division.

5th Divison took over the Dittaino bridgeheads on the 25th and the Sferro on the 30th. The Allied command plan was for Patton's 8th Army to move up on the north, for the Canadians and 78th Division to move up to the centre and for 8th Army to regroup for the final drive towards Catania, Messina and the ousting of the Axis forces from Sicily.

The gunners as usual were indispensable: 127 Field Regt RA supported 153 Bde (491 Bty - 5/7th Gordons; 301 Bty - 1st Gordons; 304 Bty - 5th Black Watch). On the night 19/20th July Major K W Pooley supported 5th Black Watch with DF to break up counter-attacks on the Sferro bridge. The field regiments and Die Hards stayed in action supporting 5th Division, 78th Division, the Canadians and the 7th Royal Marine Commando.

126 Field Regt sent a section of 25-pdrs just before the battle of the Sferro hills to US 2nd Corps to fire propaganda leaflets in HE smoke shells. Practised successfully in Tunisia using 25-pdrs, the Americans in Sicily had to 'borrow' from 126 Field. The section fired 36 shells containing about 43,200 pamphlets and leaflets; subsequently German POW were taken with leaflets in their possession having used them as safe conducts.

23

The Battle of the Sferro Hills
"Running and Dodging"

General Montgomery had pulled 13 Corps out of the line. 153 Bde was holding the Sferro bridgehead, and 7th Black Watch held the Dittaino bridgehead with 152 Bde in reserve.

For a week the Gordons and Camerons had shared the defence of the Sferro bridgehead with 5th Black Watch. There was constant patrolling activities and the *Herman Goering Panzer Grenadiers* gave as good as they got. Sferro was a death trap, stinking of death, completely overlooked by German OPs in the hills behind. German Nebelwerfer, vicious multi-barrelled mortars were encountered for the first time. Daily casualties mounted up, the Die Hards 13 in two days, the 5th Black Watch even more. Once their 'D' Coy were attacked by a 60 strong fighting patrol. Sudden long range bombardments from heavy guns added to the tension. Reliefs of course could only be made at night. It was a frustrating time.

A full scale divisional attack was now planned to cross the rivers Dittaino and Simeto and advance towards Paterno. The first objective was to get to the Sferro-Catenanuova road within artillery range of Adrano. Immediately ahead lay the line running west-east of the Sferro hills with three commanding features, Points 224, 194 and 254 commanding the river Dittaino valley. In the far distance could be seen the lofty Mount Etna.

152 Bde's objective was the Iazzovecchio ridge (point 224 and 194) and 154 Bde, the Monte Pietraperiala feature.

Brigadier MacMillan's plan for 152 Bde was for 5th Camerons to lead and take Pt 224 and the north-west sector of the ridge. 5th Seaforth would follow, reach Iazzovecchio farm, move south-east to Angelico farm and contact the left hand battalion of the Sferro garrison. 2nd Seaforth were in reserve and 7th Black Watch (154 Bde) would be attacking at the same time on the left flank. It was known that Point 194 was strongly held. From Turcisi farm after a hot windless day 5th Camerons set off down a goat track at 2130 hrs on 31st July. Two hours later with tank support they moved across the dry Dittaino river bed, behind a barrage and heavily laden. Not only weapons, entrenching tools but a day's rations of food and water were carried, so the advance rate in nil visibility was a hundred yards in three minutes. They met fierce resistance at the top of the ridge and 'A' Coy, Capt MacLeod went off the air. He had been killed on the objective. 'B' Coy too had heavy fighting, two officers were killed and only 20 men reached their objective. Battalion HQ came under Spandau fire and had to dig in at a small Wadi. Brigade sent up 'B' Coy 2nd Seaforth to help and later 'D' Coy as well. Just before dawn a traffic jam occurred in 'Spandau Alley' where Battalion HQ was under fire. At dawn 128 Field Regt helped 'C' Coy finally to clear Pt 224. The indomitable Lt Ainslie earned a bar to his MC when he and ten men, survivors of 'A' Coy emerged from the smoke screens all armed with British and German automatic weapons.

5th Camerons had taken 30 POW and buried 60 German and Italian dead, but their own casualties were five officers and 40 ORs. Alastair Borthwick, 5th Seaforth:

> The sun still blazed, water was short, cactus still had prickles, our bodies were brown and our faces black. We moved up slowly by dusty tracks and groves of unripe lemons towards the valley of the Dittaino and the Sferro Hills... Messina was still a long way away.

The plan of attack was straightforward - follow the Camerons and attack north-east to take Angelico Farm backed by six regiments of artillery and two Die Hard medium machine-gun companies.

> We lay in the sun and sweated. Was Angelico occupied or not? Would the Boche have tanks? At Alamein there had been no time, only one day out of the line, a bedlam of Recces and conferences. The battle of the Hills had been a scramble. The day before Akarit had been filled with planning and marching. At Francofonte we had jumped from peace to war in a few seconds. But here we had planned for a week. Now there was nothing left to do but think. [Alastair Borthwick]

Borthwith had taken over the Mortar Platoon after Francofonte. The Seaforth got caught up in the traffic jam. "I could hear Col Monro roaring in the darkness." All night attacks were chaotic, or seemed to be but 'D' Coy took Angelico Farm without difficulty but the large olive grove near the farm had a strongpoint and was swarming with enemy. By dawn 100 POW came trooping back. Private Graham 'C' Coy:

> In the reserve platoon, as a brengunner, I joined forces with Ptes McLoughlan and Kennedy and went into the grove. We kept on running and dodging and spraying. We could see Boche nipping about among the trees. There were Ities too. I worked up to their Spandau and hurled a grenade at it... We got 18 or 19 POW altogether, half of them Jerries.

Graham and McLoughlan were both awarded MMs. 5th Seaforth had 22 casualties including the gallant Jack Davidson.

5th Seaforth and 5th Camerons were duly counter-attacked by a battle group of *Herman Goering* infantry and tanks. The FOO of the Scottish Horse mediums had a 'field' day when 15 tanks including Tigers, some motorcyclists and lorried infantry were seen in the far valley driving nonchalantly towards the Camerons, as Panzer Grenadiers attacked Pt 224.

The Sferro counter-attack was only one of many occasions when we were saved by our artillery. We in the infantry [wrote Alastair Borthwick in his book *Sans Peur*] thank the gunners for the support they gave us in every battle. Time and again we reached our objectives with negligible casualties simply because the defences had had the stuffing knocked out of them before we arrived. And for that we thank all who co-operated with us from Brigadier Jerry Sheil down to our own particular cronies, Majors Norman Owen, Taffy Wilcox, H J Decker and captains Arthur Stobo, John Trapnell and Neil Millar.

The Die Hards had their No 13 platoon medium machine-gun with 5th Seaforth. Lt Wrampling who had joined the battalion ten hours before, at point blank range put four enemy Spandau out of action before being badly wounded. Sgt Fisher and Corp Dean led their section into the olive orchards where confused and bitter fighting was taking place and later took a heavy toll of the enemy withdrawing along the valley.

Brigadier Rennie's 154 Bde, on the left flank, plan of attack was for 7th Black Watch to move into the valley along the line of the Dittaino river bed through the 7th Argylls firm base on to the Sferro hills on the left of the Camerons, with 1st Black Watch moving on the left to capture the extreme western end of the ridge of hills. By about 0500 hrs 'D' and 'B' Coys, 7th Black Watch had taken their objectives but 'C' Coy was overwhelmed with 45 missing. The battalion also suffered 94 casualties in the battle of the Sferro Hills. The 126 Field Regt fired over 2000 rounds in support of the Black Watch and on the morning of 1st August broke up several counter-attacks.

By 1700 hrs on the 1st it was clear HD had won a considerable victory and the enemy withdrew across the river Simieto and was making for Paterno and Aderno. 7th Argylls took the high ridge of Pietra Perciata, overlooking the roads to Centuripe Muglia, during the night of 1/2nd August. 154 Bde advanced rapidly towards the mountains including Mount Spezia and then spent over a fortnight either on the hills (no shade, very hot) or orange grove, in the valley (mosquitoes and malaria) on the banks of the Simieto. Training, route marches, MT inspections, complete weapon store inspection and a lot of 'bull' ensued, visits were made to the recent battlefields at Sferro, Point 224 and Gerbini, 'unpleasant battle-scarred areas.' Reinforcements arrived, many rejoining after recuperating from their wounds.

153 Bde secured the Spezia feature and rested in the Muglia area, covering 78th Division's advance on Adrano. On the 13th they moved to south-east side of Mount Etna relieving 13 Bde of 5th Div, via Milo to Linguaglossa and Castiglione. Messina fell on the 16th and the

Sicilian campaign was over. HD had lost 1312 battle casualties in the 39 day Operation Husky (7th Argylls 223, 2nd Seaforth 194, 1st Black Watch 145, 5th Seaforth 132, 7th Black Watch 119 and 5th Black Watch 111).

51st Highland Division monument in Sicily, overlooking the battlefields of Sferro and Gerbim (Geoff Durand)

Lt Col Rebholz, CO Recce Bn *Herman Goering Division* later admitted how surprised they were at the speed of the 8th Army advance. General Guzzoni the Italian Army commander only had sufficient forces to deal with one assault area at a time and chose to counter-attack the Americans at Gela first, then switch his thrust against landings at Syracuse. There were no forces left to deal with the HD bridgehead in the centre. A large Italian force poured into Vizzini and begged to be put in the safest part of the line. Rebholz ordered them into the railway tunnel which they could defend on a one-man front in depth! Later 1st Gordons took them all prisoner! He only had sufficient forces to hold the east end of Vizzini. He covered the south and west thinly with OPs but could not engage the HD advance against this mountain fortress as his guns were being deployed on the Sferro line and were out of range. Hence the easy move by HD to the outskirts of the town. They held Vizzini until dusk as their withdrawal north was uphill and they feared the HD artillery fire. They were clear of the town well before the HD assault at midnight. Rebholz and Col Von Bonin (Chief of Staff HQ *XIV PZ Corps*) thought that had the Americans thrust north east from Gela for the Sferro area, the Axis forces might not have had time to link up on the Etna line. Vizzini was too far forward of the main German defensive position south of Etna to be held for long. They planned to hold the line of the Simeto river with a forward line on the railway running through Sferro and Gerbini and outposts on the high ground south of the river Dittaino (where the 51st HD Memorial now proudly stands). The Germans had the equivalent of two battalions plus in the area of Sferro and Gerbini supported by howitzers whose OPs were in the railway stations and on the high ground north of the railway line. Lt Col Rebholz was awarded the German Iron Cross for the defence of Gerbini. The Axis command was puzzled why HD was ordered on the defensive for ten vital days enabling the Germans to re-group and organise a brilliant withdrawal to the Italian mainland.

24

The General's Farewell
"Jocks reacted with amazement"

Good Generals think ahead and make plans for the future. General Montgomery wrote back to the CIGS, Alan Brooke on 27th July when Operation Husky was in full flow: "Wimberley has been with 51 Div for three years and commanded it for two. He feels himself he ought to have a change... He is a 1st class Div Comd. He would be quite excellent as DMT [Director Military Training] or as Commandant of the Staff College. He has great battle experience and knows his stuff well. I would replace him in 51 Div with Rennie. I think you must have a Highlander for that Division."

On the 8th August the GOC wrote: "Monty paid me a visit, broke the news, as soon as the Sicilian campaign was over, I was to go to the Staff College, Camberley as Commandant and take over from Sir Alan Cunningham. A new Commandant was needed who had had plenty of recent battle experience and I qualified under that head. I could not cavil at going for I had commanded HD now for about 2½ years which was quite a long spell in wartime." Wimberley had known his successor, Charles Bullen-Smith, GOC 15th Scottish Division in the UK, at Wellington College and liked him. His command included a number of Highland regiments which made him acceptable despite being a Kings Own Scottish Borderer! Bullen-Smith had been a staff officer in Monty's 3rd Division in the BEF in 1940. Monty then wrote an official letter:

Now that the campaign in Sicily is over I would like to tell you how well I consider your Division has done. One never imagines that the Highland Division can do otherwise than well and in this short campaign the Division has lived up to its best traditions. I have always been proud to have the HD in the 8th Army. Please tell all your officers and men how well I consider they have done.

Major JD McGregor 5th Black Watch:

No understandable reason was given. He was physically and mentally very fit and as capable of leading the Division then, as he was when the campaign started in Egypt. The Jocks reacted with amazement that their 'Tartan Tam' was leaving: the man they knew, the man they trusted. The man who had made every single one of them believe he was a Highlander, whatever else his birth certificate said to the contrary. When he came to say his farewells to the Bn on 20th August, tough battle veterans had real tears in their eyes.

Wimberley also published his own farewell, 'Order of the Day to all Ranks of the 51st Highland Division':

On giving up command of the 51st Highland Division, in which I have served for the past three years, the Division moreover, in which I was so proud also to have been numbered in the last Great War, I find it difficult to express to you what I feel.

It is naturally easiest on this occasion merely to recall to memory some of the milestones passed in the long road which we have travelled together, ever onwards, from Scotland right across Africa and into Europe.

For instance, the many tributes which your spirit, discipline and behaviour brought from those leaders best qualified to compare us with other Divisions in those now far-off days at home.

Alamein, and that moonlight night, when you went into your first battle, new and untried as individuals, but bearing in your historic tartans and your Pipes an inheritance of centuries of gallantry from your forebears, and each bearing Scotland's banner in your hearts.

Mersa Brega and its mines, and our gallant Engineers who died as we went on.

Beurat, and the rapid advance to Tripoli, when your spirit to get forward, from the leading Highlander to the very back of the Division's Administrative services, resembled a living flame.

Mareth, when you showed that the Highland Division could defend as well as attack.

The race for Sfax. That hard fight at Akarit, when you pressed through mines and wire and defences as on a field day, but paid the inevitable price for your gallantry.

The Sicilian beaches; and now Francofonte, Gerbini, Sferro and its hills, almost still reverberating with the crash of your artillery as our Gunners hammered the German infantry and tanks, and as our 'Die-hard' machine gunners fired their belts on the bullet-swept tops of San Antonio.

By your deeds, it is not too much to claim that you have added to the pages of military history, pages which may well bear comparison with the stories of our youth, telling us of our kinsmen who fought at Bannockburn, Culloden, Waterloo, the Alma and at Loos. Further, in achieving this, you have earned, as is indeed your due, the grateful acknowledgments of your Country.

All this, however, belongs to the past. All this can be summed up in one verse recently written of the Division in the Scots Press:

> Ye canna mak' a sojer wi' braid an' trappin's braw,
> Nor gie him fightin' spirit when his back's ag'in the wa'.
> It's the breedin' in the callants that winna let them whine,
> the bluid o' generations frae lang, lang syne.

It is the future which matters most. It is concerning the future about which I would therefore remind you today, and especially those thousands of you who have joined the Highland Division since we left Egypt.

No individual, no Regiment, no Division can afford to rest on its laurels. Just as your fathers in the Highland Division won their proud position as the premier fighting formation in 1917 and kept it through many weary months, so must you, in this generation, maintain your reputation to the end of the road. To do this, you must ever set your own standards, you must 'gang your ain gait'; you must choose the hard and not the easy path. Your discipline and behaviour, your saluting, your battle drill, your battle technique must continually be overhauled and be kept at the highest level, come what may.

Provided all this is maintained, then, with your national background and your great morale, you will, in due course and God willing, fight your last battle as bravely and successfully as you fought your first - proud that all must still grant to you your Alamein motto of 'Second to None.'

For myself, I can best thank you in the farewell words of my great predecessor Sir Colin Campbell, who led our same famous Highland Regiments to such glory nearly one hundred years ago - From the bottom of my heart.

The Camp Commandant presented the GOC with a wooden shield covered with all the tartans of the Highland regiments and fixed on to it all the divisional cap badges. Wimberley was Monty's guest on his last night in Sicily in a hotel in Taormina: "It was a typical act of the kindness and thoughtfulness of the little Field Marshal, I had come to admire so much. Efficiency and Duty were ever his watchwords. He could be if necessary a ruthless commander. To serve under him in war was indeed an inspiration and in his generalship we had complete confidence." Later Monty sent on 22nd September to Wimberley a copy of his booklet. 'Some notes on High Command in War,' "To Major General Wimberley whose skilful and determined leadership of the magnificent Highland Division played a large part in the victories we gained in Africa and in Sicily."

The problem was that his successor would inevitably be judged and assessed against Wimberley's superb and inspirational leadership in the North African and Sicilian campaigns. And Bullen-Smith an excellent training general had not seen recent action and he was not a Highlander.

25
Limbo in Sicily: "prayer for the dead"

It was to be another three months before the HD was on the move again as they were tasked as garrison of the Messina area of Sicily. So re-organising, resting, arms and equipment maintenance, the running of training cadres took place.

There were parades galore. The 'Highway Decorator' tradition continued even if its architect was no longer there to see the results. A Divisional Assault-at-Arms was organised up the coast at 'Bydand Bay' and Brigade Sports meetings were held. The Sicilians were happy to field football sides to compete with HD battalion teams. The Syracuse Municipal Band also gave concerts. The Balmorals were in their element under Sgt Felix Barker, but there were other 'competitive' concert parties, ENSA shows, film shows, football matches, dances with the nursing sisters of 98th General Hospital. 128 Field had a concert party with three pianists and a ballet scene in which the Italian piano player had no idea how to stop! The pipe bands were much in demand and Highland dancing was encouraged.

Fresh fruit, vegetables, even ice cream, and much 'vino' made for more enjoyable cuisine. Interesting trips were made to climb Mount Etna to see the inactive volcano craters and bathing parties were popular.

HD helped the Italian campaign get off to a good start. The artillery of 30 Corps was deployed to support the landing of 13 Corps crossing the Straits of Messina. The HD Field Regts supported 5th Division's landings on the southern toe of Italy sending FOO's across the 4000 yards of water. The large artillery programme of 500 rounds per gun was fired on the afternoon of 2nd September from near Spadafora. The landings were only slightly opposed! The Die Hards fired as a regiment, 48 medium machine-guns in all, most unusual, 14 belts per gun on a timed programme on the line of the road (in Italy) from Villa San Giovanni to Torre Cavalla. Their fire covered bridges over the mountain streams. A number of white flags could be seen waving on the mainland. 128 Field Regt, due to the extreme heat, on 3rd September lost five guns due to prematures. Sgt Frank Simpson fired off the last shell from his gun after cease fire which saved his gun. The training manual was amended to read 'Cease Firing - Empty Guns' another lesson learned.

However HD did have a presence in the Italian campaign. The four companies of RASC moved across the straits, engaged on lines of communication duties. The intrepid Major Desmond Skinner, OC 563

Corps Coy drove into Rome and painted a large blue HD sign on the side of the Vatican wall. 7th Black Watch were sent over for a four day, totally peaceful, defensive position in the hills near Reggio.

Five days later came the welcome news of the unconditional surrender of Italy. In practice nothing changed. The Axis forces were now the usual, tough, uncompromising German forces unencumbered by a fairly useless ally.

The Army Commander visited and at a parade on 25th September presented medals won in Africa and Sicily. Many decorations were awarded to the HD veterans: 128 Field received two MCs, three MMs and Lt Col WA Sheil a bar to his DSO. The Argylls received two DSOs (the late CO Lt Col Mathieson and Capt Buchanan), one MC, no less than three DCMs and five MMs. 1st Gordons CO Lt Col Fausset-Farquhar a bar to his DSO, five MCs, five MMs. And 5/7th Gordons two MCs and eight MMs (two for stretcher bearers).

A number of HD management left, besides the GOC; Lt Col Jack Stephenson CO, the Die Hards left to obtain infantry training with 7/10th Argylls prior to promotion. Major AJ Hughes took over command. Brigadier MacMillan returned to the UK promoted to Commander 15th Scottish Division and was replaced by Lt Col JA Oliver DSO. And Lt Col I Cathcart took command of 7th Black Watch.

Winter quarters were moved to when the weather broke. On 9th October the Die Hards moved to Acireale. The Sicilians had warned HD that one night 'The Rains will Come,' and they did, a drenching downpour followed by a tremendous electric storm. Rumours grew stronger every day of a return to the UK.

On 11th October, "In a long column the battalion [5/7th Gordons] marched down the hill from Augusta through the old Spanish gateway and across the narrow causeway which connects the town with the mainland." They were on their way to a remembrance service in a Zeppelin hanger on the hill:

> Eight hundred voices sang the words of the 98th Psalm and bowed their heads during the prayer for the dead. Then the CO came to the table and lifted a book from the drumhead and began to read. It was the Battalion Roll of Honour and for five minutes the hangar was absolutely silent as he read the names. It were as if every man there wished to hear every one of those hundred and twelve names to catch one last glimpse of the men who had been their friends and had given their lives in the two campaigns somewhere from Alamein to Sferro. The last name was read. He lowered the book and still no one moved. Then the silence was broken by the sound of the pipes playing 'Flowers of the Forest' and from a distant bugle came the solemn, haunting strains of 'The Last Post.' [Felix Barker]

On Alamein Day 23rd October the Highland games were held in Syracuse Stadium and the massed pipe bands played Retreat. But HD were now definitely marked for Home; advanced parties were detailed. Anti-tank guns, portees and carriers were handed in. Earlier, 30% of all HD vehicles had been handed over to 13 Corps for use in Italy.

A week before departure, Major General Bullen-Smith and many members of HD unveiled a Celtic Cross memorial in stone on the Gerbini battlefields. It commemorates the loss of 224 officers and other ranks killed in the Sicilian campaign.

The Highland Divisional Farewell to Sicily by Hamish Henderson:

> 'Then fare weel, ye banks o' Sicily
> Fare ye well, ye valley an' shaw,
> There's no Jock will mourn the Kyles o' ye
> Puir bliddy bastards are weary'

26

Homeward Bound
"solid half crowns, water-taps and baths"

The HD advance parties from all units under command of Lt Col Fausset-Farquhar set sail on 23rd October on HMT *Dunnottar Castle*. Their convoy of 20 ships put in at Algiers and after an uneventful journey arrived at Greenock on 4th November.

The American ship USS *Argentina* of 20,700 tons carried the whole of Brigadier Murray's 153 Bde when she and 16 others in convoy set sail from Augusta on 9th November. 127 Field Regt RA, a Field Coy RE and 174 Field Ambulance were aboard this 'dry' ship. Only two meals per day were served cafeteria style with a complete meal on a multi-purpose tray. 'A' Coy 5th Black Watch volunteered for cookhouse duties with pleasing results. Lifebelts were worn all the time because the convoy route to Oran and the Straits of Gibralter were under constant U-boat threats. At one stage the Navy had 25 escorts to make sure HD reached Liverpool on 27th November. 152 Bde sailed on the USS *Edmond B. Alexander* and arrived at Liverpool on 25th November. The Die Hards sailed on the *Dominion Monarch*, as did the RASC companies. Major Roy Mumford's wife lived a quarter of a mile away from Liverpool port but for security reasons he could not contact her. Geoff Durand, 128 Field Regt RA:

> The SS *Nea Hellis* (ex *Tuscania*) had been used for carrying bananas and the sardine approach in the ship was general. In the Firth of Clyde, through the boom defences we saw RMS *Queen Elizabeth* and *Aquitania* moored nearby. We were the first troopship back from the Middle East. A brass band played

welcoming music for us on the quayside. This was Glasgow. We may be a Glasgow Regiment but by 2300 hrs we were on a train to Ashridge Camp, Tring, Berkhampstead. We had our disembarkation leave there.

The convoys were greeted by GOC 30 Corps, Lt General Oliver Leese and by Major General Bullen-Smith who had gone ahead by air. Special trains were waiting on all ships and main Div HQ was in Amersham, Buckinghamshire.

Alastair Borthwick, 5th Seaforth recalls the wartime posters at Gourock, and the great ugly unbelievable tram cars on the outskirts of Glasgow: "Soon a donkey must appear between the train lines, carrying well over its rump a dirty old gentleman with an umbrella, followed at a decent interval by the dirty old gentleman's wife, on foot, with no umbrella but a great deal of luggage. Surely all these puddles bred mosquitoes." And toast, sound, solid half crowns and water taps and baths. Even the sparse rationed food of late 1943 was found to be acceptable.

The Highland Division were back - not at home - still in a 'foreign' country, in a semi-circle round the north of London from Slough, Aylesbury, Berkhampstead to Watford, St Albans and Hertford.

Hard on disembarkation leave followed Christmas and the New Year, so little serious training took place until January 1944. New battledress was issued and so was the coveted North Africa Star ribbon.

There were many changes in command. Lt Col Ralph Carr who had been wounded at Alamein and Mareth became CRE. Brigadier DH Haugh briefly commanded 152 Bde until in June 1944 Brigadier AJH Cassels succeeded him. Lt Col WAS Sheil was promoted to be Brigadier CRA. Two Brigadiers, Gordon MacMillan and Thomas Rennie were promoted to command divisions - 15th Scottish and 3rd British respectively. Lt Col James Oliver took command of 152 Bde, and then 154 Bde. Lt Col AM Man now commanded the Die Hards, Lt Col Angus Rose command of 7th Argylls, Lt Col JDC Anderson 1st Gordons (until May when due to ill-health was succeeded by Lt Col WA Stevenson). Lt Col 'Wallaby' Bruton became AQ and his successor as CRASC, Lt Col ESA Nicholls, immediately threatened to post away his 8th Army soldiers.

Early in the New Year General Eisenhower, Air Chief Marshal Tedder, and General Wimberley came to visit HD. On 13th February, Monty now GOC-in-C 21st Army Group, with General Crocker GOC 1st Corps (in which HD now found themselves) inspected the Division. He said how pleased he was to have 51st Division under his command again. His complete confidence in the outcome of the Second Front was infectious and undoubtedly raised morale. Queen Elizabeth inspected 'her' battalions on 23rd and the Black Watch pipes and drums played her favourite tune 'Scotland the Brave'. On the last day of February the

King came and inspected training on Stoke Common. A number of Gordons were his estate workers from Ballatur. HRH Princess Royal on 20th February inspected units, and an exhibition of sewing and tapestry done by the St Valéry prisoners of war. Training with tank squadrons often Guards Armoured Brigade with 'new' Churchill tanks, bridging, river crossings, gas and intelligence duties, sniping courses, mine lifting and laying, patrolling, TEWTS (Tactical Exercises Without Troops); anti-tank platoons fired their new 6-pdrs on the range at Foulness in Essex.

Route marches were frequent as Monty demanded very high standards of fitness in his new command. Portly officers (and a few men) were sent elsewhere. The Middlesex practised firing their big support mortars - a new and deadly weapon. Reinforcements arrived who were frequently in awe of the bronzed Desert veterans and all units were soon up to strength. Later on detachments were sent to practice street fighting in the bombed, devastated Limehouse and other areas in the East End of London. The Gordons and others worked with deadly flame-throwers on a field-firing range near Harlington.

A popular addition to the strength were between six and ten young Canloan officers posted to every infantry battalion training for 'Overlord,' the new codename for the Second Front. They might have been on 'loan' but many of them, poor devils, never returned to Canada. Many were to be killed in action during the next year. In 5th Black Watch they were Captain Barr, Lts Cowan, Campbell, Miller, Richard and Stewart. In all 65 young Canloans served with HD in north-west Europe, 12 were killed in action or died of wounds, seven were awarded MCs, two won MIDs, one a Belgian Croix de Guerre, one the Order of Leopold, another the Order of Orange (Dutch).

A certain amount of training - perhaps not enough - was carried out in tactics to be used in close, wooded countryside with small fields, but there were few such areas available. Night attacks were practised. Since Alamein this was always a key 'Monty' tactic. Wireless procedures were changed and the new Americanised phonetic alphabet had to be learned. New signal equipment arrived, new LCVs, the HP No 19 sets, HP No 12 sets and for the gunners the new 22 sets in lieu of the No 11 sets they had used for so long. Exercises 'Curb' and 'Snaffle' in February and March were designed to test procedures in the field. Every unit carried out experiments and practice with the waterproofing of all vehicles including carriers to wade three or four feet of water without 'drowning.'

The gunner regiments still with faithful (but new) 25-pdrs sent officers and men on courses at the School of Artillery on gunnery, survey training and signalling. All guns of course were calibrated. Exercises took place at Hunstanton, Redesdale ranges, Salisbury Plain,

Larkhill and Thetford battle area.

Early in April the Division moved to East Anglia with the training emphasis on river crossings, night advances and patrolling. The Gordons preferred the beer in Amersham to that in Southwold and weekends in London were drastically reduced. Street fighting practice in the East End was popular since Piccadilly was within easy marching distance.

The Die Hards were reorganised with five companies HQ, 'A' (Mortar) and 'B', 'C' and 'D' machine-gun companies. And a new non-Scottish unit joined HD. The original 51st Recce Regt had been disbanded in North Africa and now 2nd Derbyshire Yeomanry were to lead HD into action - when there were wide open spaces to move in! Lt Col RH Palmer was their CO. They usually fought a squadron to a Brigade (often in an infantry role!). Their armoured car troops consisted of three Humbers (later Daimlers) with 37mm cannon and 7.92 Besa machine-gun, plus two Humber Light Recce Cars. In addition there was a Carrier Tp with seven Bren carriers, PIATs and 2" mortars and an Assault Tp with five armoured half-tracks. Finally RHQ had available eight 6-pdr anti-tank guns and six 3" mortars. A very powerful addition to HD's strength.

The final invasion exercise 'Operation Fabius' took place during May, a complete rehearsal by the Division of the move from the Invasion Concentration Area to the Invasion Marshalling area. All trucks and carriers were loaded exactly as for the actual operation. On 10th and 11th May loading and landing exercises took place at Lowestoft, partly for the benefit of the Navy. But veterans from the Sicily landings ably demonstrated how loading and unloading on to LCTs should be done! On 16th May Major General Bullen-Smith briefed all his senior 'managers' about HD's role in Overlord.

Along the Southend on Sea to London main road a series of camps had been erected specifically for the marshalling of the invasion army. With a barbed wire perimeter, tents and a few huts they resembled prisons. A group of Italian prisoners of war watched the 5th Camerons at their camp in Snaresbrook, with amazement and amusement at the Jocks incarcerated behind the triple Dannert wire fence. On 17th May the whole of HD went into 'prison,' 5th Black Watch into S1 camp near Tilbury, 5th Seaforth into S6, 7th Black Watch into S3 near Purfleet and so on. Inside the sealed up camps were canteen and cinema facilities and up to 26th May, 24 hour passes were granted.

The secrecy for 'Overlord' was almost total. Until the very last minute formations did not know exactly where they were going. It was made known that HD would not be in the main beach assault. TAC Div HQ and 153 Bde Group would land on D+1, followed by 4th Armoured Bde, 152 and then 154 Bdes on the beaches near Oustreham at the mouth of the river Orne. HD would be the immediate follow-up force to 3rd British and 3rd Canadian Divisions who would assault the beaches.

The Infantry battalions would land in three 'flights', 60% for the first (on D+1) with four rifle companies, 'S' Coy less half the carrier platoon, and TAC Bn HQ with essential transport. The second flight (on D+7) with 25% including the remainder of all the fighting elements of each battalion. Finally the third flight of 15% (D+14) would be the 'A' and 'Q' elements.

The first flight was sub-divided into a transport echelon under the CO and a walking echelon loaded with full equipment respirators, tools, ammo, a 24 hour ration pack, greatcoat and blanket - a very heavy load particularly for Bren gunners and 2" mortar men. Not of course forgetting an 'anti-louse' shirt, underclothes, Tommy cooker, water steriliser, 200 French francs and on the voyage, lifebelt, anti-seasick chewing gum, 'vomit bags' and waders!

Lt Col Walford briefed the officers of 5th Seaforth on 28th May, a hot sunny day, as Alastair Borthwick recounts:

> We went into a big black hut. The entire wall facing the door was covered by a gigantic map. It was the same old story. Our marshalling area across the Channel was called 'Edinburgh' or 'Chicago' or some such name and all we knew of the beach on which we were expected to land was that it was called 'Nan'. All the vital questions of 'when' and 'where' were still unanswered.

So HD set off once again to war - somewhere 'over there'. 5th Camerons in HMTs *Cheshire* and *Lancashire*; 7th Black Watch in the liberty ship *Fort Brunswick* and LSI *Isle of Jersey*, 7th Argylls on *Maid of Orleans*, 128 Field Reg RA on liberty ship *Hannibal Hamlin*. All part of an immense armada well guarded by the Navy and the RAF.

27

The Killing Grounds in the Normandy 'Triangle' - June

The 5/7th Gordons were the first battalion of HD to set foot on French soil in Operation Overlord. At sea, maps and final instructions were unsealed by the officer commanding troops on each craft and the plan of attack was revealed to the men. The large town inland was revealed to be Caen, and the landing beach, Courseulles-sur-Mer. Lying offshore a great mass of shipping was seen, vast battleships, busy little destroyers, flak (AA) ships, barrage balloons, LCTs, LSIs, LCIs, liberty ships and overhead the waves of aircraft hammering the beach defences. By late afternoon on D-Day, 6th June the Gordons had waded through several feet of water carrying their 70 lbs weight kit. By 8pm they were all ashore (less transport) and 153 Bde concentrated at Ranville four miles inland. Lt Col 'Chick' Thomson OC 5th Black Watch was by chance acting as Brigadier since Brigadier 'Nap' Murray's ship (with the battalion 2i/cs and Bde HQ) was in the queue of ships waiting to unload. 3rd Canadian Division by this time were several miles further inland.

5th Camerons landing by LCT off HMT *Lancastrian*, D+1 at Juno beach

The CRE, Brigadier Ralph Carr sailed from Tilbury on LST 3002. The civilian dockers and crane workers, of course, clocked off at 5pm, but the mechanical equipment of the Field Park Coy completed the loading. Carr on arrival off Courseuilles drove his own armoured Recce car ashore in a foot of water on 8th June:

> The beach littered with the usual bric à brac of drowned vehicles, damaged craft, knocked-out tanks, a few dead bodies and a number of POW. The Jocks are busy now at their old pastime of slaughtering Germans and doing it quite effectively.

The GOC landed on D+1 from HMS *Hilary* and HD was ordered by 1st Corps to capture a German radar station still holding out near

Douvres-la-Delivrande. 5th Black Watch then had their first engagement in Normandy backed by CLY Shermans against the North Shore Regiment of Canada who were sheltering in the German dug outs in woods. Nearly twenty casualties were needlessly caused, shared between HD and the Canadians. The Radar station held by some 200 Germans then held out for another ten days. The *8th Grenadier Regt, 716 Division* defended 'Radar' wood and station with great skill. 5th Camerons arrived to keep an eye on the German strongpoint whilst 153 Bde moved forward by Hermanville to the 6th Airborne Pegasus Bridge.

Lt Col Walford, CO 5th Seaforth was in temporary command of 152 Bde. His battalion had spent many frustrating hours on board four miles offshore.

"Ahead was a low ridge with a small town below it, fat farming country, neat and peaceful like the coast of Devon before the war," wrote Alastair Borthwick, "Ships were everywhere. The whole sea crawled... This monstrous regatta, this mass of five hundred vessels was spread over only seven miles of a bridgehead already more than fifty miles long." As 5th Seaforth arrived on D+2 on Nan beach, Courseulles-sur-Mer, Pte Willie Thain was sitting in the cab of his ammo truck at the front of the LCT. He saw several bodies floating in the tide and thinking one was still alive jumped down to help. A naval officer saw Willie apparently about to 'chicken out' and pointed a loaded revolver at his head with, "Soldier, get that f—ing load of ammunition off my ship. Now." In Willie's own words: "That f—ing load of ammunition went up that beach like a scalded cat." His mate James Younie: "Regretfully Willie was badly wounded a few days later." TAC Div HQ set up shop at Colombiers on D+2. The CRA and CRSignals arrived perched on top of a three ton vehicle for a half mile 'swim.' By nightfall Main Div HQ arrived, a mile away from TAC HQ, 2nd British Army.

HD was now concentrated around Colville on the right flank of the bridgehead on both sides of the river Orne. 153 Bde was ordered to enlarge the bridgehead on the night of the 10th, D+4, with 152 Bde in reserve and 154 Bde providing a firm base at Basly. The main attack would be on Touffreville with 5th Black Watch, 'C' Coy Die Hards and their Major Pearson directing the 14" guns of HMS *King George*, leading from Ranville north-east to Breville. The Die Hards had 'C' Coy with 153 Bde, 'D' with 152 Bde and 'B' with 154 Bde who had landed on the 10th June. 153 Bde was temporarily under command of 6th Airborne so 1st Gordons guarded the bridges over the canal and river Orne at Benouville and 5/7th Gordons were in reserve on Periers ridge.

On the 8th [D+2] I became a Derbyshire Yeoman and was sent to 4 Tp 'C' Sqn in a field at Benouville. The Tp CO was Lt Millington. I [Tpr Leslie

Philpott] made up the crew of Corporal 'Chalky' White and 'Geordy' Simpson. I had never heard of the DY and was pleased to find them a decent lot. Since several of them wore the Africa Star, I decided they should know a bit about keeping your head down. One Tp mounted a guard on Benouville Bridge which they told us Jerry was trying to destroy with frogmen. 'Wee Jock', 'Tich' Read, Harold Pearson, Jock Dawson and 'Taffy' Pritchard helped us novices a great deal.

The Divisional artillery were arriving battery by battery and half of 128 Field Regt supported the Black Watch attack from Blainville and Colleville, whilst 126 Field arrived near Hermanville on D+6. *346 German Infantry Division* with artillery and tanks were defending the Breville area. From St Aubin the Black Watch (under command of 3 Paratroop Brigade) crossed the two canal bridges and the river Orne and at 0430hrs Sunday, 11th set forth on their first bloody battle in 'bocage' country. Sunken lanes, small fields, apple orchards, very thick hedgerows and small fields meant difficult tank country, difficult for RA FOO's to find height for their OPs: in fact excellent defensive country. Quite soon enemy mortar bombs rained down on 'A' Coy. By 0900 they were down to platoon strength with all their officers casualties except Lt McDonald. Their OC was wounded four times and the 2i/c Capt Andrew killed. 'B' Coy trying to work round Breville to the south and 'C' making a left hook were pinned down by withering fire. Lt Col Thomson without tank, and little artillery support, was ordered to withdraw to the start line and dig in. 'D' Coy and 'HQ' Coy were holding the nearby Chateau St Come and that evening the survivors of 'A', 'B' and 'C' dug in defensive positions round the chateau. 11th June was a bad day for the Black Watch with 50 officers and men killed. But there was more to come. At 1500 hours on the 12th a very heavy enemy barrage descended on the battalion's positions and then a German infantry battalion supported by tanks and SP guns firing AP and oil bombs, made their successive onslaughts on the Black Watch. Nine Bren gun carriers and all the anti-tank guns were put out of action. The fighting went on for three hours. A company of Canadian Paratroops arrived to take over 'D' Coy section and a decisive fire plan from the six inch guns of HMS *Arethusa*, 12 miles away landed slap in the centre of the milling German troops and tanks with devastating effect.

In their first week in Normandy the Bn lost six officers and 92 ORs killed, 11 officers and 198 ORs wounded, a total of 307 casualties most of them on the 11th and 12th. Unbelievably on the 13th the RAF inflicted ten more casualties, including four killed. Appreciative letters were received from Brigadier H Murray and Major General Gale, GOC 6 Airborne and 'Breville' became a well deserved battle honour for the regiment. The 2i/c Major Dunn, the Adjutant Capt McIntyre visited all the RHU camps seeking reinforcements.

The Die Hards sent No 10 Platoon with four Vickers machine-guns to help in the defence of Chateau St Come with 5th Black Watch: "Early in the morning Jerry mortars knocked-out our section, and two guns killing and wounding most of us [Private Denis Daly]. I survived the stonk with Ginty Riley and Mathewman. We made our way back to the security of the chateau. Later in the day Jerry laid down a heavy barrage before attacking in force." Daly later noticed some soldiers clambering over the Middlesex carriers parked behind the chateau. He had left a lot of cigarettes in his vehicle and shouted at the soldiers to clear off, "Shouts of 'Achtung Englander' ensued accompanied by bursts of gunfire." The company commander Major Pearson placed the remaining Vickers at the top of the staircase in the chateau firing through a shell hole in the wall. Tommy Latham the platoon signaller fired the Vickers and helped hold off the attack, earned an MM. Sgt Fred Addison took a PIAT, used it vertically as a mortar to break up another counter-attack from the stables. He too earned the MM. Most of the Black Watch officers were by now casualties and the NCOs took over. Daly's rifle was split in two and his shoulder badly bruised: "The following morning despite firing yellow smoke canisters RAF Typhoons attacked the Die Hards. They gave us a going over. It took just one week to turn a green kid into a very wary campaigner."

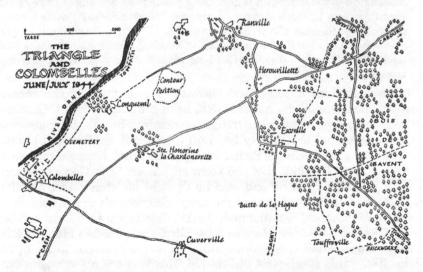

When 5/7th Gordons reached Touffreville on the evening of the 11th it was empty having been cleared by the Airborne. 1st Gordons then occupied the brickworks and 5/7th the village but large scale enemy infiltration started before dawn on the 12th and at one stage or another on this critical day each company was surrounded and Battalion HQ rudely assailed by Spandau parties. At noon the Germans withdrew having caused 28 casualties. Lt Col J Hay was awarded the DSO after this action. Sgt Aitkenhead, 'B' Coy was taken prisoner, killed his guard, hid in a cornfield, then a farm, under British artillery fire and rejoined his unit. He was greeted by: 'Is that you Sgt Aitkenhead? Aye, I ken't they could never kill *you*.'

The Provost Sergeant, Sgt Willie McPherson, when Bn HQ was attacked by 30 enemy with machine-gun, .345 machine pistols and mortars took charge of the signallers, batmen and regimental police. With grenades and stenguns they fended off the attackers who left 13 dead or wounded behind, and four Spandaus. McPherson was awarded the MM for a good morning's work. Two days later both Gordon battalions were withdrawn from Touffreville, now in a dangerous salient, losing over 30 casualties. Jeff Haward, 12 Platoon 1/7th Middlesex were supporting 5/7th Gordons:

> It was getting light but our observation was obscured by smoke from the burning corn and bursting shells. Out of this at 200 yards came running PZ Grenadiers firing machine pistols throwing stick grenades and screaming their heads off. I thought it must be a bad dream and my stomach felt full of lead. A wire fence held them up for a few seconds. Our four Vickers opened up and the Grenadiers were mown down. I remember grimly hanging on to the trigger grips and firing whole belts non-stop. The nearest Grenadier was 12 yards in front of my gun. Next six MK IV tanks moved down the road from Cuverville towards us. The 17-pdr anti-tank at our side was the best. It fired six rounds and knocked out four tanks and a half track. The 3" mortars of 5/7th Gordons played a big part in stopping the enemy.

Later a Gordons officer asked Haward to collect ID off the enemy dead in front. Hoping for a nice watch, he approached a 'dead' German officer with a luger and entrenching tool nearby, "In a flash he jumped up, raised the tool to chop my head off'." After an undignified brawl, Sgt Haward's No 2, Ginger Richardson (a little bomb happy after being in the siege of Tobruk), shot the German officer. "The Gordon officer was laughing his head off and said he thought we were doing a waltz in No Mans Land! It was one of the longest 30 seconds in my life."

Operation 'Smock' was the task for 152 Bde to capture Demouville, by 2nd Seaforth and Ste Honorine by 5th Camerons. Ste Honorine la Chardonette, a small village surrounded by orchards stands in the open plain, 4000 yards south-west of Breville. This was the objective for 5th Camerons who had been 'watching' the Douvres Radar station. The barrage at 0420 on the 12th June came down on the Camerons! Although the area could be seen by the enemy OPs 2000 yards away in the factory chimneys of Colombelles, an industrial suburb of Caen, the village was captured by 0700 hrs. Heavy shell, mortar and machine-gun fire came in at about 0830. 'D' Coy facing east reported a counter-attack with infantry and 14 tanks. Sgt A MacKenzie's 6-pdr anti-tank gun hit three of them and the rest retired, for which he later received the MM. Nearly all the battalion wireless sets were knocked-out as shells, mortar bombs from Nebelwerfers exploded in the trees, causing many casualties. Withdrawal seemed inevitable, started at 0945 and was completed an hour later. Major Cairns OC 'C' Coy and 15 men were left behind by mistake still fighting vigorously as Divisional and enemy 'stonks' rained down on Ste Honorine. The Battalion then took over the defences of Longueval, a 1000 yards north-west of Ste Honorine. Cairns and Capt Yellowlees, the MO received MCs, CSM Clelland, L/Corp Monley and Pte Sands the MM. Reinforcements of five officers and 53 ORs arrived to replace the heavy casualties.

127 Field Regt RA, Benouville June 1944 (Capt M V Sim)

Fraser Burrows was a platoon commander in 'B' Coy 5th Camerons:

The set piece attack was launched from Longueval, overlooked by the Boche, so a concentration of tank support would have been detected. 'B' and 'D' duly arrived on the start line, 'D' being heavily shelled before the attack timed for midnight. We were all established in the village by day break with only the battalion's 2-pdr anti-tank guns as protection against the counter-attack which came in the morning. Despite three enemy tanks destroyed by our own 2-pdrs we were ordered to withdraw to our original start line. The panzer tanks were very close to be brewed up by our little 'pop' guns. This was the first time 5th Camerons had ever voluntarily given up captured territory and the Brigadier was very upset. He was fired thirteen days later. In hindsight an attack launched from Herouvillette with tank support might have succeeded" [it did on 23rd June].

Because of the failure of the Cameron attack, and the huge defensive fire programmes that the Germans were putting down, the 2nd Seaforth attack was abandoned. They dug-in north of Ste Honorine and 5th Seaforth came into the line between 2nd Seaforth and 5th Camerons.

153 Bde had been simulating an attack on Sanneville to draw attention away from Ste Honorine. The division had moved to the area of the bridges across the river Orne and its canal by the 14th and two days later a heavy counter-attack supported by tanks came in against 153 Bde.

Padre Tommy Nicol and CQMS Ed Meekison 5th Black Watch set off to the Para HQ to locate the graves of 'A' Coy killed at Breville. On foot laden with armfuls of wooden crosses they located the temporary graves, carried out their sad task and at dusk the enemy brought down a barrage of fire on the two of them. A few hours later at 0425 hrs the Germans attacked along the whole front east of the river Orne and got within a few hundred yards of 'D' Coy, fought off by Major JO Wright's men. The main onslaught fell on 1st Gordons now around Escoville. Divisional artillery, the Die Hards 'A' Coy heavy mortars and the Derbyshire Yeomanry between them knocked-out four MK III tanks and two armoured cars. All day confused fighting went on in the hedgerows and orchards and Escoville was taken and retaken. A 61 Anti-Tank Regt 17-pdr knocked-out an SP gun and a MK IV tank. Later in the day the enemy were streaming north through the woods towards Breville when L/Sgt Fraser 5/7th Gordons pumped in 30 shells from his anti-tank 6-pdr and hit and brewed three enemy tanks. Sgt Willie McPherson CMP:

> The German tanks had broken through, only about three hundred yards from us. I prepared myself for the POW camp... Fraser gave the order to fire and the leading tank went up in flames. Nice work, Jack - a real brew up. A second tank swings round past the first one, its guns trained on our guns vainly trying to knock it out. I begin to feel down-hearted again - this second tank still advancing 400-300-200. 'By God, Jack you don't know how I've been sweating but there's another lovely brew.' From out of the black smoke there emerges an armoured car. 'Stand by, lads! Load, Range - On target - Fire!' And the last threat for this attack is over. But that gun crew - heroes all.

Willie McPherson was killed on 29th August. 5/7th Gordons suffered heavily, seven KIA, 24 wounded and 40 missing.

The 1st Gordons were dug in along hedgerows near Escoville with enemy infiltration shooting up battalion HQ. A platoon of 'C' Coy was over-run. Fighting continued throughout the day with many DF targets called down by the gunner FOOs. By midnight the enemy withdrew having caused many casualties including six officers and 30 ORs.

HD Div HQ moved to Ranville and had a very unpleasant trying period of offensive/defensive battles. This triangular Orne bridgehead was shelled, mortared and bombed, day and night, and there were heavy casualties. It was difficult country, thickly wooded with orchards, hedges, hay fields and corn fields. The RE work was mainly opening and maintaining the vehicle and tank routes, removing the enemy mines and laying our own protective mines, bull-dozing in of tanks, guns, headquarters, burying dead cattle, livestock and sometimes Germans too. The armoured bulldozer was invaluable; the mechanical section of 239 Field Park Coy often operated right up into the front line. [Lt Col Ralph Carr, CRE 51st HD]

All three divisional field regiments were now in action with FOO's out with all battalions and most companies. Capt Bannerman 126 Field Regt was killed supporting 6th Airborne attack on the Breville crossroads, and in the Escoville counter-attack by the Germans, the regiment fired 180 rounds per gun. Geoff Durand, 128 Field Regt:

Our infantry experienced devastating mortar fire especially from the German Moaning Minnies, a six barrel rocket propelled mortar which had a terrible effect on our troops. To counter this we became involved in a counter mortar drive with special equipment called a Four Pen Recorder. A job for the surveyors, as four microphones were set up in front of the infantry and wired back to our recorder which was in a dug-out about half a mile behind the infantry. The operation was hazardous, sniped at by the enemy, resented by the PBI since the activity might give away their locations. The instrument marked a graph, then read the determined mortar positions by co-ordinates. Regimental targets then shelled the enemy mortar sights in the area of Escoville and Herouvillette where our infantry suffered most casualties.

The Derby Yeomanry had a frustrating time, like all the Recce regiments in the British Army, in the bridgehead. Unlike the desert there was no space to lead, roam, harass and destroy. DY guarded bridges but took part in the bitter fighting for the villages of Escoville and Herouvillette, being employed mainly in an infantry role. In four days casualties were about 50 including the CO, Lt Col RH Palmer, but three MCs and four MMs were awarded. On 2nd July Lt Col WP Serocold took command.

By 14th June the Supply Column (RASC) was in position fully maintaining the division. CRASC had landed at 0730 at Graye-sur-Mer on 8th June and joined Div HQ at Cresserons. Over the next few days the four companies faced varying degrees of chaos and due to shelling from German long range guns their main depots were moved several times. They suffered almost as much from allied aircraft as from enemy action. The companies now renumbered 525, 526, 527 and 458 were reorganised on 21st June to a commodity basis (rations, ammunition, petrol etc.).

The next attack was by 152 Bde, again on Ste Honorine on 23rd June. A silent night operation by 5th Camerons from Le Bas de Ranville backed by Die Hard heavy mortars and a squadron of 13/18th Hussar Shermans. Although the two leading companies came under heavy Spandau fire the ill-fated little village was taken (or retaken) by 0400 and Major Wormald's tanks were in position. The code word 'Haggis' for success was sent to Brigade shortly after 0600. At dawn snipers and Moaning Minnie bombs caused more casualties. From Cuverville the enemy sent in waves of counter-attacks losing three tanks at 0700 and at 0930 with no less than 35 Mark IV tanks, and a final substantial attack at 1100 hrs. A company from 2nd Seaforth and another from 5th Seaforth arrived to help but by noon the enemy had had enough, leaving 13 tanks and two half-tracks behind. It was an all arms victory. Hussar tanks, divisional artillery. 61st Anti-Tank Regt guns, the Die Hards and of course the determined Camerons and Seaforth. A final counter-attack at 1630 was quickly dispersed.

During the two battles for Ste Honorine the battalion suffered no less than 230 casualties. Lt Chalmers won the MC and Sgt M Fraser the MM. The Hussars Major Wormald won an immediate DSO. A few days later the popular Lt Col 'Sandie' Monro was posted back to the UK and Major HW Cairns took command. Corporal GA Lleitch, 'I' Section, 5th Seaforth discovered that the top branches of an enormous elm tree near the Pre Baron farm made an excellent OP. Richard Fleming, OC 'D' Coy:

> The fame of our OP spread quickly. Before mid-day our line of elms was like a rookery with a different OP in each. We had our 'I' Section, 'D' Coy snipers, an FOO from 127 Field Regt, the Mortar platoon even a desperate naval gunner from HMS *Arethusa*. Life was intolerable on board for him through lack of targets." 5th Seaforth were in Le Bas de Ranville for three days close to the Benouville bridges over the Orne. It was the high water mark of the airborne drop and 60 corpses, German and British were still lying in the nearby cornfields. Under fire from heavy 150 and 210 mm guns and mortars the Seaforth were underground for all the time, losing 20 casualties. Lt AFS Hector joined the battalion on the 15th and was dead an hour later. The Seaforth then spent ten more 'peaceful' days in Longueval until the 26th and relieved 2nd Seaforth in Ste Honorine, defenders there since the Camerons success.

On 14th June 154 Bde were put under command of 6th Airborne to defend the vital captured Orne bridges with 7 Argylls in the Bois de Bavent ridge, the southern point of the bridgehead to the east of the river. It was close country with scrub, small orchards, thick hedges and in places dense forest. The enemy were active and infiltrated at night. There were limited fields of fire and patrols were difficult in close wooded country. Until 9th July the Argylls, 1st and 7th Black Watch rotated defensive positions under fire with a constant drain of daily casualties.

The whole of 154 Bde was heavily shelled on the night of Saturday, 24th June. The 7th Black Watch in their slit trenches were deluged with shells as was the road leading back to Ranville and the Orne bridges. 'B' Coy fired 20,000 rounds of small arms ammo and the mortar platoon over 1000 3" bombs. Capt Porteous of the Argylls led carrier convoys throughout the night, up steep tracks, twisting among the trees to rush mortar bombs up to the Black Watch. By 0430 the enemy fire ceased but the battalion lost 42 casualties and their MO was killed. The enemy observation posts in the Colombelles area commanded the area and they brought down concentrations from Nebelwerfers at the drop of a hat. On Monday, 26th as the Black Watch moved back into reserve - companies dispersed, 'A' Coy, lost three officers and their CSM to 'Moaning Minnies'.

Although the RAF had now almost total command over the Normandy bridgehead, there were occasional Messerschmitt raids and also some leaflet raids. On Bannockburn Day (24th June) 5th Black Watch were showered with leaflets calling on the Allied forces to surrender before the now deadly V-1s (and later V-2s) destroyed London and the main city centres. And two days later Monty unleashed another grand slam attack on Caen with support from 600 guns. But it was several days before 3rd British and 3rd Canadian troops fought their way into the suburbs.

For several weeks the tall factory chimneys at Colombelles, harbouring enemy OPs were bombed and shelled to little effect. The area between Breville, Ranville, the river Orne, the Bavent woods with a wide base from the Caen road, Cuverville and Touffreville was known as the Triangle. Brigadier James Oliver had visited 5th Camerons with Lt General Crocker, the Corps Commander. He and Lt Col John Hopwood CO 1st Black Watch took their VIP across an open field where they thought they would probably get shelled. They were and had to lie flat to avoid the shell fragments. Oliver told Hopwood, "it will do the Corps Commanders a lot of good to have a first hand taste of conditions in the front line."

5th Seaforth spent five days and nights in Ste Honorine, which is described by Alastair Borthwick:

> Once a douce little place with its seven or eight big farms and huddle of smaller buildings round them. The village had been abandoned completely and fast. The walls were down and the windows in and the contents of the houses were ragged heaps where pigs rooted. Dust from the shellbursts lay

thickly over half eaten meals and burst mattresses. There were 29 dead cows in one farmyard, 11 in another all killed by shrapnel. They had lain in the sun for twelve days. Hens were plastered on to the walls like pats of mud. The place was a shambles

So passed the first three weeks in the killing grounds.

28

The Normandy Bridgehead: July - the 24 hour raid

The GOC Major General Bullen-Smith visited 1st Black Watch on 30th June and a few days later Brigadier Harvey Haugh 152 Bde was relieved of his command and replaced by Brigadier AJH Cassels, a Seaforth Highlander. Cherbourg had fallen to the Americans and Operation Epsom had forced a bridgehead over the river Odon. HD watched the RAF heavy bombers partially destroy Caen on 7th July. The German defenders had withdrawn from the centre but the Canadians and 3rd British finally battered their way into Caen on the 10th. HD were now ordered to mount an attack on the notorious Colombelles village, a factory suburb with its dominating high chimney OPs. It lay two miles north-east of Caen and in the event was a very difficult objective. It was planned as a 24 hour raid for 153 Bde plus 7th Black Watch. 1st Gordons had sent 'A' Coy along the towpath from Longueval on the 9th to test the defences. It was a hornet's nest. Although a factory building was found to be empty, when the fighting patrol left a severe barrage of heavy mortars retaliated. At 0100 on 11th July 1st Gordons set of on the right, 5th Black Watch on the left with 7th Black Watch to follow through to secure the factory area and protect the sappers as they destroyed the two tall chimneys. Tremendous artillery support launched the 153 Bde night attack. 'B' Coy 1st Gordons cleared some houses on the outskirts but heavy fire caused casualties. Lt Robertson took command as the OC and 2i/c were wounded and withdrew the weakened Coy to reorganise at 0345 at the cemetery. 'D' Coy were checked too but 'A' got on to their objectives, so Lt Col Stevenson ordered 'C' in reserve to take the towpath route and link up with 'A.' The sappers could not get their vehicles up.

On the north-east outskirts of Caen several tall chimneys gave the Germans excellent observation over our activities. I arranged for a large quantity of explosives for the divisional sappers for the demolition of these chimneys and an armoured bulldozer was also made available. 153 Bde was sent to take the factory by a night attack on the 11th July. Unfortunately information was scarce, the area strongly held with infantry and armour, thoroughly defensively prepared. It was nearly a disaster. There were heavy casualties before retiring. [Lt Col Ralph Carr CRE]

'B' and 'D' Coys were withdrawn back to Longueval. About 0500 'C' and 'A' were mopping up the south-west corner of Colombelles; an hour later the CO was wounded and Major Cumming-Bruce took command. At 0810 'A' and 'C' to their surprise were ordered to withdraw back to Longueval and then to Ranville. When Major Martin Lindsay joined the battalion as 2i/c a few days later Cumming-Bruce told him that "the defences were much stronger than anticipated and the attack failed miserably. The continued shelling had made a number of men 'bomb-happy.' They lacked offensive spirit as a result of being too tired, too much use having been made of the Divison. They had lost twelve officers including three company commanders and 200 men in 35 days of fighting 'without achieving very much.'"

Maj Gen Bullen-Smith and Brig Murray, TAC HQ, Normandy

On the left were 5th Black Watch supported by a Sqn of 148 Regt RAC tanks and two platoons of 61 Anti-Tank 17-pdr guns. By 0330 hrs all objectives were secured - the crossroads and north-east corner of the Colombelles factory with eleven supporting tanks in hulldown positions. As the Gordons attack had failed, the Black Watch were now surrounded on three sides. The hardness of the ground made digging in difficult and the predictable counter-attacks came in. By 0700 five Tiger tanks had closed to within 300 yards and later ten Shermans were knocked-out. Casualties were mounting and Brigadier 'Nap' Murray agreed to withdrawal, completed under smoke screens by 0930 hrs. Throughout the action the German OPs on the factory chimneys had total control of the battlefield and the Black Watch suffered 128 casualties, including 71 killed or missing.

Major Alexander Brodie, 'A' Coy 5th Black Watch addressed his company before the Colombelles night attack:

> I told them while I would not hesitate to shoot any one who ran away. I expected them to shoot me or any officer or NCO who ordered them to pack in [ie surrender]. To my surprise this rather frightened them and soon after Bill Johnstone [the Coy 2i/c] told me that our two stretcher-bearers had disappeared. These had both been at Breville and no doubt their courage had been worn away. By making off before or during a battle, men add to the difficulties and danger of those they leave behind. They may have to carry extra loads of ammunition and stores and will certainly get less sleep during operations because their turn to be sentries will come round more frequently. I found weariness and lack of sleep the worst of the strains of war. The establishment of a rifle company was about 110 of which about 15 were cooks, drivers and storemen, so the company should have about 95 to go into action. In fact, companies were very lucky if they numbered 60, all ranks. So anyone running away caused bitter feelings.

Brodie was a colourful character, well-liked by his men for his reckless bravery. Under shellfire he helped manhandle a 17-pdr anti-tank gun for it to be towed back. He was badly wounded and earned the MC for his exploits.

Lt Col 'Chick' Thomson who had been CO since December 1942 wrote a report about the disastrous 'raid' on Colombelles. He made it clear that hundreds of vantage points other than the factory chimneys afforded good observation of the area; that the right flank was unguarded, and that the supporting Shermans had been knocked-out (leaving the massive German tiger tanks masters of the battlefield). A week or so later Lt Col Thomson was posted back to the UK to command 10th Black Watch and was succeeded by Lt Col Bill Bradford.

By mid-July morale was very low in most of the British Army. But some of the 'German' units were not much better. Alastair Borthwick was now IO of 5th Seaforth, who were within a few hundred yards of *858 Grenadier Regiment*. Their strength was between 300-350 of which

60% were German, 25% Polish and 15% Russian. Many of the Poles and Russians deserted: "The Poles gave our gunners some beautiful targets." On 18th the Seaforth went into an attack during 'Goodwood,' to retake the Triangle, a small wood-enclosed area two miles east of Escoville. Two crossroads at the southern apex were strongly held as shown on air photographs. The whole British and Canadian armies watched the awesome bombing of the German village and strongpoints of Cagny, Touffreville, Sannerville, Bourguebus and a score of others. "The Jocks were all standing grinning at the sky. After weeks of skulking in trenches here was action - action on a bigger scale than any of them had dreamed was possible," recalls Alastair Borthwick. Their supporting barrage started at 0645 and 'A' Coy of the Die Hards threw 2500 4.2" mortar bombs into the attack. H-hour was at 0745. Helped by Crocodile flame-throwers (Churchill tanks towing a large oil drum on wheels), the Seaforth captured all their objectives taking 80 POW and killing 60-70 for the loss of 11 KIA and 51 wounded. Then the Camerons and 2nd Seaforth came thorough and dug in astride the Troarn road.

154 Bde then took over Demouville, 153 Bde the Ranville area and 152 Bde followed up 11th Armoured Div to consolidate the ground won. A cloudburst on the 20th brought Goodwood to a sticky end. The author's Black Bull Division lost 126 tanks on the 18th and another 65 on the 19th. For the next ten days the Seaforth battalions and 5th Camerons had a miserable time in and around the Triangle, not only from the Germans infesting the Bois de Bures with non stop shelling, but from swamped doovers or slit trenches (which often had three feet of rainwater in them); from night bombers and also the ferocious Triangle mosquito!

> We used to count the stings. On the average each of us had twenty on the back of a single hand at any one time. Before the day had healed the itch, darkness brought fresh multistrikes. They caused more discomfort and loss of sleeping in the Orne bridgehead than ever shelling did,

Alastair Borthwick wrote. They not only liked Highland blood, but that of 3rd British and 43rd Wessex divisions a few miles way. And presumably the violent blood of the Panzer Grenadiers, a few hundreds of yards away! A meagre consolation for the foul weather was an Army authorisation for an issue of rum. 7th Black Watch occupied smashed up Demouville and Le Poirer then Cagny and came out of the line on 25th July to Anisy for three days. A rest, thence to the Bois de Bavent, their old 'hunting ground'. Frenouville was the thoroughly unsatisfactory home for 1st Black Watch on a forward slope with little concealment. Their mortar platoon was given targets named 'Brimstone,' 'Corruption,' 'Hail' etc., which was perhaps indicative of their mood at the time: on the 25th they moved back to Cazelle where their Pipe Band played in the pleasant fields.

The Argylls moved from Ste Honorine to Cuverville on the 19th, well dispersed but met heavy shelling, 'C' Coy alone suffered 28 casualties but the battalion acquired 60 German POW. A patrol from 'B' captured 35 in the cornfields along with much valuable booty! Then to Cagny to relieve a Guards battalion until going back to rest at Le Landel on 25th. Mobile bath units, a change of clothing, leave to Bayeux and ceremonial guards plus concerts and Retreat programmes by the Divisional massed pipes and drums helped to relieve the monotony - and restore morale.

Herouvillette was 'home' to 5/7th Gordons until 22nd July. Their CO Lt Col JEG 'Scrappy' Hay was wounded in the head and at the end of the month Lt Col Blair Imrie from the Black Watch took command. The MO Capt JC Thom was killed by a direct hit on his slit trench and at his burial the pipe major played 'Lochaber no more.' The battalion had a week out of the line camping in a cornfield south of Douvres with rest, cleaning up, drill of course, PT, football and visits to a mobile cinema.

Reinforcements poured in, some veterans from disbanded units, some rather 'green.' Private Stanley Whitehouse an Oxfordshire and Buckinghamshire LI man, was part of No 6 Beach Group. He landed on D-Day and was in action for the next five weeks before transferring to 1st Bn Black Watch in mid-July. In 'B' Echelon he and 'Shorty' Les Shorthouse saw 64 'big packs' laid out in neat rows on the ground. "As there were 64 of us I assumed they were ours." They weren't. 64 Jocks had been killed in the last few days and personal items were being taken out to be sent back to the next of kin. Stan noticed there was traditional bad feeling between the Black Watch and the enemy, particularly the SS. The previous day stretcher-bearers had been shot while retrieving wounded comrades. Stan was told by his 'B' Coy officer. "There is no such thing as 'bomb happiness' [battle fatigue or shell shock] in the Black Watch." Just as a young Cornish lad 'Mushty' began crying and sobbing, fervently hoping he would be sent back. 'Shorty' was sent off as a runner to contact 'A' Coy at night. He heard voices with words ending in 'och', 'uch' or 'ich' and assumed they were the Jocks of 'A' Coy. They weren't. "Bloody hell they were Jerries. One spotted me. I had to open fire." Almost by mistake Shorty shot the three Germans, silenced their machine-gun and earned the MM. Little Wally Walters was detailed to guard a large captured SS man and take him back to battalion HQ for questioning. "Hands Hoch, yer bastard," as little Wally looking very businesslike motioned the SS man forward with his rifle. On the way back to battalion, Wally was strangled.

Major Martin Lindsay, 2i/c 1st Gordons, recalled an evening in July out of the line:

we had Retreat with 'the Road to the Isles,' the 'Skye Boat song' and all my favourite tunes. It was a brave display, the pipe band marching and counter marching in a tiny paddock beside the main road, with ammunition trucks and ambulances slowing down to see what they could while passing. For guest at supper was [Lt Col] Maurice Burnett CO 127 Field Regt RA which had supported 153 Bde from El Alamein. He talked about the problem of the gunners, very occasionally, firing short, landing shells amongst their own infantry and how difficult it was to find out, who was responsible. One must be philosophical when it happens and forgive the occasional human error as the benefit one receives from the guns is so immense. Burnett said that our superiority of artillery is about 40 to one. The enemy guns were usually immobile having only one tractor to about four guns.

It was true that the German artillery (excluding the 88mm anti-tank gun) was usually subdued by the massive deployment of British field guns, but the mobile, ubiquitous 'Nebelwerfer' multi-barrelled mortars inflicted enormous damage on British and Canadian infantry.

July ended with HD being complimented by 8th Corps Commander (to 1st Corps Commander): "My thanks to the 51st Highland Division for the wonderful work they have done in removing the minefields and so enabling our armour to pass through," during Operation Goodwood.

29

Morale and the Leadership Crisis

When General Montgomery withdrew his three famous Desert Legions (51st Highland, 50th Northumbrian and 7th Armoured) from the Middle East to lead his 2nd British Army into the heart of Normandy, he was confident they would continue their victorious march. 'Epsom,' 'Jupiter,' 'Mitten' and 'Charnwood' and now 'Goodwood' had not been successful and casualties had been heavy. Many of the Whitehall warriors were demonstrably unhappy with the apparent lack of progress in Normandy. In his heart of hearts Monty was desperate to capture Caen and launch the breakout that would drive towards Paris.

By mid July Monty had despatched a 'for your eyes only' cable to CIGS Alan Brooke which read: "Regret to report it is considered opinion Crocker, Dempsey and myself that 51st Division is at present not - NOT - battleworthy. It does not fight with determination and has failed in every operation it has been given to do. It cannot fight the Germans successfully; I consider the divisional commander is to blame and I am removing him from command. Bullen-Smith has many fine qualities but he has failed to lead Highland Division and I cannot -

repeat, cannot - therefore recommend him to command any other division. I consider he would be able to perform the duties of Dep. of Infantry but you may consider that an unsuccessful divisional commander is not - repeat, not - the man for that job. He would command a District or a Training Division; I consider best man to put in 51st Division in its present state is [Major General TG] Rennie, and I have confidence he would bring it up to its former fine state. Can you send Rennie over at once to report to me on arrival?"

Lt General Brian Horrocks, perhaps Monty's ablest Corps Commander wrote:

> Another disturbing feature was the comparative lack of success of the veteran 7th Armoured and 51st Highland Divisions. Both of them came again later on and finished the war in magnificent shape but during the Normandy fighting they were not at their best. The danger signal comes when the troops begin to say 'Is nobody else fighting this war?' The 7th Armoured and 51st Highland Divisions after being lionised in the UK, came out to Normandy and found themselves faced with an entirely different type of battle fought under different conditions of terrain. And they began to see the difficulties all too clearly. A racing enthusiast once described this condition 'like an old plater who won't go in the mud.' All the more credit to them, they eventually staged a comeback and regained their Middle East form.

The Prime Minister, Winston Churchill was fully aware of the problem and wrote to the War Office (CIGS and Secretary of State for War): "It is a painful reflection that probably not one in four or five men who wear the King's uniform ever hear a bullet whistle, or is likely to hear one. The vast majority run no more risk than the civil population in southern England. It is my unpleasant duty to dwell on these facts. One set of men are sent back again and again to the front, while the great majority are kept out of all fighting, to their regret." Well, perhaps!

The morale in HD was low, as indeed it was in every 2nd Army division which had suffered heavy losses for so little to show for it. The CRE Lt Col Ralph Carr wrote home:

> At the end of six weeks we were very tired, even the gunners and sappers. There was no let up. Pinned up in our little corner under steady shellfire by day, and air attack by night, every 24 hours brought its trickle of casualties. Sleep was difficult, chiefly because we have lived in our own gun line for so long. After the Caen battle we found ourselves relegated to holding the shattered ruins of villages, splintered leafless woods smashed in our previous six weeks fighting, reminded at every turn by the sights and smells of our hastily buried dead caused by our fruitless endeavours, you can imagine a certain depression setting in.

On 24th July he wrote:

I had liked this campaign the least of any I had taken part in after five years of battling. There were some very unsatisfactory features to it as far as we are concerned. I can only hope that it won't go on for very long. All was not well with the Highland Division.

Major DFO Russell 7th Black Watch:

The ups and downs of morale are almost inexplicable - possibly being in a holding role after almost continual advances and attacks as the battalion had become accustomed to throughout the North African and Sicilian campaigns had something to do with it - but during the whole of this period, the morale of the battalion was at its lowest ebb which made the task of competing with day to day troubles and worries even more difficult. The enemy although he seldom showed himself seemed to be well equipped with mortars and the battalion was almost continuously under mortar fire.

When Lt Col DB Lang took command of 5th Bn Cameron Highlanders at the end of July, he was their fifth CO in seven weeks. Lt Col 'Sandie' Monro was posted to the UK. His successor Major HW Cairns was wounded on 22nd July. Then Major CAH Noble was wounded in an incident when the Brigade Major was killed and the Brigadier slightly wounded. and Major PM Hunt took command until Lt Col Lang arrived. In the first three weeks of the campaign the battalion had 17 officers and 204 ORs casualties. The loss of the young fighting leaders, section, platoon and company was a terrible blow to morale.

During an attack a Platoon or Coy Commander had plenty of things to concern them. The private soldier had nothing to think about except where the next hostile shell or bullet was coming from. Nothing was easier in a night attack, but to stop, tie a boot lace and disappear. In Normandy this became more and more prevalent. We dealt with this in a number of ways; no breakfast for a start; no NAAFI rations (ie no cigarettes) for a week; a threat to inform their next of kin of their behaviour. The scorn of their peers was also a very effective deterrent. I had one Jock in Normandy who was marched into battle with a bayonet up his backside. [Capt Fraser Burrows 5th Camerons]

Captain Ian Cameron 7th Argylls:

Not a day passed without the battalion area being subjected to heavy shelling and mortaring and although our casualties were not heavy, there was a continual drain on personnel. In former campaigns the 51st Division had always been used aggressively and wherever there was an attack HD always took part in it. This was the first time that the battalion had to sit for lengthy periods in a defensive position without launching an attack and this became very monotonous. In addition the Division was not used as a Division but had battalions attached to other divisions here, there and everywhere... It was a period of very considerable strain and we had to keep a very high degree of alertness all the time. Sometimes the Bn would have to 'stand to' for two or three hours at night in anticipation of an attack.

Peter Parnwell, Intelligence Section, 7th Argylls:

I felt that the battalion was almost at war with itself as with the enemy. The officers with several notable exceptions, seemed second-rate and lacked any skill in man-management or in establishing a rapport with their men. Frequent changes in the more senior ranks did not help. The majority of the men had fought in the Desert and Sicily and with some reason felt they had done their share. Any orders that involved life-threatening activity were ignored or watered-down, especially if given by young officers without battle training.

Major Alexander Brodie, a regular officer, joined 5th Black Watch at the end of June to command 'A' Company, which consisted of very young English cockneys. Ed Meekison was CQMS and the 2i/c was Bill Johnstone, a Glaswegian.

The NCOs were inexperienced and had arrived since Breville where the battalion had suffered badly. The few soldiers who had survived Breville were no help. They had been thoroughly frightened and had lost their friends. If I had been more experienced, I would have had them posted but I was still feeling my way, so I lacked the confidence to ask for this to be done. [Major Brodie]

Jocks were reporting sick for a variety of reasons including malaria from the Middle East mosquitoes. Indeed four 7th Argyll officers were evacuated to the UK with malaria. Shellshock, battle exhaustion or a state of 'bomb-happiness' cases passed to the RMO in the RAP, mostly genuine, some not. Pte Stanley Whitehouse, 'B' Coy 1st Black Watch recounted a grisly story:

'Banger' Brown and Jock Jarman were the first 'trotters', ie deserters. The CMP caught them, returned the couple to Stan's platoon both handcuffed. They had then been taken out on patrol, still manacled, into 'no mans land', and then a second patrol. On their return, during the night a supporting tank had pulled into the platoon position by mistake and one track went over the prisoners doover crushing the two 'trotters'. For them the war was over.

Alastair Borthwick recounted:

We had been in the line for a long time, continuously under fire and doing (as it must have seemed to many) absolutely nothing. And yet here we were, still in the same old doover, getting nowhere. The enemy mortars had our range and casualties were mounting. We were all bone-tired. When a man sees his friend killed in an attack he can understand the need for it and accepts it: but bridgeheads and buildings and Army plans are abstractions too vague to be comprehended when he is sitting in a trench and seeing, day after day, four or five or six of his mates being carried off or buried. It is to the credit of the men that none of them ever did ask why, that they did accept the situation even if they did not understand it and held on uncomplainingly until the end.

Captain Lionel Aitkenhead, 128 Field Regt joined Divisional HQ on the 'Q' side and wrote: "It might have been different if we had remained in the 8th Army and after a short rest continued up Italy, as with the rests after the end of the Western Desert and the Tunisian campaigns. Instead we had six months in the UK, saw our loved ones and were stationed mainly in the Home Counties. We became perhaps too soft and relaxed - and perhaps justifiably were lionised by the British public - their African heroes." Aitkenhead went on to explain:

> Our role was primarily to hold the left flank of the bridgehead on the right back of the River Orne with 6 Airborne. This resulted in the Division being spread out along the perimeter in a defensive role most of the time until the breakout. In this role, the units were faced with a considerable amount of shelling and mortaring from relatively strong enemy forces with occasional night air attacks from the odd plane or two with the enemy indicating the position of their front line with flares. This produced a small but almost constant trickle of casualties which was depressing. On at least two occasions, offensive action was taken by the Division alone with unsatisfactory results. The first was the 152 Bde attack commencing with the 5th Camerons having to take Ste Honorine. I remember looking at the battle plan and seeing the other Bns of the Bde were to pass through to objectives further on with the 153 Bde to repeat the pattern followed by 154 Bde. It seemed to me the Division was proceeding on along their line towards Berlin. The attack of course failed at the first hurdle. The second was the attack by 153 Bde on the factory at Colombelles without success and with heavy casualties. In retrospect, it seemed that the factory would really have needed a Corps to take it. The feeling was that in order to obtain results, orders to the Division had not simply to be carried out, but analysed as to whether the tasks were within the capability of the Division and the timescale allotted.

On 26th July General Montgomery interviewed the GOC, Major General Charles Bullen-Smith, an emotional scene as reported by Lt Col Kit Dawnay, Monty's LO: "'You must go, the men won't fight for you,' and 'You will go home now.' Charles came out with tears pouring down his face. Monty deeply moved said; 'If I don't remove you, Charles, men will be killed unnecessarily. You must go.' That was all."

Bullen-Smith's popular successor Major General Thomas Rennie DSO MBE had commanded 5th Black Watch in the Desert and 154 Bde in Sicily, before being appointed to command Monty's old division, 3rd British, the 'Iron-Sides.' He had been wounded on D+6 and was now fit to return to duty.

It is probable that the new GOC was fortunate in the timing of his appointment. Perhaps if he had succeeded Douglas Wimberley after 'Operation Husky' in Sicily, he would have inherited all the problems already mentioned, but for a variety of reasons things started to get better. The HD were now - in August - to be fighting as a division, not in penny packets. They would be attacking in a well-planned offensive action (Totalise). They had absorbed and integrated hundreds of young, 'green' but eager troops (mostly Scottish) who were not as cautious as many of the desert veterans justifiably had become.

And they had a Black Watch Highlander to lead them! Lt Col Ralph Carr CRE writing home: "I am sure we shall go from strength to strength." And within a short time Monty was writing to the CIGS: "Bullen-Smith could do nothing with 51 Div so had to go. Thomas Rennie is there now and the Division is quite different under him."

Gen T G Rennie

30
Breakout in August: Operation Totalise - "hammer and tongs"

On 31st July HD was relieved and came out of the line to Cazelle, north-west of Caen. The HD divisional rest camp by the sea had opened on 26th June, providing reasonable food, rations, NAAFI beer, some unofficial cider and calvados, sea bathing, ENSA and Balmoral concerts, mobile bath units, cinema shows, inter-company football matches, regimental games. Sun, relative peace, predictable 'bull', mail from home and the first issues of Piobaireachd, the HD newsheet giving up to date news from home towns in Scotland - all helped morale. The Padre of 5th Seaforth had "discovered a camembert factory, so fresh cheese and milk were now on the Jocks' menus" noted Alastair Borthwick. Div HQ had some canine favourites. Capt Locke's dog Maggie a 'bomb happy' bitch from Ranville produced pups called Gazelle, Boville and Ben which went with Div Signals all the way to Bremerhaven. Ten per cent of each battalion were allowed day leave into Bayeux. 1st Gordons 2i/c Major Martin Lindsay felt, "the confidence we now all had in the future was wonderful. It was the product of faith in the [new] generalship, in our own Division and in Second Army. Nor could morale in any Division have been higher. Another source of strength was the magnificent type of man that you get from Scotland, whether he comes from the glens or the straths, the fields or the coal faces, the towns or the cities."

5/7th Gordons received 46 reinforcements from the Duke of Wellington's Regt on 6th August and 1st Black Watch, 100 from the Oxfordshire and Buckinghamshire L.I., but not enough for 7th Black Watch who were reorganised on a three company basis. In 154 Bde 5th Camerons disbanded their Carrier platoon and distributed many highly trained men into the rifle companies. Scout platoons from 15 to 30 men, organised into sections of four to six men were armed with anything from a sniper's rifle to a Vickers 'K' type sub-machine-gun.

Capt ALK Aitkenhead was posted from 128 Field Regt RA to Div HQ to become Staff Captain RA: "I was under the tutelage of two very well known Divisional characters, the DAAG Major Jock Gray (Gordons) and DAQMG, Major Geordie Ross (Seaforth) both shortly to be promoted and appointed AA and QMGs. I was immediately nicknamed 'the stooge.'" The wisdom of Solomon was needed to decide the responsibility of allocating jeeps, in short supply to replace those 'written-off.' He doubled the Die Hards indent for Vickers machine-gun ammo and that was very popular. Capt Ian Cameron 7th Argylls became G3 at 154 Bde HQ: "Many of my friends in the battalion since 1940 were long since dead but the spirit of the battalion was the same. Staff work at brigade gave me a better idea of what was happening within the brigade as a whole." Another change took place at 5/7th Gordons: "On 31st July the new CO, HCW Blair Imrie [formerly 2i/c 7th Black Watch] arrived. He was five years younger than me [Major Martin Lindsay] but had five times more battle experience, having fought through the desert campaign and out here since D-Day."

Monty now planned two massive break out operations which involved an immense amount of planning to get the appropriate formations in the right places. Operation Bluecoat had started on 30th July with 8 and 30 Corps thrusting east to take Vire and capture Mt Pincon. 2nd British Army's main objective was Argentan and 1st Canadian Army's, Falaise. HD now came under command of Lt General GG Simonds' 2nd Canadian Corps. They moved by TCVs from Cazelle/Augerny through devastated Caen on 6th August to Cormelles and Bourguebus.

The new GOC held two Divisional 'O' Groups for senior and junior officers with a sand table of the terrain eastwards down the Caen-Falaise main road. Air photographs had shown that the enemy had prepared two considerable defence lines, the forward one fully manned, the second prepared, dug and ready for occupation when necessary. An armoured column would break through the first line and expected to take the second line with some rapidity. Tilly-la-Campagne was a key objective. On 7th August General Rennie sent out a message to be read to all troops. In it he wrote:

> The Highland Division is about to take part in a battle under command of the 2nd Canadian Corps. This may well prove to be the decisive battle in France. The Division has an enterprising part to play, well suited to its particular characteristics. The battle also bears a strong resemblance to some of those great battles in North Africa in which the Division added laurels to its reputation of the last war. In Africa we fought side by side with Australians and New Zealanders. Now we are with Canadians and it is a coincidence that during the closing stages of the Great War we were also fighting beside a Canadian Corps. The Highland Division fought at El Alamein which great victory was the turning-point in our fortunes. Now we are to take part in what may be the decisive battle of France. The success of the battle depends on the determination and offensive spirit of every Commander and Soldier in the Division and in the 33rd Armoured Brigade and other units with the Division. Good luck to every one of you.

A third conference was held by HQ Div Signals to ensure that signal standards in a move from static to mobile operations would be of a high standard.   Wireless silence was imposed to conceal HD movements.   Lt Col James Cochrane OC Div Signals had set up a signals School in the battered Cazelle railway station for 74 'students,' replacements for the heavy casualties suffered by regimental signallers in the first seven weeks of bridgehead fighting.   Cochrane described Operation Totalise:

> 33rd Armoured Bde joined us for the operation. New and quite revolutionary tactics in the use of armour had been introduced by Lt General Guy Symonds GOC Canadian 2nd Corps, using Priests [105mm SPs without their guns], infantry carriers and White Scout half tracks to carry the infantry supported by tanks right through the enemy defences by night and into their back areas where the infantry debussed and took the enemy from the rear. 154 Bde were given the task of the armoured thrust to the wooded area of St Aignan-de-Cremesnil, five miles from the start line. 152 Bde were ordered to take Tilly attacking on foot and take advantage of 154 Bde's barrage, and confusion caused by the passage of 154 Bde's two armoured columns, one on each side of Tilly.   Div HQ would go to Cormelles, TAC HQ to Bras and Brigadiers Oliver and Cassels would site their Bde HQs near Bras.

Many specialised 'Funnies' of General Hobart's amazing 'Zoo' collection would support the attack - armoured bulldozers, flails, Avres, Crocodile flame-throwers and Fascines for filling the enormous bomb craters en route.

At 2300 hrs, 7th August RAF heavy bombers led by Pathfinders pulverised the enemy defences.   The divisional artillery fired 600 rounds per gun in a massive barrage.   Monty's Moonlight, searchlights bouncing their beams off clouds and Bofors firing red tracer illuminated the HD centre lines.   The gunners fired green smoke on to the objectives to guide the advance.

Brigadier Harry Scott was of OC 33 Armoured Bde (who were going to be HD's 'big friends' for months to come) which consisted of 144 and 148 RAC and the Northants Yeomanry.   154 Bde's two columns were successfully navigated into the infantry debussing areas, by-passing the strongpoints at Tilly and Secqueville and then occupied positions at St Aignan-de-Cremesnil, Cremisnil and Garcelles, by 1st Black Watch, 7th Argylls and 7th Black Watch respectively. Each column was four vehicles abreast   with vehicles about 20 yards apart laterally.   The routes to the startline had been lit with lamps on five foot pickets, right - green and left - amber. Much training had been done beforehand at Anisy, Couvre Chef, Epron and Lebisey which certainly paid off. The advance was led by Sherman tanks, troops of Sherman Flail tanks, an RE party; Avres, armoured bulldozers, tank HQ Squadron, another squadron of tanks, the infantry column and finally the reserve squadron of tanks - nose to tail at the start they stretched for 600 yards.

The weather was warm and sultry, the dust indescribable and the familiar noises of Nebelwerfers and Spandaus started up.

The 1st Black Watch column strangely enough encountered no enemy DF and with good navigation by the Northants Yeomanry arrived 800 yards short of St Aignan by 0315 hrs. A typical little Normandy village with thick stone walled farms, apple orchards and surrounded by thick hedgerows, it was subjected to an artillery concentration (Brimstone). By 0600 the Black Watch were digging-in waiting for the expected counter-attack which also came in on the Argylls. 'A' Coy were attacked by infantry supported by tanks getting to within 300 yards before the Northants Yeo knocked out four Tigers and seven MK IVs. During the attack on St Aignan the battalion lost 11 KIA, 43 wounded and 15 missing and five officers became casualties. But the Black Watch took 82 POW, four anti-tank guns, many mortars and machine-guns. 7th Argylls suffered a counter-attack and had 23 casualties. During the day the Northants Yeo lost 18 Shermans which they considered to be a fair exchange. The divisional artillery were superb and many DF tasks were fired.

Supporting 154 Bde was 126 Field Regt RA. Captain WJ Brown:

> Again the guns held the enemy at bay and beat off innumerable counter-attacks, before moving themselves into a more advantageous position. It was near Bourguebus a most depressing area. A no mans land for many days, it was littered with dead and with abandoned equipment. Every field was torn by shellfire and the farms were mounds of rubble.

7th Black Watch with 148 RAC followed 7th Argylls. An anti-tank gun knocked-out a 148 RAC Sherman at a gap on the railway line blocking the column. Garcelles was reached at 0500 and taken despite Spandau posts in houses and gardens. Lt McAllister knocked out three machine-gun posts before being killed. Unfortunately the battalion was not fully dug-in by dawn and very heavy shelling and mortaring cost 52 casualties. The anti-tank platoon under Sgt Ross knocked out a MK IV tank and an anti-tank gun. Major DFO Russell:

> The casualties were very light for an advance which penetrated 6000 yards deep into enemy held country. Morale was higher than it had been since our landing in France. The battalion was getting back to its old form of the Desert and Sicily days - 60 prisoners were also taken.

So 154 Bde had done their stuff, were on all their objectives on time and seen off a formidable counter-attack. Against all the odds *1055 Infantry Regt* defended Tilly-la-Campagne, almost to the last man. Battered by the RAF and Corps artillery, surrounded and bypassed by the armoured columns of 154 Bde, they continued to fight and give 152 Bde a bloody nose. 2nd Seaforth's first quick assault on Tilly failed, so Lt Col GLW Andrews then ordered a second attack simultaneously from two sides. 'D' Company lost direction in the dark and arrived at the wrong place. Heavy fire caused many casualties so Brigadier Cassels ordered Lt Col Walford to send 'D' Coy 5th Seaforth to take the railway level crossing. This attack failed with 21 men killed or wounded out of forty including Capt Grant Murray. In a hopelessly confused situation just after dawn a tank squadron from 33 A/Bde attacked Tilly from the south. By 1050 on the 8th a little ragged column, dirty and red-eyed of 30 brave, resolute German infantry surrendered. In this savage little battle Seaforth casualties were about 80 but they captured altogether 150 POW including five officers. 5th Camerons had an exhausting night and day clearing the Lorquichon crossroads and Secqueville woods in stifling heat and finally occupying Poussy two miles further south. This village attracted German DF fire wounding 14, but swarms of bees were almost as annoying.

153 Bde who had provided the firm base for HD in Totalise now came up in support, 5/7th Gordons putting two companies into Poussy. They drew shellfire and in the afternoon spotted certain objects in front which might have been tanks or dummy tanks. They proved to be the latter! From Garcelles Secqueville 1st Gordons attacked and took at 1700 Secqueville-la-Campagne helped by a barrage and Crocodiles taking nearly 100 POW by nightfall.

Major Martin Lindsay 2i/c 1st Gordons led the battalion across cornfields:

> 500 fighting men well dispersed. Then I heard the awful groaning of Moaning Minnies, looked round to hear the crack and see the burst as some 20 smackers landed behind, luckily between two companies. We crossed the stubble and entered a leafy lane. There I found the General [Rennie] a tall, rather heavy figure wearing a Tam O'Shanter with the red hackle of the Black Watch. The General was looking very glum. 'I'm afraid there will be not much artillery to support the attack [on Secqueville]. The Americans have bombed our gun lines near Caen and Colombelles with 48 Fortresses.'" Lindsay found the MO, Bert Brown and Padre, Ewen Traill tending 20 wounded Gordons in the RAP, a mill in the village square of Garcelles.

General Rennie moved TAC HQ to Garcelles Secqueville at noon on the 8th, to be followed by main Div HQ the next day. About 1400 the Polish Armoured Div Shermans passed through heading for Roberts Mesnil and St Sylvain where 88mm anti-tank guns gave them a very sticky time. The Poles reported that they had taken St Sylvain, but their second and third attacks all failed. So 154 Bde, were ordered to clear the extensive woods around St Sylvain and 'retake' the small town. Supported by 144 RAC tanks 7th Argylls led in a silent night attack towards the south-east of the village followed by 1st Black Watch. 'D' Coy 7th Argylls met intense Spandau fire and casualties mounted, but by first light on the 11th 40 POW had been taken. During the day three determined German counter-attacks came in each with about 200 infantry but were beaten off. 2nd Derby Yeomanry came up to thicken the defence, as did 'A' Coy 5th Black Watch. Heavy shelling and mortaring took their toll and the Argylls lost 97 casualties including eight wounded officers, among them Lts White and Twinbarrow who had joined the battalion the day before. 1st Black Watch were tasked with the capture of the right-hand sector of the St Sylvain woods, behind a barrage from four Medium and three Field Regts of artillery. By 0430 the battalion was on its objective capturing 70 POW for the loss of 12 casualties. For the next three days extremely heavy shelling fell on the Black Watch well dug-in causing 20 casualties per day. Major Benson:

> 30 tanks of Polish Armoured Div moved into 'D' Coy's area where they milled about for an hour attracting considerable shell and mortar fire. After a two hour Recce towards La Bu-Sur-Rouvres they withdrew through the battalion area attracting more shell and mortar fire.

The Germans remained extremely active. They slaughtered the Polish armour and the Canadian armour too, one tank regiment losing 53 out of 65 tanks. *12th SS Division* were formidable opposition.

Totalise ended on 10th August. HD had done everything asked of it and for the next three days acted as a firm base for the Polish Armoured Division and also protected the flank of the Canadian Corps attacking south towards Falaise. Brigadier H (Nap) Murray came to say farewell to 153 Bde on the 12th before leaving to take command of 6th Armoured Division in the Italian theatre of war. Major John McGregor, 5th Black Watch: "We were all sad to see him go. He had led the Brigade with great skill and during the early days in Normandy he maintained morale, despite the difficulties of having his three Battalions under other peoples' command." Lt Col Cumming-Bruce took command of 153 Bde until the arrival of Brigadier Roddy Sinclair.

The work of the Divisional Engineers was described by the CRE, Lt Col Ralp Carr:

> During Totalise 275 Field Coy RE was with 152 Bde, 276 Field Coy with 153 Bde, 274 Field Coy with 154 Bde. In the advance there was an RE platoon with each infantry Bn. All three field companies were under my command as was 239 Field Park Coy with a strong Mechanical Equipment section with the invaluable bulldozers, some armoured... The RE work was clearing the route or road where bombs and shells had made it impassable, as well as demolitions and mine clearance.

Hostilities resumed on the 14th with 5/7th Gordons attacking the south-east sector of St Sylvain to secure a wooded ridge but although successful lost 53 casualties including six officers. Sgt Birley took over command of 'D' Coy when all their officers were 'hors de combat'. Pte Hutchinson performed nobly as a stretcher-bearer under fire. 1st Gordons at St Sylvain now under command of Major Martin Lindsay had their HQ in a cow barn before later taking over the main German HQ in the main street. In two days about 2000 shells landed in the town causing 50 casualties. The 1st Gordons company commander noted that all the Poles were drunk when position take-overs were needed. "There was a great clatter of transport and a huge column of dust as the last of the Poles, driving much too fast left the town. Sure enough down came the shells.

La Bu-Sur-Rouvres defenders had kept the Poles at bay so 5th Black Watch needed a set piece attack on the 14th, aided by 148 RAC and some Canadians. 'D' Coy came under heavy Spandau and mortar fire so CSM Bill Fraser with Coy HQ stalked the machine-gunner and led a charge killing or capturing the machine-gun crews. Although the Black Watch lost 40 casualties including two officers of 'C' Coy they captured 200 POW, six anti-tank guns and six mortars. 148 RAC Shermans were invaluable in the attack and Brigadier James Oliver sent his congratulations.

When 5/7th Gordons took St Maclou in a night attack on the 16th from Percy en Auge, Major CF Irvine and the battalion *transport team* did most of the fighting. For the loss of five casualties the little town by the river Dives was easily taken. The IO captain in creditable German telephoned on a captured line to the local German HQ, and announced that 'the Englishe Schweine' had arrived and demanded surrender. St Maclou was a 'liberation' town with greetings of flowers, cider and bottles of wine. St Pierre-sur-Dives fell to the 5th Camerons on the 16th taking 50 POW and were also greeted in Gallic fashion as 'liberators.'

Capt WJ Brown 126 Regt RA on leaving St Aignan on the 14th: "The Regt had an hour of misery with bombs from our own heavy bombers showering down on the village, quickly a mass of blazing vehicles and exploding ammunition. We were fortunate to escape with comparatively few casualties." With the Canadian Corps continuing to make progress on their axis south of Caen, HD's main attack changed from a south-east direction to a more easterly drive for the river Seine, via Lisieux. 152 Bde had captured St Pierre-sur-Dives and seized crossings over the river. At once 153 Bde passed through, whilst 154 Bde concentrated in reserve at Magny-la-Campagne.

7th Black Watch with Shermans of Northants Yeo found a small bridge over the river Dives and headed for the high ground at Le Godet. Unfortunately the forward companies came under heavy mortar and shellfire and Panzers knocked out ten of the supporting tanks. The Black Watch attacked again after dark and were held up by SPs and a determined rearguard. But 154 Bde kept pushing ahead towards St Julien le Faucon.

In blazing hot weather, close and windless, 5th Seaforth moved from

La Bu-Sur-Rouvres to attack an elongated wood a mile west of Blatigny, on the 14th, the next day marched 3½ miles south-east to a large wood on a plateau. Several little villages including Favierès were ensconced in the woods, and the Derbyshire Yeomanry were involved in clearing the area. Prisoners told Lt Col Walford after six Spandau teams had opened up, there were at least 300 of their comrades in the woods. 'A' Coy's wireless had died, 'B' were being held up by a strong position astride the main road. Lt Col Walford was desperate for tank support and toured the countryside in his jeep begging or stealing stray tanks as he went along. Eventually anti-tank guns and four 'stray' tanks were rushed up to the lead companies at dusk, but another two 'strays' were knocked-out by an SP gun. 2nd Seaforth came up in the night to cover the right flank.

When daylight came the enemy had gone! 5th Seaforth then moved to join 5th Camerons in St Pierre-sur-Dives waiting for 49th Polar Bear Division to arrive.

Every forward unit in the British and Canadian Army was thoroughly bombed, dive bombed and strafed by the RAF and USAAF (occasionally the Luftwaffe too) in the period 16-20th August. Bright yellow silk triangles, yellow smoke signals, khaki uniforms, the white identification cross on most vehicles, all were totally ignored. A flight of five Spitfires attacked and kept on attacking 5th Camerons HQ destroying vehicles and all their wireless sets. The Argylls were bombed in Clamesnil by RAF Lancasters - their raid went on for 3½ hours. 1st Gordons lost 13 out of 15 trucks on 14th to an Allied bombing strike and 5/7th Gordons were bombed in Fierville. Lightning's cannon fire destroyed 152 Bde HQ. They wounded Brigadier Cassels, killed the BM John Thornton and an LO Douglas Morone and wounded Lt Col Andrews, CO of 2nd Seaforth.

Alastair Borthwick helped dig out the wounded which included Jimmy Watt, DAA/QMG and two other LOs. What else? A French family of four in a farmhouse were all killed, he remembered; "There are still men who claim that the strafing by the Lightnings was the most terrifying single experiences they have every had. The fact that our own planes were doing it, made it ten times worse." General Rennie and Harry Cumming-Bruce (acting Brigadier) twice had to get into a ditch to avoid Typhoon strafing. Martin Lindsay, 1st Gordons, heard Cumming-Bruce talking to the General on the telephone: "The one thing I cannot afford is to have the RAF operating anywhere within 50 miles of me." On the 15th the Gordons watched the Lancasters bombing the gun lines behind. "For one hour this went on and everybody was powerless to stop it."

The opposition had given 7th Black Watch a hard time and now they did the same to the Argylls on the 17th with mortars, SPs and 88mms.

In thickly wooded country short of St Julien in a long and exhausting day they lost 77 casualties including their CO Lt Col Meiklejohn DSO, wounded in both legs and eight other officers. Early on the 18th, 1st Black Watch passed through and captured St Julien, the enemy having withdrawn. The RAF out of control again attacked the Argylls on the 19th and 20th despite yellow smoke candles and yellow Celanese triangles on all aircraft. The speed of the Allied advance was given as an excuse. The 1st Black Watch was strafed no less than five times by Typhoons on the 18th.

"The absurd thing", noted Major Martin Lindsay, "was no direct ground to air communication which could have stopped [the RAF bombing] at once. The channel of communication was Division-Corps-Army-Army Group-Supreme HQ-Air Ministry-Bomber Command-Group-RAF Station (or something very like it). So no wonder it took over an hour to get through." General Rennie warned the Air Liaison Officer that 40 LAA Regt would fire on the RAF planes.

"The three opposed crossings of the rivers Dives, Vie and Touques at Lisieux were obstacles successfully overcome by culverting and bulldozing or Bailey bridges (such as the 110 foot triple/single at St Pierre). HD always had two bridges capable of taking Sherman tanks. The advance was fast. It was difficult to keep up the supply of bridging equipment. The roads were littered with enemy transport, blocked by felled trees and telegraph poles booby trapped with mines and charges. The mines were hard to detect through the foliage." [Lt Col Ralph Carr, CRE].

The crossing of the little river Vie was the responsibility of 153 Bde. At St Maclou 5/7th Gordons had received 65 reinforcements from the South Staffs and at half an hour's notice were ordered to attack Grandchamps on the night of the 18th, repair a bridge over the Vie and establish a bridgehead. The unpleasant night march was in pouring rain, and despite heavy shelling 5/7th Gordons made their river crossing. Their popular CO Lt Col Hew Blair-Imrie was killed in that action. He had joined the Black Watch before the war and had been 2i/c 5th and 7th Bns before taking up his recent command on 30th July.

5th Black Watch passed through 5/7th Gordons to get on to a hill east of the river near La Butte code named 'Ben Nevis' and then occupy another ridge on their left, 'Ben Lomond.' Unfortunately battalion TAC HQ was struck at 0200 on 19th by a salvo of eight shells, wounding the CO Bill Bradford in the arm and legs, killing their signals officer and Major Ken Aitken, FOO of 127 Field Regt RA. All their wireless sets were knocked-out, but soon after dawn the 2i/c Major George Dunn arrived with replacement sets. By mid-day Point 150 was taken. The enemy lost 42 men and 12 Spandaus were captured, but at a cost of 49 casualties. General Rennie sent a message "Well done, 5 Black Watch."

152 Bde now passed through. 5th Camerons found two blown bridges over the river Vie, 'B' and 'D' Coys forded it and held a bridgehead and with Shermans of the East Riding Yeomanry had a successful day on the 20th. Parallel to the Lisieux road, they advanced nearly six miles through St Fressard-la-Chere to their final objective, 'Lobster.' Tank/infantry co-operation on a troop/platoon level was excellent against small rearguard ambushes. The Camerons then rested from the 22nd to 26th at St Pierre-des-Ifs, not only absorbing 60 reinforcements, training, route marches, zeroing rifles on a range but enjoying freedom from shellfire, the local wines, good food and listening to their Pipes and Drums. The Sappers had built a new bridge over the Vie at Grandchamps on the night of 18/19th, that and the crossroads were in full view of the German artillery on the steep and rugged hills to the east.

Alastair Borthwick, 5th Seaforth: "David Purgavie was killed there. The assembly area was under mortar fire. It had been fought for by 5/7th Gordons before we arrived. It was strewn with corpses and the smell of death was everywhere." 5th Seaforth were also happy with their East Riding Yeomanry tank support: "They were to fight beside us many times. We established a tremendous liaison with them. Before the war ended Humphreys' [Major Phillips] boys had practically been adopted into the battalion." La Corne crossroads was captured in a silent attack after dusk without artillery support although a burst of Schmeiser killed CSM McLeod and three other Seaforths. They dug-in. Then the 'retreating' Germans launched an attack at breakfast time. 'B' Coy spotted a hundred infantry filtering down the hedges a couple of hundred yards away. Breakfast stopped abruptly. Sgt Lachlan MacKintosh 'C' Coy: "They sounded like a lot. They were yelling their heads off, as if they were half crazy or drunk." 'C' Coy fired 8000 rounds of ammunition and the ERY tanks destroyed two occupied houses and machine-gunned all the hedges. But 30-40 Boche infantry were found dead within 30 yards of the Seaforth trenches. The next day a magnificent old brigand, Monsieur Fernand the local butcher led a Seaforth patrol into St Pierre-des-Ifs. "Give me two men with the little machine-guns and I assault the village myself," he cried. In the village of La Pommeraye, on the 22nd, a nice looking farmer's wife seized Lt Col John Hopwood, CO 1st Black Watch and showered him with kisses saying, "We will celebrate - please wait." She walked into the orchard and with a spade carefully dug up a bottle of 'vieux calvados.' Major Benson:

> This was handed round and we all partook. After nearly two weeks of the recent heavy going, nearly always on the move and little sleep, I do not remember anything tasting better. It was wonderful. It continued like this until we got to Le Havre. A marvellous euphoria among the Jocks and local

inhabitants.

Lisieux, the main objective, fell on the 22nd to 153 Bde. 5/7th Gordons despite receiving a complete new reinforcement company of East Lancashire Regt could still only muster three rifle companies. Now commanded by Major du Boulay, they led into Lisieux to establish a bridgehead over the river Touques which flows through the town. On the far side SS troops in houses put up determined resistance and Pte Redican though wounded in both legs kept up covering fire with his Brengun. He was recommended for the VC but received the DCM. 1st Gordons, also weak in numbers were next ordered at 0830 23rd August to clear the SS troops out of eastern part of Lisieux.

Martin Lindsay, temporarily CO 1st Gordons had occupied La Forge Vallée a large stud farm owned by Sam Ambler. He then drank champagne in a huge cave with about a hundred refugees. 22nd August was his 39th birthday. The next day Harry Cumming-Bruce, the acting Brigadier ordered up 1st Gordons into the badly bombed Lisieux - a famous religious centre. The SS snipers killed Murray Reekie, OC 'A' Coy and Spandau had destroyed half of Jim Robertson's 'B' Coy. "Meanwhile the Hun got a light mortar into position and we had yet a few more casualties, bringing them to five officers and 40 ORs for a most ineffective day's work," wrote Martin Lindsay. He was not happy with his tank support from 144 RAC, but 7th Armoured Div arrived at 1500 in pouring rain:

> So there we were in some sort of defensive position what was left of us. We had lost 15 officers and about 150 ORs since the breakthrough started on 8th August. The remnants of the four rifle companies were now amalgamated into one composite company. I brought up the Pipe Band, the Pioneers and as many drivers and clerks as could be scraped together, under the transport officer to thicken us up. I felt very low indeed as I thought of the day's miserable failure.

The next day Brigadier Sinclair arrived to command 153 Bde, Cumming-Bruce went back to command his battered 1st Gordons. And Lt Col GD Renny took command of 5/7th Gordons who were billeted near a nunnery outside Lisieux. The Pipe Band played retreat on the 16th and the Mother Superior presented the pipers with a dozen bottles of cider (not calvados). Reinforcements arrived but in the main were from non-Scottish regiments. Some were very disappointed at not being able to don the kilt.

After Lisieux Tom Renouf left the Tyneside Scottish to join No 7 Platoon, 5th Black Watch. There he met another 19 year old friend Alex Corris who had joined the army on the same day and place:

> I remember the sheer exhaustion and battle weariness that showed on the faces of my new comrades. The battalion was battle seasoned. It had fought its way from El Alamein and despite heavy casualties, a few of its

number wore the much respected Africa Star. My new section leader was Corporal Chapman, a fine soldier who won our confidence and respect immediately. An efficient but kindly person, neat and smart in his turnout but very understanding. He looked after us like a father figure but at the same time controlled us as a fighting unit.

After the capture of Lisieux the Canadian Corps pushed north-east towards Rouen and the Seine leaving HD to 'mop up' and cross the river Risle towards Bourg Achard. Capt Fraser Burrows, 5th Camerons who had been wounded at El Alamein was convinced he would not survive in Normandy. He was duly shot up and wounded by Spitfires after Totalise. After his recovery his previous CO Lt Col Ronnier Miers had Fraser transferred to 9th Bn Seaforth, a training Bn for young soldiers based in Dumfries-shire. "Miers policy was to replace officers and NCOs with battle experience before and send abroad people who had spent most of the war years sitting at home." A policy after Winston Churchill's heart!

'Mopping up' often meant clearing determined little rearguard opposition as every day minor roads, hamlets and farm houses had to be cleared.

> A pleasant sunny day. The farther we moved the less we felt threatened. We travelled past a roadblock of felled trees and through a minefield of six or eight anti-tank mines laid in the road. Everything was so tranquil. We approached another roadblock climbed over the trees and a burst of machine-gun fire opened up on us from the woods ten yards ahead. We moved like lightening. I [Tom Renouf, 5th Black Watch] found myself lying behind a sawn-off tree stump. There was more fire, the bullets kicked up the earth first to the left, then to the right of my tree stump. I wriggled to keep out of the line of fire.

In order to tackle the Schmeisser fire Renouf felt in his pouches for a grenade. First was a tin of sardines, secondly a tin of bully beef and finally a grenade! Tom became (walking) wounded but the badly wounded Corporal Chapman and 'Ginger' died in the ambulance going back to Bayeux. A few weeks later Renouf was back with his platoon; "Out of all the members of No 7 Platoon only one of the members, the platoon Sgt 'Nick', survived but he had been wounded twice."

Lt Col Ralph Carr CRE described the August break-out as he wrote home on 28th August:

> We have just completed three weeks of the most gruelling fighting which the HD has ever experienced. We have lost just under 2000 casualties taken as many POW and advanced 80 miles. We started off with the big 'set piece' attack with the Canadians on the [German] defensive ring astride the Caen-Falaise road. In the great attack which lasted a night and a day we broke through the crust - we drove a spear into him and then in the next four or five days 'waggled it about' enlarging and deepening the hole - the Alamein technique again. Then came another great thrust and we were

through and into the mobile war. We were still up against formidable unbroken German formations fighting desperately to prevent their comrades in the Falaise pocket being cut off, determined to try and 'seal off' our advance - to control it, slow it down, finally to halt it. They had ideal country, hilly, wooded with a series of difficult river lines. However, we went at him 'hammer and tongs' and forced river line after river line, but he exacted a price for every yard.

Major General Rennie's own message to his Division was as follows:

In its advance from Tilly to Lisieux, the Highland Division has played a major part in the Battle of France. During that advance the Division for fifteen days fought continuously in its most intensive period of fighting in this war. We sustained some 1761 casualties but took over 1600 prisoners, in addition to killing and wounding a very large number of Germans and to over-running great quantities of German equipment.

The Canadian Army Commander has congratulated the Division on its 'fine aggressive work', and it is to that aggressive work that we owe our success. The German is no good when his tail is down, and we undoubtedly kept it down. Great scope for revenge lies ahead both south and north of the River Seine. Remember that on 12th June 1940 a portion of the Highland Division, including its Headquarters, 152 Brigade and 153 Brigade, were captured by a large German force at St Valéry-en-Caux, due north from our present position.

We of the Highland Division must not rest till we have freed our kith and kin of the St Valéry Highland Division and avenged their misfortune to the full.

31

Return to St Valéry

HD were spared the horrors to be seen in the Argentan-Falaise corridor as British, Canadian, Polish and American forces converged and smashed the German *Seventh Army*. The Allied air forces turned the corridor into an awful slaughterhouse. More than 40 German divisions had been destroyed in Normandy, but 20,000 desperate Germans did escape the pocket, plus 24 tanks and 60 guns which were eventually ferried across the river Seine. Paris surrendered on 25th to the American/French forces and General Patton motored at great speed through Brittany to the Meuse and the Moselle rivers. It was an amazing triumph for Monty's (and Eisenhower's) men despite some doubting Thomases in the Allied top brass.

During the advance from Colombelles to Lisieux, TAC Div HQ was highly mobile and often moved two or three times during the day. The advance was made on a single axis and the GOC and CRA fought the battle by day on the wireless sets in their jeeps and in the evening returned to TAC Division HQ by which time the signals lines were laid to the fighting units, the Field Regiments and the 'next for duty' Brigade. The GSO1 moved Main Div HQ if necessary twice in a day to come up near to TAC Div HQ or even join them in the evening. The CRA leapfrogged his field regiments right up into the HQ area of the brigade doing the advance. Most of the 'teeth' units rarely know, perhaps rarely care about the immense complexity of the controls needed to keep about 15,000 men doing 'the business.'   Provided rations, ammunition and mail came up promptly and casualties are sent back quickly and efficiently, the fighting teams are relatively happy to keep 'bashing on.'

Lisieux had been badly smashed by the RAF and was full of mines but the beautiful Basilica of St Therese was scarcely damaged and an RC service was held there in the week that HD spent nearby. The locals, despite the damage were quite friendly and provided eggs, butter, milk, cider and calvados. 5th Black Watch after two major attacks at Bretteville (Ecajeul on 17/18th) and La Butte (Grandchamps on 19/20th) moved to a rest area two miles east of Lisieux, absorbing large drafts from the Depot and from the Tyneside Scottish. 1st Black Watch found a very pleasant large orchard on the high ground west of Lisieux with a friendly farmer keeping them well supplied. On their departure he presented a fine goose to battalion HQ. 5/7th Gordons started their few days out of the line in a nunnery and when they played Retreat on the 26th the Mother Superior presented the pipers with a dozen bottles of cider.

On the 25th, 154 Bde continued the advance eastwards reached Marolles and the next day to St George-du-Vievre. The Division concentrated there and then crossed the river Risle. 152 Bde then came through and reached the river Seine by first light on 28th. The Die Hards enjoyed themselves with excellent shoots on barges laden with enemy troops escaping from the Falaise pocket. The Derbyshire Yeomanry had its first chance in its reconnaissance role when the advance started after 'Totalise,' and Yville on the Seine was their latest objective. The three gunner regiments leapfrogged with their brigades and moved at least daily to provide their usual support. 126 Field Regt RA occupied two positions south of St Sylvain, then Condé sur Ifs, Thieville, St Pierre, Vieuxpont, St Julien-le-Faucon to the orchards of La Boissière. Thence to Appetot, Touville, Francourt, La Halboterie (1000 yards from the Seine) and La Greve south of the du Clair bend in the Seine. Capt WJ Brown:

> The banks of the Seine showed the aftermath of an Army in disorder. This
> was no retreat, no orderly withdrawal. Panic had run rife - the RAF had

reaped a rich harvest. Bodies of horses and men littered the banks, the roads and the fields. Motor and horse-drawn vehicles abandoned had piled up in unutterable confusion and the loot of the German army, wrenched from the homes of France was scattered wide.

In the 7th Black Watch area near Anneville they counted eight tanks, eight SP guns, 12 Field guns, 18 Nebelwerfers, 380 wheeled vehicles, 80 half-tracks and innumerable horse-drawn vehicles. Four small patrols were sent across the river Seine - 200 yards wide - by boat to Duclair. On the 31st in pouring rain a skeleton battalion crossed the river.

152 and 153 Bdes were clearing the Seine bend up to Duclair. Both the Gordons Bns were in action with Lt Col Renny's 5/7th Gordons clearing difficult pockets around Yville under mortar fire on 28th and 29th, needing Wasp flamethrowers to persuade the Boche to leave - presumably by swimming. 1st Gordons from Yville then cleared with 5th Black Watch the wooded Forêt de Mauny loop of the Seine. A succession of artillery concentrations went down on minimal opposition. 1st Gordons captured "Poles, Mongolians, Jugo-Slavs an 'Eskimo' or two not a Hun amongst them" according to Major Martin Lindsay. He and Reid the officer mess cook 'found' two cases of brandy, six bottles of red wine, a wireless set and an alarm clock. There were some problems. Eight sappers were blown up clearing a roadblock of booby trapped trees near the Seine.

5th Black Watch lost 20 casualties capturing Maunay crossroads and chateau. Major Mirrielees who had joined the battalion on the 25th was killed four days later. Lt Col Bill Bradford wounded in the arm and legs at La Butte was wounded near Maunay in the neck. Sgt Monty Mendel, Intelligence Section from pre-Alamein days went 2000 yards forward of the battalion, behind the enemy lines and sent back by wireless valuable reports, later he was awarded the Croix de Guerre. 1st Black Watch captured a POW, an Italian called Luigi who was promptly enlisted as an officers' mess waiter. Lt Col John Meiklejohn CO 7th Argylls was wounded and evacuated and command now went to Lt Col Donald Nicoll (Black Watch from 49 Polar Bear Division).

5th Camerons motored from Lisieux to Bourg Achard on 26th and on 28th pushed patrols out towards the Seine. In Le Landin 60 POW were taken by 'C' Coy and the battalion consolidated on high ground a mile from the Seine. All available fire power was deployed on the Germans seen trying to cross; the Camerons anti-tank 6-pdrs; the 17-pdrs of 'K' Tp 61 Anti-Tank Regt; machine-guns of 'D' Coy 1/7 Middlesex, and the faithful 492 Field Bty RA plus the battalion snipers of the Scout Platoon. There was only one ferry left to the retreating enemy within small arms range; 'Every time a coconut,' it was too easy!

All unknown to the Division back at TAC HQ 21 Army Group General Montgomery wrote to General Crerar GOC Canadian Army saying that all Scotland would be grateful if the Highland Division could capture St Valéry-en-Caux.

On 1st September 2nd Derby Yeo led 152 Bde supported by the tanks of East Riding Yeomanry directed on St Valéry. They crossed a Canadian built bridge at Elboeuf and by noon followed by Div TAC HQ went through Rouen.

Private James Younie: "'C' Coy [5th Seaforth] leading was passing through the town. The local inhabitants were so pleased to see us they were throwing fruit and all sorts of things at us. One young lady threw an orange and it struck our Coy CO Major Findlay Shirras very hard on his nose. I was very sorry for him." The Derby Yeomanry armoured cars had scouted ahead of the column. The civilians they met claimed the Germans had left St Valéry-en-Caux two days previously.

5th Seaforth covered 80 miles that day and occupied Veules-les-Roses on the coast by nightfall, having cut the Le Havre peninsular.

> None of us will ever live such a day again. Though we live to be ninety we will never do it. During their first hours of freedom after four years of German occupation, the French went mad. These people who crowded the village streets and walked for miles across the fields to line the roads for us, were happy and excited but behind the flag waving and the cheering and the singing was a profound thankfulness. We were mobbed in every village. Gigantic streamers announced 'Welcome to our brave Liberators.' Others said 'God Save the King' in letters three feet high. There were flags in every window and in every hand, speeches of welcome were made and cognac offered. We left each village with bouquets piled on the tanks of our motorbikes. It was a tremendous day,

wrote Alastair Borthwick. The Seaforth noticed vehicles of the old 51st HD lying by the roadside still with the Stags Heads and Highland Brigade colours visible on their mudguards. Lt Col Walford had been a company commander at St Valéry, one of the few who got away at the surrender. He found his old company shield and sign in a farmhouse. Major AN Parker led 'D' Coy 5th Camerons into St Valéry and their CO Lt Col DB Lang [now General Sir Derek Lang] who as adjutant 4th Camerons had been captured and afterwards escaped, was received by the Mayor in the centre of the square. Capt Dawson also led a patrol of 5th Seaforth into the town - so it may have been a dead heat.

General Rennie halted his TAC HQ at Pissy Poville seven miles beyond Rouen for the night. Main HQ joined them in the middle of a dark night in torrents of rain. The GOC chose the place 'for the name only.' On the morning of the 2nd Rennie moved HQ into the Chateau at Cailleville where in June 1940 General Fortune and his staff were forced to surrender. The Brigade groups went into the same areas in which the 1940 Brigades had fought their last battle. During the remainder of the day visits were made to the town, to the military cemetery where each grave of the 'Eccossais Inconnu' was scarlet with geraniums in full bloom, contrasting with the white wooden crosses. There were a large number of German soldiers' graves there as well. Battalion orders of the day explained to the reformed HD the significance of St Valéry and parties were shown the bridgehead battle and the West Wall defences. Lt Col Bradford, 5th Black Watch visited three cemeteries (Hondetot, Angiers) with well tended graves of the 1st Bn. There was a notice in St Pierre, 'Honour to the Black Watch who fought here with courage in 1940.'

Last Post at St Valery

"3rd September was declared 'St Valéry Day,'" wrote Lt Col James Cochrane, OC Div Signals, "which will ever bring memories of General Rennie meeting some of his staff in the Town Square by accident that morning and describing to them the scene at which (as at that time GSO II to General Fortune) he had been an unwilling participant. He told of how Rommel watched the Division march past its commander in that very same square into captivity while from the heights round the town the splutter of German machine-guns could be heard firing on the Jocks on the beaches, and of his own successful dash from the marching prisoners."

The Gordons celebrated at Veules-les-Roses. At 10.30 a battalion memorial service was held. "It was most moving when Harry [Cumming-Bruce, the CO] read out the list of 133 officers and men who had been killed or died of wounds. The names seemed to go on for ever and I [Major Lindsay] feared that this long casualty list would come as a shock to the large new draft that arrived a few days before. At the end the buglers blew the Last Post and Reveille most beautifully and the Pipe Major played the Lament. It was held in the courtyard of the principal hotel and the remaining standing room was taken up by the French." The Mayor had tended, as the village doctor, 300 British (and French) wounded on 12th June 1940, mainly of the Duke of Wellington's Regt.

At 1500 a dance for all ranks in the village hall and then speeches by the CO to the mayor and citizens. "Harry said just the right thing: how pleased we were to be there and how grateful for the succour they had given our wounded four years ago, how brave they had been under our bombing, how much we admired de Gaulle's resistance movement and how with their help, we were going to liberate the last metre of French soil and give the German his desserts." In the evening the pipes and drums played Retreat in the village and the officers dined at the Hotel de France.

At 1600 the massed pipes and drums of HD played Retreat at the GOC's HQ at Cailleville. Major Benson 1st Black Watch:

> Thomas Rennie dressed in his Black Watch kilt - battledress blouse - Tam O'Shanter with Red Hackle and the General's badge fastened just underneath the Hackle, tall, dark, sombre and extremely smart stood beside the French Mayor. Retreat was played on cut grass about the size of two football fields with a background of hardwood trees all in full leaf and a chateau in the background. All the old favourite tunes were played."

The Divisional Pipe-Major then played 'The Flowers of the Forest.' On 3rd September General Rennie addressed HD:

> This is a very great occasion in the history of our famous division. Here at St Valéry on the 12th June 1940, a portion of the Highland Division, including its Headquarters, 152 and 153 Brigades, was captured by a large German force.

> That magnificent Division was sacrificed in a last effort to keep the French in the war. True to Highland tradition the Division remained to the last with the remnants of our French Allies, although it was within its capacity to withdraw on Le Havre.

> The Division drew on St Valéry the German 4th Corps, a Panzer and a Motor Division - in all six Divisions - and thereby diverted this force from harassing the withdrawal of other British troops on Le Havre and Cherbourg.

> General Victor Fortune ordered the surrender of the Division at St Valéry when it had run out of ammunition and food and when all prospects of

evacuation, which had been carefully planned by him, had failed.

That Highland Division was Scotland's pride; and its loss, and with it the magnificent men drawn from practically every town, village, and croft in Scotland, was a great blow. But this Division, then the 9th Highland Division, took its place and became the new 51st Highland Division. It had been our task to avenge the fate of our less fortunate comrades and that we have nearly accomplished. We have played a major part in both the great decisive battles of this war - the Battle of Egypt and the Battle of France - and have also borne our share of the skirmishes and those costly periods of defensive fighting which made these great victories possible. We have lived up to the great traditions of the 51st and of Scotland.

I have disposed the Division, as far as is possible, in the areas where it fought at St Valéry. General Victor Fortune had his HQ here, 152 Brigade held the sector to the west, and 153 brigade to the east. The Lothians and Border Horse held the sector to the south. The 154 Brigade and 'A' Brigade ('A' Brigade was at that time operating with the Division) embarked at Le Havre.

I hoped by disposing the Division in that way to make it easier for some of you to find the graves of your relatives or friends who lost their lives with the St Valéry 51st. You will find at St Valéry and in the village cemeteries around, that the graves of our comrades have been beautifully cared for.

We have today playing with the Pipes and Drums of the Highland Division those of the Scottish Horse. There are also officers and men of the Lothians and Border Horse at this meeting.

32

Operation Astonia: Capture of Le Havre

Field Marshal Montgomery now decided on a massive all arms attack to capture the important port of Le Havre, which was defended by 16,000 German forces under Colonel Eberhard Wildermuth. Using forced labour, a huge labyrinth of deep concrete bunkers and pill boxes harbouring 76 field, medium and AA guns had been built. Extensive deep minefields protected the whole perimeter although the main coastal batteries were sited to fire out to sea. The Navy, mainly the gunship HMS *Erebus* would bombard the town (until the coastal batteries hit it and forced a withdrawal) the RAF bombers would carry out two massive drops before the 10th September which caused - regrettably - very heavy loss of civilian life. The defenders were relatively safe in their bunkers.

49th Polar Bear Division would attack Le Havre from the left flank (south-east and north-east) and HD from the right (north-west and north). 33rd Armoured Bde were under command, the East Riding Yeomanry with 152 Bde, 144 RAC with 153 Bde and Northants Yeomanry with 154 Bde. In addition Funnies from 79 Armoured Division were to play an important role in the minefield breaching with Flail tanks, and scissor bridges to gap anti-tank ditches.

HD concentrated in the Criquecot area ten miles north-east of Le Havre, with Main Div HQ at St Martin-du-Bec and TAC Div HQ about 1200 yards away from the German forward posts. General Rennie suggested to Corps that HD main attack should be put in from Montvilliers, six miles north-east and a simulated attack from Octeville in the northern sector. The divisional artillery moved up, 126 Field to Mannie Villette and dumped 500 rpg for the supporting barrages.

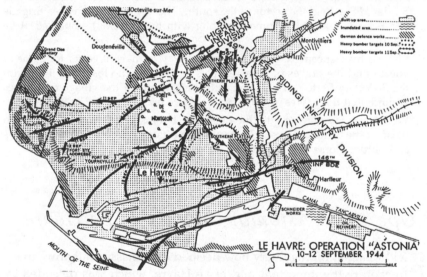

152 Bde would attack at 2300 on 10th September, and on their left 153 Bde at 0400 on the 11th. The Polar Bear attack went in at 1745 hrs after a very heavy air bombardment.

5th Seaforth moved up along the coast through Fecamp to Beaumesnil, twelve miles north of Le Havre and stayed there a week. Air photographs and information from French civilians showed exactly in great detail, the extent of the problem - the gapping [Ale, Rum and Gin] of the very professional defences (wire, minefields, anti-tank ditches and formidable pillboxes). 5th Seaforth would use a 49 Div gap, pass through and turn right (west) to attack and capture the strongpoint 76 on the high ground east of Fontaine-la-Mallet. Alastair Borthwick:

> The usual column trudging along resignedly in the darkness, heads down,

steel helmets and rifle muzzles making a frieze against the night sky - a column immensely patient, almost apathetic, storing up nervous energy for the demands of the night. A black night of low cloud, no wind and three searchlights to light us on our way...

The Polar Bear gap (two others were incomplete, because flail tanks had bogged down or blown up) was a natural and easy target for the German artillery and mortars. For 700 yards it wound over the fields churned up by the Funnies, tank support carriers. The tank tracks were two feet deep in the gap centre line. The strongpoint garrison surrendered, 80 of them with six large guns, banks of rockets, mines and wire. James Younie was the 'C' Coy jeep driver, and arrived at 0930 as a stonk killed Major Douglas Findlay Shirras MC and his batman, Pte Austin. Younie drove their bodies back for burial in a small wood. But at 1530 he was told to drive an advance party forward. He and his three passengers were blown 20 feet in the air when the jeep hit a mine. They survived but a tank officer and crewman standing nearby were killed. Younie had a badly bruised back and a dent in his chin, but the new company commander, Major Paterson needed the replacement jeep - and Pte Younie to drive it.

The battalion took all their objectives by 0300 relatively unopposed - the non-stop shelling which lasted throughout the night and the morning, only ceasing when two other gaps had been established, caused 20 KIA and 30 wounded.

2nd Seaforth advance was delayed by the lack of cleared gaps but took all their objectives, with a total bag of 1244 prisoners by the end of the two day battle. Lt Col DB Lang had briefed 5th Camerons before they assembled at St Barthelemy. 'D' Coy under Major Parker led followed by 'C' Coy; both were initially held up as the Avres had not succeeded in making a crossing through the minefields. Many flails were knocked-out so both companies crossed the minefields and anti-tank ditch without 'Funny' help. Casualties were heavy due to shelling. Major MacNab 'C' Coy and Capt Milne, the IO were killed and many others wounded. Fontaine-la-Mallet was cleared by 'B' Coy and at 0700 'C' moved into the woods near Freville.

Before 'Astonia' began the Gordons and others had been entertained near Fecamp by a concert party whose star was Gertrude Lawrence. The Benedictine liqueur sold by the abbey in Fecamp was perhaps equally popular! In the attack on Le Havre 1st Gordons led 153 Bde in their follow-up role but at 0500 on 11th were held up in the traffic jams in the gaps so the rifle companies went on alone, through Rum, taking 80 POW in Fontaine-la-Mallet. Another 100 Germans were taken in the Forêt de Montgeon. The Polar Bear division had also made significant inroads into the Le Havre defences - the end was in sight.

By the end of the battle 1st Gordons for 14 casualties collected a total of 600 prisoners and much equipment and loot was found in the bunker and coastal defences. "They lined up in front of me. [Major Lindsay 2 i/c] "There you are, the Master Race, help yourselves." And the Jocks soon had a fine collection of watches, fountain pens, pocket knives and French francs.   The 5/7th Gordons got 50 cases of champagne in the Citadel (Fort Sainte Addresse) - Bollinger '34 or '37. The garrison blew up a naval gun which caused a breach in the walls of the fort and so 250 POW were taken. Soon every Jock was smoking a Wehrmacht cigar! Pte Stan Whitehouse 1st Gordons was deputed by his Sgt Edmonds to guard a liqueur store, 'a veritable Aladdin's cave.' Some time later he had sunk half a bottle of orange Dutch Curacao liqueur and was in a helpless condition. Crafty Sgt Edmonds had been organising a smugglers run selling the captured Wehrmacht rum to the local café owners. The spoils were considerable, £25 to each of the 'smugglers' whose pay was 21/- per week.   Stan was shown the German cemetery with 2000 graves of those killed by the RAF bombers who had dropped bombs with fuel oil around barges of an invasion fleet. The screams of the burning Wehrmacht were heard by the citizens of Le Havre.

5th Black Watch followed up behind the Gordons later on the 11th and despite shelling which caused 18 casualties, by the end of the two day battle, had collected over 1000 prisoners. Corporal Stacey of 'B' Coy escorted a batch of 500 back to the Divisonal cages. His six men and one machine-gun were ably assisted by the French Maquis as extra guards.

On the coastal part of the attack 154 Bde organised a deceptive plan. 61st Anti-Tank Regt sited guns at St Sulpice which fired on Octeville. Two composite forces, 7th Black Watch/Northants Yeo, a mobile column and 'Grayforce' of 2nd Derby Yeo armoured cars with 'A' Sqn Northants Yeo mopped up the coastal area capturing 1200 and 200 POW respectively.

On 13th General Rennie sent a message to HD telling them of another important task successfully accomplished in close co-operation with the Polar Bears division. HD captured 122 officers and 4508 ORs for the loss of 138 casualties. The Polar Bears lost 301 casualties and nearly 7000 POW were taken. The main losers apart from the German garrison, were the French civilians who suffered heavily. 'Astonia' was over - a typical well-planned, brutal set piece Monty operation - and very successful. Whilst the Channel ports were being invested and captured, the three armoured divisions, Black Bull, Desert Rats and the Guards had been streaming north to capture Antwerp, Ghent and Brussels. On 17th September Monty's rather optimistic message went out: "Today the Seine is far behind us. The Allies have removed the enemy from practically the whole of France and Belgium except in a few places and we stand at the door of Germany." The 'Great Swan' had caused great euphoria. Major Martin Lindsay 1st Gordons: "We greatly feared that the war in Germany might be over while we were back there [Villainville] and out of it. Having travelled so far since 1939 we all wanted to be in at the death." Prophetic words indeed.

Most of HD then spent two weeks in limbo in the Le Havre area, apart from the gunners 'visiting' Calais and 154 Bde investing Dunkirk. Most of HD transport was lent to the RASC supplying 2nd Army in the north, attacking Arnhem, liberating Antwerp and Brussels. 5th Camerons stayed at Hecqueville, 5th Black Watch at Beaurepaire, Gordons near Etretat, Die Hards at Bordeaux St Clair. Training cadres, inspections, football matches, local dances, Balmoral concert party in action, Battalion Games and a few sneaky visits to Paris. Major John McGregor, 5th Black Watch recalls that on one parade for the massed Pipes and Drums at the ceremony of beating retreat (very good for the 'Auld Alliance') there were 10 Pipe Majors, 120 Pipers and 56 Drummers taking part.

Sgt Jack Cheshire, 1st Bn Gordon Highlanders had spent five years with the 1st Bn Oxford and Buckinghamshire Light Infantry. He was detailed in Criquecot to provide a ceremonial HQ guard in full Highland dress. So he chose six men under Corporal Harold Wareham, all ex Ox and Bucks who could *only* carry out light infantry drill at light infantry speed (i.e. rather fast). After half an hour of frustration the RSM gave up, Cheshire's guard was dismissed. "After this the light infantry men never did an HQ guard: us Ox and Bucks boys were not as green as we looked!"

After the model two day battle Div HQ were back at Criquecot with 152 and 153 Bde resting nearby and 154 Bde left to garrison Le Havre. The artillery regiments were vital to HD in defence and attack, masterminded by the CRA Brigadier 'Jerry' Sheil. Capt Aitkenhead was his Staff Captain RA:

> I knew about his qualities of leadership, his 'eye for country' and his ability to size up a situation in an instant. I found him a good master. Presented with the essential facts he gave swift and sound instructions and left me to get on with it. In major battles lasting up to a fortnight arranging for the dumping of ammunition for the opening attack was the easy part. I spent about an hour with him each evening after he had been out and about all day in his jeep. He would brief me on the course of the battle and give me a guide as to likely ammo requirements over the next two or three days. To have ammunition available at the right place and the right time was the tricky part in a war of movement. I was intrigued with the work of the Army Photographic Interpretation Section and also by the RAF officer at HQ RA known as the Weatherman who produced the meteor telegrams - a kind and elderly (to us!) science teacher from Fife. If pressed he would return to his caravan and redraw his isobars to see if he could improve the

weather! Intelligence ensured that we were kept up to date with the military situation and the War Map was always on display.

33

More Channel Ports: Boulogne, Calais and Dunkirk
"swanning days are over"

On 13th September the three gunner regiments and HQRA were quickly called away to support the Canadians attacking Boulogne. It was a long and wearisome trek of 160 miles before the harbour areas around Cormon were reached. 128 Field Regt stayed at Montreuil and went into action the next day (14th).

> The enemy held Wimereux and Mont Lambert from which we were shelled by German 88mm guns but our counter measures were completely successful. The final POW bag was 140 officers and 5100 ORs. We captured three of their guns. Boulogne was liberated on 23rd September and the Canadians thanked us for quick and excellent support.

Wrote Geoffrey Durand, 128 Field Regt. 126 Field Regt's gun positions were at Conteville, five miles east of the port. 300 rpg were dumped for the main attack by 3rd Canadian Division on 17th September, after the usual RAF heavy bomber attack. The Boche was stubborn and isolated strongpoints held out until the 23rd. Calais was next on the list, and torrential rain made the short journey unpleasant. The approach road was difficult in full view of the German garrison manning the coastal and light guns of Cap Gris Nez. So smokescreens were put down to shield the roads. Near Wissant the three field regiments poured 450 rpg on to the defenders at 1000 hrs on 25th after another RAF pounding. Calais was finally liberated by the Canadians on 27th September. The Field Regts then had four days out of the line.

Some 170 miles away 15,000 Germans were still holding out in Dunkirk. Its 56 mile perimeter was being guarded by the 4th Special Service Brigade and orders were now given to Brigadier Oliver's 154 Bde to relieve them. 1st Black Watch left on 25th September and the move took two days via the Forêt de Crecy to a concentration area north of St Omer. In a defensive position the three forward companies covered a frontage of three miles with battalion HQ in Loon Plage. The only battery of 25-pdrs was limited to 20 rounds per gun per day, and after a truce on 3-6th October for an evacuation for French civilians, the battalion mortars fired up to 2000 bombs per day. In their two weeks outside Dunkirk the battalion lost 16 casualties. Major Benson drove round the battalion positions each day in his jeep with Pte Ogg. Once a large covey of partridges was spotted and the 2i/c tried to blast them with his Sten gun. Nothing happened as the Sten catch had not been moved forward!

Pte Stan Whitehouse:

> Our role at Dunkirk was merely to lay siege to the town and tie down its garrison. The Germans had ringed the whole area with a deep collar of mines and miles of barbed wire effectively sealing themselves in. It was a 'stand off' situation although they shelled us and we retaliated. The French Maquis were active, installed in farmhouses with enormous ancient looking machine guns. One was a glamorous young lady, a courier, flitting about the country lanes on her cycle, constantly ogled by sex-starved squaddies!

The 'S' (Specialist) Platoon tried to sweep a six foot wide lane through a minefield in the dark. Someone trod on a 'S' mine wounding Lt Soulsby, two sergeants and killing Sgt Percy Edmonds; "Old Edmonds had been killed within sight of those same Dunkirk beaches from which he had been rescued four years earlier."

The 7th Argylls held the line around Bray Dunes Plage. The three carrier platoons of 154 Bde were put into a mobile unit, 'Campbell Force' disposed from Bergues to Spycker. The German patrols were aggressive. One penetrated the Argyll's HQ and caused three casualties, and 'Campbell Force' was also attacked. The small town of La Panne over the Belgian border was a rest centre. Brigade HQ was at Wormhoudt, twelve miles from Dunkirk. The two day truce negotiated by the Red Cross allowed 18,500 civilians to 'escape' over the bridge at Grande Mille Brugge.

7th Black Watch area at Ghyvelde was largely under flood water caused by the German defenders who on the 17th sent in a strong fighting patrol supported by heavy shelling and mortaring. They were quite successful, took some Black Watch prisoners and set fire to houses in the main street. 'B' Coy Die Hards were brought in as extra support and the mortar platoon was kept busy. On 8th October the Czech Armoured Bde relieved 154 Bde who returned to HD in the Eindhoven area, via the WWI battle grounds of Abbeville, Bethune, Ypres, the Menin Gate, Courtrai and Brussels.

On 25th September Div HQ moved to Wirwignes six miles east of Boulogne. Lt Col James Cochrane, OC Div Signals:

> On 28th September one of the most enjoyable moves ever made by HD was begun. Iteghem 35 miles north-east of Brussels was the concentration area. Div HQ arrived there after a journey through a very happy liberated Belgium. The Signals Officers Mess was in the Burgomeister's house and 'A' Mess Div HQ went to M Hanson's Chateau.

On 2nd October HD relieved 15th Scottish Div on a wide front from

St Odenrode to Eindhoven guarding the supply corridor to Nijmegen.

Market Garden had come and gone - a glorious failure but a huge salient had been gained - a spring board for the future. "Swanning days are over. The winter campaign in Holland was designed to consolidate our gains, open the port of Antwerp and prepare the ground for the spring offensive," wrote Alastair Borthwick. Col Walford, 5th Seaforth had earned a bar to his DSO and in the 16 days the battalion spent at Olland near St Oedenrode, Major Richard Fleming the 2i/c encouraged the Seaforth snipers to show their deadly skill: "The snipers are a law unto themselves, they submit only to the fatherly will of CSM Davidson, apart from that, they go their own ways regardless of what the rest of the battalion does, what Standing Orders say." L/Corp Matchwick won the MM when he and five others made up a sniper patrol and in a noisy fracas with rifles, grenades, a Sten that didn't work, a revolver and a captured Spandau killed four and captured three. "The woods were fair hotching with Jerries. There was shooting all over the place." The opposition were from a parachute battalion.

153 Bde left Normandy on 28th September and via Amiens and Cambrai entered Holland on 1st October to take over from units of 15th Scottish Division. Between St Oedenrode on the river Dommel and Fratershof were 5th Black Watch on the right, 5/7th Gordons in the centre and 1st Gordons on the left. New reinforcements with no battle experience were given a gradual initiation. 'B' Coy 5/7th Gordons was made up to strength with RASC drivers and RAMC personnel. 21st Army Group was facing a scarcity of front line troops and 50th Tyne Tees Division and two tank brigades were shortly to be disbanded.

7th Black Watch were based opposite Oirschot held across the Wilhelmina Canal by the Germans. 1st Black Watch were on their right and 7th Argylls beyond them to their right. 154 Bde's main role was to protect the large airfield at Eindhoven from enemy patrols who might cross the canal. Here they stayed in miserable autumn weather until a Dutch Brigade relieved them on the 17th. Two days later 154 Bde were in the line again at Koevering with 7th Argylls on their right and 1st Black Watch on their left.

On 20th October just before dawn an enemy patrol, 20 strong infiltrated 'C' Coy HQ 1st Black Watch, "and captured about six of our lads. They tipped two Jerry cans (of water) over the Brengun carriers to set them on fire." Pte Stan Whitehouse saw a crowd of mingled Black Watch bonnets and hackles and German helmets:

> I assumed our boys were escorting prisoners to the 'pen' and called out 'where are you taking that lot?' A signal for pandemonium. Firing began with bullets zipping past us followed by shouts and screams. We opened fire on the Germans silhouetted against Monty's Moonlight and easy targets.

Eventually honours were even. 1st Black Watch had 13 casualties (including friendly fire) and the Boche lost 13.

Major JE Benson 1st Black Watch:

> We generally found that newly joined drafts of officers and Jocks provided they survived the first three weeks, had a much better chance of surviving. They got battle experience in simple things and of course they learnt a lot in those (three) weeks by talking to their NCOs and fellow Jocks. Quite a lot of them only had staff experience not having been at the 'Sharp End.' But proper battle experience could only be gained by experience under active service conditions, and one was lucky indeed if you were well experienced without being hit.

Benson reproached himself for not alerting young 2/Lt Viney who on his first patrol stood too close to a Northants Yeo 'Firefly' when its 17-pdr muzzle blast killed him instantly.

152 Bde spent nearly three weeks in the line near Best just north of Eindhoven. 2nd and 5th Seaforth were in Best and just north-east of it. 5th Camerons were to the right of 5th Seaforth and 2nd Derbyshire Yeo in an infantry role were on the right of 5th Camerons. It was the perfect training area, closely wooded but with no natural features for defences and ideal for patrolling, raiding and the deployment of various weaponry. Several battalions delegated control of minor, low key offensive operations to their 2i/c. Major RM Munro, 5th Camerons with a large air photo of the area deployed snipers, forward gunner and mortar FOOs, Recce and fighting patrols. Sometimes Brens were used, or 2" mortars, even PIATs, anti-tank guns and supporting AA Bofers in a ground role. Six young Canloan subalterns on 25th September joined 5th Camerons from AA or coast artillery units. They were brave and all became casualties before the war ended. Ross Le Mesurier, Bruce Ellker, Archie Fox, Bob Hackness, Evatt Merchant and Bill Neilson. "Bill Agnew was there when we arrived but three others had already been wounded, Lew Arnett, John Pennington and Joe Pearce." The Die Hards enjoyed themselves with their medium machine-guns and 4.2" mortars and borrowed 'C' Coy of the Manchesters, as their own 'B' Coy was busy outside Dunkirk.

The gunner regiments rejoined from helping to bombard the Channel ports via WWI battlefields Colombert, Hazebrouck, Ypres, Menin, Courtrai, Oudenarde to Alost and then through Mechlin to St Oedenrode on 4th October.

An HD leave camp was opened in Eindhoven for a 24 hours rest with baths and clean clothes and later on 17th October four day leaves started to a rest camp in Antwerp. Every form of generous Dutch hospitality was showered on the Jocks. The Balmorals and ENSA performed, cinemas and cafés were popular. Well-deserved decorations now 'arrived' for actions up to mid-August. 1st Black Watch were awarded two MCs and eleven MMs. They were pleased too that 'their' Gunner FOOs from 126 Field Regt, Major Riach and Capt Cameron who had supported the battalion since landing both received the MC. Lt Col Harry Cumming-Bruce received the DSO for his time spent commanding 153 Bde. Major George Dunn 2i/c 5th Black Watch was awarded a bar to his DSO, CSM Fraser a DCM plus three MMs. Lt Col Walford 5th Seaforth was awarded a bar to his DSO as was Lt Col Hopwood CO 1st Black Watch.

34

Operation Colin: 23 October-1 November

Field Marshal Montgomery now planned a massive drive to try and force the enemy out of Brabant to clear the area up to the mouth of the river Maas and open the port of Antwerp. Lt General Neil Ritchie's 12 Corps would drive due west to clear the province of Brabant and the area round the river Scheldt. The 1st Canadian Army would advance northwards from Woensdrecht towards Roosendaal and link up with 12 Corps at Moerdijk thus cutting off all, or most of, the German *15th Army*. Four divisions, 53rd Welsh, 7th Armoured, 15th Scottish and HD would take part in the battle in Operation Colin. Jack Didden, author, historian and schoolmaster who lives in Drunen has written the definitive study 'Colin - 51st HD in Brabant.' 53rd Welsh aided by 7th Armoured would capture the key town of 's-Hertogenbosch held by the German *712 Division*. HD would attack north from the St Oedenrode area, capture Schijndel, St Michielsgestel, Boxtel, Esch and Vught villages and small towns south-east and south of 's-Hertogenbosch. This area was held by *59th Infantry Division* (with the *Bloch* and *Gramse* regts) holding the line Eerde to Liempde between Boxtel and Veghel.

In the event Operation Colin would take nine days of more or less constant action, rather more than 2nd British Army had planned. Thick woods, many canals, and poor marshy country unsuitable for tracked vehicles caused delay - and the defence fought rather well. Starting from Eerde 153 Bde were on the right (northern) flank, and 152 Bde on the left (southern) flank starting north of St Oedenrode - both supported by Shermans of 33 Armoured Bde. Travelling in Kangaroos 154 Bde would follow through to exploit in the centre.

For Colin additional RE support came from 12 Corps. Two extra field Coys (262 and 263), Engineer Assault Sqn (16), an RASC bridging Coy (35) with its Bailey bridge folding and assault boat sections. The CRE's main task was to open up and maintain two separate class 40 (ton load) routes for tanks, initially a temporary Class 40 bridging by the ARE Sqn.

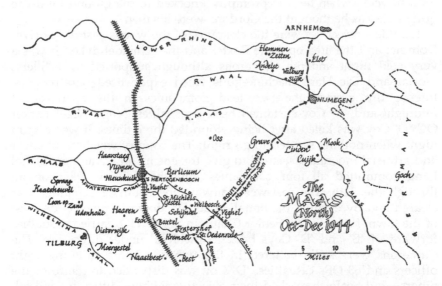

Operation Colin

Zero hour for the silent attack of 153 Bde was midnight 22/23rd October. 5th Black Watch on the left to tackle Schijndel and 5/7th Gordons on the right to capture Wijbosch. It was to be the second anniversary of their baptism of fire at El Alamein. The Gordons started first, 'B' Coy walked through a minefield and Sgt Stevens stormed an enemy post with great éclat. 'C' Coy HQ used grenades against bazookas and 'A' and 'D' took Wijbosch with 35 POW losing in the process 20 casualties. 5th Black Watch went through the Gordons at dawn with tank support from 144 RTR, a smokescreen and a creeping barrage. Their CO Lt Col Bill Bradford arrived alone in the small town of Schijndel as his two companies in the lead lost their way in the thick smokescreen. The enemy had pulled out beforehand and the battalion settled into a silk stockings factory. 1st Gordons started with a ration of rum and by noon had secured the south-west corner of the town. Their CO Lt Col Cumming-Bruce had set up a rota for his three brave company commanders, Bruce Rae, Bill MacMillan and Jim Robertson who had fought in every battle since El Alamein, so that in turn they were sent off to run the Divisonal rest camp in Antwerp. A reasonable place to be for LOB (Left Out of Battle).

Private Jack Tough, 'D' Coy 5/7th Gordons went into his first action near Veghel on the anniversary (23rd October) of the battle of El Alamein. 'C' Coy was leading towards Wijbosch. On the far side of the village 16 Platoon dug-in. Out of the darkness came a German soldier on a bicycle; "when he was promptly knocked to the ground he made quite a fuss as he thought the Gordons were his men."

152 Bde's objectives were the clearance of the woods east of the river Dommel and the area opposite Boxtel and the Schijndel dyke. It was a very cold night and 5th Camerons although supported by artillery, mortar and Die Hard machine-guns faced experienced paratroopers. Intense fire greeted the two lead companies in the open, about midnight and 'A' Coy sustained heavy casualties. Major Nigel Parker OC 'D' Coy was killed after being wounded three times. It was a grim night when nothing seemed to go right. The country was bare of cover and artificial moonlight seemed to give the enemy an advantage. Lt Col Lang committed all four companies and the fighting went on all through the 24th. The east-west railway line south of Schijndel was cleared and by evening the battalion settled down in pinewoods west of the town. Padre Smith, Senior Chaplain at Div HQ, carried casualties forward of 'B' and 'D' Coys back to the RAP under direct fire. The Camerons were sadly battered in the two day battle suffering eight officers and 63 ORs casualties. 'D' Coy was disbanded to reinforce the others. 2nd Seaforth reached their objective without difficulty, and 5th Seaforth found Olland empty, the Germans having withdrawn nine hours before the attack. Helped by advice from a crashed Dakota pilot called Joe, a tall thin priest and an extremely fat dumpy priest wearing a steel helmet, the Seaforth were told that Liempde was clear. At 1830 the battalion moved in TCVs towards Den Dungen, entered the next day without opposition. The road was clear up to the Zuid Willems Vaart where the bridge was blown.

The GOC knew that the two night attacks had gone well despite 5th Camerons painful engagement with the parachute troops so he sent 154 Bde into the attack. The Argylls cleared the woods between Zuid-Willemsvaart Canal and Schijndel slowly because of mines. 6 Platoon, 'B' Coy, 1st Black Watch were shelled by friendly fire after a Lysander spotter plane reported enemy close ahead. "I think we'll try and shift the Jerries some other way, if you don't mind," Lt Yates told the FOO. At about midnight on 25/26th the Argylls sent patrols out to try to surround the enemy in front of Pte Stan Whitehouse's section. At dawn, "the Germans were through 5 Platoon's position. Eight had been killed - three on the wire, five as they dashed between the slitters. Lt Danny White was among the dead. In the poor visibility his own men had cut him down. A popular lad and a fine soldier."

Typhoons and accurate RAF bombing had softened up the enemy defences. 7th Black Watch set off at 1130, cleared minefields and by

1600 had reached the blown bridge at St Michels Gester. Pioneers and sappers started work on Class 9 and 40 bridges. Before first light on 24th 7th Black Watch followed by 1st Black Watch were across the Dommel. Private John Tough 1st Black Watch saw the sappers building a bridge under fire. "They received a terrible pounding with mortars and 88mms. When they were finished, they came running up the road towards us in quite a state. They had some casualties and were very upset." The Black Watch incurred 17 casualties from this heavy shelling. The GOC arrived to congratulate both Black Watch battalions and Major Small, 'A' Coy, and Major Lowe, 'D' Coy, of the 7th Bn who made a bridgehead to make the vital bridging possible. The CRE Lt Col Ralph Carr had great responsibility for the organisation of a dozen bridges over the Dommel, Hal, Munsel, Esch and other water barriers.

Still on the 24th, 2nd Seaforth tried to cross the Dommel north of Boxtel but were delayed by intense machine-gun fire. By 1445 they were across and found Munsel and at dusk Boxtel empty. Lt General Poppe had withdrawn his troops and over a hundred airborne troops who had escaped from Arnhem were now rescued. 5th Seaforth in Den Dungen found "the streets were crowded and orange streamers and banners everywhere but the biggest crowd" wrote Lt Alastair Borthwick, the IO, "...was crammed into the square opposite the Townhouse, cheering Allied pilots and paratroopers who had been kept in hiding until that morning." 2nd Derbyshire Yeo had a sticky time at the crossroads south of Den Dungen where two companies of the *Gramse Bn* with anti-tank guns beat them off. 7th Bn Black Watch pushed 'A' Coy on to seize the bridge at Halder two miles ahead, blown of course, but 40 POW went into the bag. The bridge at Hal was blown literally under the feet of 1st Black Watch. They caught 90 POW and the Argylls 35 in the woods. For the time being 7th Argylls came under command of 153 Bde and 5/7th Gordons under 154 Bde.

Major Martin Lindsay and Bert Brown, MO 1st Gordons played a strange game of golf at Schijndel with three clubs between them as the Germans had stolen the rest. There were only four playable holes, the rest being in a minefield. In front of the fourth green the GOC was holding a conference with all his commanders, "so this was too much for us."

Meanwhile the German defenders received their first armour support, ten SP guns of a Sturmgeschutz Coy. At first light on the 25th 1st Black Watch patrols pushed out from their bridgehead towards Vught, met a counter-attacking battalion with SPs and anti-tank guns who knocked-out five carriers, taking their crews prisoner.

Captain WJ Brown, 126 Field Regt RA:

> With the infantry pushing on night and day the commitment of the gunners was a heavy one. 'Mike' and 'Victor' targets by day and harassing fire by

night provided the Regt with incessant employment. Target records were again a nightmarish task for the Regt and Bty Command post staffs. On the 23rd morning 126 Field Regt fired 300 rounds per gun and moved forward again into action near the badly battered village of Schijndel.

Soon positions were to be occupied at St Michels Gestel, Udenhout, Loon op Zand and Kattsheuvel.

Lt Col James Cochrane, OC HD signals:

> For the first time we were fighting in areas with a good system of underground cables. It had never been possible up to now to use the overhead PTT cables during the campaign owing to their complete destruction by bombardment. A strange thing was that the Germans were not very successful in destroying Dutch Post Office exchanges (apart from 's-Hertogenbosch). The others were in very good order. Dutch PO officials came out of hiding and gave great assistance.

Stan Whitehouse 1st Black Watch and eight rather bitter ex-Tyneside Scottish lads (six Geordies, two Welshmen), under Corporal Grainger went off on patrol through woods to recce a bridge:

> Ambling towards us following our trail were a dozen Germans about thirty yards away, nonchalant, carefree with weapons slung over their shoulders. Violent bursts of Sten fire came from our left and the unrelenting fire chopped the Germans down. Now the rest of us fired into the groups sending the field grey figures milling around and stumbling. Within seconds it was over. The Germans blew the bridge and three POW were taken back by Whitehouse's patrol. L/Corp Aichinson in his lilting scarcely understandable Geordie dialect said. "We didna really know how many were aboot, did we? There might have been mair of the buggers behind 'em. Yer better to shoot the bastards while ye can. Ah knew they would have shot us - ay've seen 'em.

Major Boyle OC 'D' Coy, 7th Argylls supported by wasp flame-throwers and Shermans of the Northants Yeo resumed the attack over the Halsche Water towards Vught. At a road block three tanks were knocked-out, snipers were active and enemy shelling and mortaring was very heavy. Half way to Vught a pitched battle ensued as the Argylls met an enemy counter-attack head on. Prisoners were taken on both sides, but an enemy SP and anti-tank gun were destroyed. It was an exhausting day and no progress could be made at all, casualties were heavy. The next morning 7th Black Watch came through under a heavy concentration and by 1330 on 26th Vught was captured. The 200 POW taken included some of the notorious German 'Green Police' guards of the ill-famed concentration camp near Vught. The tanks of 7th Armoured Division passed through HD during the night but were held up at Loon op Zand.

Further south 5/7th Gordons at dawn on 25th in thick fog were counter-attacked by an 80 strong patrol. Capt Brayley's 'C' Coy saw them off inflicting about 40 casualties including 24 POW. Major Muir's 'A' Coy surprised and captured a patrol and the rest of the enemy company arose from ditches and surrendered! Their company commander missed the early morning battle and with his servant, both on bicycles rode into the Gordon's lines unaware of the situation. They were late for the battle having spent the night with lady friends. 5/7th Gordons took 70 POW that day for the loss of 23 casualties. By the end of the 25th, 154 Bde had pushed well over the Halsche Water and 2nd Seaforth and 1st Gordons linked up the two bridgeheads south-east of Esch. In the early hours of the 26th 1st Gordons attacking towards Oisterwijk lost ten casualties in 'C' Coy including their indomitable Major Bruce Ray. He was shot twice in the chest, once in the jaw and his life was saved by stretcher bearers who got him back to the RAP. At dawn on the 27th the Gordons got their revenge; artillery and tank shells smashed the wretched village and 25 Germans covered with dust and plaster were only too glad to surrender. 144 RAC supported 2nd Seaforth and 5th Black Watch towards Haaren. The latter had a stiff battle on the 26th to take Esch, again the next day at Eind and Haaren - their fourth action in Operation Colin. 153 Bde now had 1st Gordons in Oisterwijk, 5/7th Gordons in Holeind and Black Watch in Haaren. Their position was halfway between Tilburg and 's-Hertogenbosch, and twelve miles away from the main HD objective, the river Maas.

'C' Coy, 5th Camerons, Battle for River Maas, late October 1944

To the north 152 Bde were also thrusting towards Vught, a key road centre. 5th Camerons led and cut the Vught-Tilburg road on the evening of the 26th, and then mopped-up south of the Aftenvaterings Canal. 7th Armoured Div were badly held up by the waterlogged fields and flat polder country and made little progress. On the 27th no HD unit was involved in serious fighting and 153 Bde planned to take Loon op Zand, holding up the Desert Rats advance.

The German *15th Army* had been given permission to withdraw to Stellung Zwei (the second line of defence), Loon op Zand was a key position defended by an infantry battalion and five 75mm anti-tank guns. So General Rennie decided that a two brigade attack was required, 153 Bde from the south, 152 Bde due north and then turn west to cut off the defenders retreat. Fifteen regiments of artillery belted the wretched *256th Volksgrenadier* (who had replaced the original depleted garrison). 2nd Seaforths failed to cut off the retreat because of minefields, thick woods and the fading light, but 5th Seaforth captured 80 POW and two of the anti-tank guns.

1st Gordons were ordered to take Loon op Zand, then 5th Black Watch would pass through and capture Horst. From Haaren to Oisterwinjk the Gordons advanced through the village with feeble resistance with only two casualties. The CO Lt Col Cumming-Bruce politely knocked on the door of a house to ask questions and out tumbled seven perfectly good German soldiers who surrendered to him. His 2i/c Martin Lindsay described his CO: "Harry, a slightly stooping, unmilitary figure, wearing spectacles with a near-white frame above an old-fashioned fair moustache, a Tam O'Shanter and a short gabardine coat with a black sheepskin collar; the unique immutable Harry." Unfortunately that night Battalion HQ in a council school with acres of glass were heavily shelled causing thirteen casualties including Capt David Martin, the new adjutant, John Frary, the Signal officer, John Inglis, their FOO and Waters, 'I' Section. 5th Black Watch reached Loon op Zand at dark and were heavily shelled. Confused fighting took place in thick pinewoods and at one stage the battalion was cut in two. For an hour very heavy firing ensued but with friendly tanks appearing in total darkness the enemy were driven clear. The next day Horst was taken despite serious opposition with a line of anti-tank guns causing Sherman losses. By 1500 on 29th 5th Black Watch had been in battle continuously for 14 hours and were happy to see 5/7th Gordons come through heading for Kaatscheuvel. In the meantime 15th Scottish Div had captured Tilburg, three miles south of Loon op Zand. 7th Armoured Div would now exploit westwards south of HD. On the night of 28/29th, 152 and 153 Bde were clearing the wooded areas round Loon op Zand and 154 Bde were directed on Gertrudenberg with 1st Black Watch moving towards the Hooge and Waspik canal bridges -

both of course blown.

The PIAT (Projectile Infantry Anti-Tank) was a heavy cumbersome weapon, four foot long that fired a rocket-shaped 2½lb bomb and was effective, if on target, on most enemy tracked vehicles up to 100 yards. The one-off lightweight German bazooka was a more effective (disposable) weapon as our tank crews were well aware. Private Stan Whitehouse 1st Black Watch on 28th October volunteered for a spell with the PIAT in No 7 Section led by Lt Bernard and Corporal Holland. Bernard was rather small with a pencil moustache who often asked his section for advice, "But for all that he was a gentleman through and through," recalls Whitehouse. Sitting on the edge of their water-logged 'slits,' "My heart gave a flutter as I saw a German helmet, then another and a third against a sliver of silver skyline." A metallic clicking was the sound of the useless Brengun with a broken firing pin. L/Corp Fitzsimmons and the Bren team further up the road were now of little use. "A mighty explosion erupted down the lane followed by weird shouts and screams. A long burst of the dreaded Spandau raked the front of my 'slitter,' hurtling my small pack, pouches and pistol over my head away into the night." Whitehouse fired an acquired Schmeisser, and a little later his PIAT, with no sign of activity from 6 or 8 sections. He was physically attacked by a huge German soldier pointing a bazooka at Whitehouse and the PIAT bomb loader, 'Popeye'. After a ferocious battle, 'Popeye' fired his only shot of the night. Then to everyone's surprise 16 wounded Germans walked in to give themselves up. "Hey, Popeye, I (Stan Whitehouse) was 18 yesterday. Put a drop of rum in that brew."

HD was now only five miles from the river Maas. 153 Bde were sent north towards Kaatsheavel and Sprang. A 5th Black Watch carrier patrol reported the road was clear and by 1030 1st Gordons moved into Sprang without opposition on 30th October. On a wall was chalked 'We will come back, Tomy.' Kaatsheavel was the objective for 5/7th Gordons which they took without much trouble bagging 30 POW. In the barrage of 8000 shells on the unfortunate village 28 Dutch civilians were killed. General Rennie now ordered 154 Bde to outflank the opposition; 7th Black Watch towards the Maas via Nieuwe Vaart and Kapelle and 7th Argylls in Kangaroos to Gertrudenberg. 153 Bde rather unexpectedly moved eastwards in TCVs to relieve 53rd Welsh Div as the garrison in 's-Hertogenbosch captured a few days earlier. Major John McGregor, 5th Black Watch: "The town was like a miniature Venice but without the bridges most of them blown by the Germans who were now dug in on the northern bank of the Aftwaterings Canal with a clear field of fire."

Pte Patrick Adams, 174 Highland Field Ambulance, all 6ft 6in of him drove an Austin ambulance, then a captured German one with a wooden steering wheel. He noticed the eagles above the gates of Vught Concentration Camp and saw the gas ovens for the cremation of the unfortunate inmates. On leave in Antwerp with Pte Trevor Edwards their theatre was bombed by a V-1 which demolished a nearby cinema killing many troops. At St Oedenroede he presented the nurses and the 20 stone matron of the local hospital with (looted) silk stockings.

Waalwijk, 31 Oct. 1944. Major Bill Field. 492 Field Batt. RA; Capt Tony Lamb, Adjt; Lt Col Derek Lang, CO 5th Camerons (Ross Le Mesurier)

On the last day of the month 152 Bde were plodding through sand dunes north from Sprang towards Waalwijk where 5th Camerons received a tumultuous welcome just as the enemy shelled the main square. The German High Command ordered the bulk of their surviving forces back across the Maas but the Fuehrer personally ordered *59th Division* to stay south of the river behind the Afwateringskanaal and a regiment of *256th Division* to make a stand around the Keizersveer bridge. 1st Black Watch moved from Zandschel towards Waspik. "The Bn reached Waspik in Kangaroos. Eight of us [Pte Whitehouse and Section, 6 Platoon 1st Black Watch] crammed into the converted Sherman tank with just the driver and machine-gunner up front." Mines on the road were exploded by the leading tank. 'B' Coy dismounted: "Pte Eddie Head and his mate were looting gory bodies caught by the mine blast and scattered around the crater." Stan Whitehouse put PIAT bombs into houses:

> The blast was colossal flushing out three Germans. Sgt Baxter was shot through the lung with blood and froth coming from his lips, another veteran - one of the best - to fall by the wayside. Slowly the platoons old,

seasoned campaigners were being whittled away. Major Bob Anderson, our beloved company commander was shot in the chest and critically wounded while leading an attack on nearby houses, invalided home with OBE, MC and Bar.

SPs and anti-tank guns caused casualties. Major Riach their FOO brought down DF fire. Major Benson 2i/c:

'C' Coy on a two platoon front after difficult confused fighting cleared the long main street killing several Germans. Lt Cox had secured the bridge in spite of heavy Spandau fire under cover of 2" mortar smoke but was shot in the stomach and later died. We received magnificent support from Major Gray Skelton's 'A' Sqn 1st Northants Yeo. Later in the afternoon 7th Argylls passed through us. During Colin we lost four officers and 49 ORs (mainly at the Hooge bridge) but we took over 70 POW and much equipment.

Raamsdonk was well defended and on 31st, the Argylls had 80 casualties before they reached the centre of the village, including 23 KIA. Bazookas knocked-out supporting tanks and enemy shelling, mortaring and Spandau fire was intense. After hours of severe fighting the Argylls were exhausted. At 1530 the 7th Black Watch came through in Kangaroos. They then completed a fine performance by knocking-out and capturing five SP guns. During Colin they lost 53 casualties, half of them in the final phase to Hooge bridge. 7th Black Watch, Major DFO Russell noted also captured five 20mm Flak guns and cut the enemy's escape route at Gertrudenberg five hours later taking 200 POW: "The scene of this encounter presented a remarkable sight, the German SP artillery and our own knocked-out Kangaroos all being in the closest proximity in the positions in which they had met their end." By 2100 the Black Watch had achieved all their objectives. Lt Ian Donaldson in his Kangaroo actually rammed an SP gun and machine-gunned its crew. Casualties during the long day were 32. Major Hugh Forster, OC 297 Bty 126 Field Regt gave invaluable support to 7th Black Watch. He carried their CO, Lt Col Cathcart in his half track affectionately known as 'The Barouche'. The handling of his guns during the Black Watch attack down the Raamsdonk road, five miles to Gertrudenberg was masterly. The Divisional artillery had put in huge concentrations to demolish a counter-attack launched by the enemy across the river Maas.

By the end of the 31st the area west of 's-Hertogenbosch and the Maas villages of Waalwijk, Sprang, Waspik, Raamsdonk and Raamsdonksveer were in HD's hands. So Operation Colin was over and apart from one last section the area south of the river Maas was secure - at a cost.

Major Lindsay wrote:

...the badly wounded Bruce Rae was the last remaining of the twenty rifle company officers who came out with the battalion on D-Day. That is what was so superlatively gallant about these chaps. They would go into battle time after time, knowing perfectly well that they were dicing against the mathematical odds. For an officer to go into a dozen actions without being killed or badly wounded was like a coin coming down heads six times running. He knew that his luck could not possibly last, yet he would die of shame were someone else to take his place.

35
Operation Guy Fawkes

Planning now started to turf the German *59 Division* out of the 'island' six miles long, four miles wide immediately west of 's-Hertogenbosch and north of the 40 yards wide Afwateringskanaal. 153 Bde were still in 's-Hertogenbosch and 154 Bde in Helvoirt and Vught. On 1st November 152 Bde went to Cromvoirt (2nd Seaforth), Winkelse Hoek (5th Seaforth) and Loons Hoekje (5th Camerons). The Divisional plan for Operation Guy Fawkes to start on 4th November was for assault crossings to be made over the canal with its 30 foot high banks from the south, with 152 Bde on the right (east) and 153 Bde on the left (west).   An armoured force of tanks, Avres and 2nd Derby Yeomanry would attack along the north bank of the canal at 2030 on the 4th. Behind a tremendous barrage by eleven field regiments, 5th Camerons were soon across heading for Drunen where the hideous barrage had killed 32 Dutch civilians. 5th Seaforth found Groenwold empty and 2nd Seaforth took their objective, the crossroads at Drunen. Twelve Crocodiles [Churchill tank flame throwers from 141 RAC (the Buffs)]were split among the assaulting battalions, plus 90 tanks of 33 Armoured Bde. It was believed that six enemy battalions held the Island, but they turned out to be two with low morale.

The snipers of 5th Seaforth had previously killed nine Germans, including five dead drunk on looted Schnapps. The Seaforth advance across the canal in 16-man assault boats had 'B' and 'D' Coys over in seven minutes flat. Tanks and Crocodiles were blasting flame, smoke and HE across. Then came the Drunensche Dyke a thousand yards ahead where 'B' Coy caught a platoon of defenders in enfilade. Pat Grant's Bren gunners destroyed them and soon Groenwold was taken with 80 POW. At midnight a German RQMS drove into the Seaforth area with his company mail, two enormous cans of hot soup, hot-boxes full of rissoles and sausages, baskets of fresh farm butter, cigarettes and cigars. The Germans also left on the ground 32 casualties, seven bazookas, ten Spandaus, an AA gun, two mortars and a medieval crossbow! 5th Camerons got across on the left flank without a casualty, soon captured 90 POW and by 2100 moved along the Bund into Firenwold. And yes, the Camerons were also visited by a German quartermaster dispensing a hot meal for his (absent) troops. Later Wolfshoek, Elshout and Heusden were all cleared.

Codeword 'Spade' was the plan for 1st Gordons and 5th Black Watch to begin crossing 40 minutes after the Cameron/Seaforth assault. The Gordons with Crocodiles took Nieuwkuijk, the town in flames and the church in ruins. Brigadier Roddy Sinclair and the Derbyshire Yeo rescued Major Lindsay when his jeep went up on a mine, thence to Brigade Casualty Clearing Point, then Divisional Advance Dressing Station, and Casualty Clearing Station outside Eindhoven. In his ward were eleven non-battle casualties (pneumonia, bronchitis, bladder trouble, rash, food poisoning, and a Sten gun accident). 5th Black Watch despite their leading boat being bazooka-ed captured a wood, a road junction and linked with the Gordons at Haarsteeg.

Sgt Howard and his carrier driver Denis Daly, 10 Platoon of the Die Hards supported 5th Black Watch at the Hoogemaasdijk crossing. They carried four Vickers medium machine-guns with ammo across two miles of fields to the southern reverse slope of the canal bank. Their task was to protect the Crocodile flame throwers and tanks (who in the event were unable to climb the steep canal bank). They had to keep the enemy infantry pinned down as the BW attacked and also fire on the enemy guarding the locks to prevent their opening and flooding the area. No 10 Platoon fired 42 belts of ammo (10,500 rounds), whilst 11 and 12 Platoons carried their Vickers and 72 belts of ammo across to protect the assault on Nieuwkuijk.

The fearsome Crocodiles belching flame had caused many enemy to surrender. 5/7th Gordons assembled south-west of Nieuwkuijk and suffered ten casualties forming up but by dawn on the 5th were in Vlijmen. The obstacles were roadblocks mines and boobytraps. The pioneer platoon were kept busy helping the sappers to lift mines. Lt Taylor, IO was badly wounded when his jeep went up on a mine but the Germans had gone completely. Sunday 5th November saw the end of Operation Guy Fawkes with the capture of the Island. The Queen's Bde of the Desert Rats arrived early on the 6th to take over. With overwhelming firepower it had been an easy operation - well planned and executed - against the spent force of *59 Division*.

The GOC issued a message for HD:

We of the HD with 33 A/Bde can look back with satisfaction on the successful operation just completed. During the period 23rd October to 7th November HD by its thrust from Schijndel to Gertrudenberg and its activities east and north of 's-Hertogenbosch cleared an area of some 300 square miles of Holland, denied the Germans their brigade escape route and captured or annihilated most of their rearguards south of the river Maas. The operations included assault crossing of two rivers, the forcing of the narrow causeway from Waspik to Gertrudenberg and the assault crossing of the Aftwaterings canal. The casualties of the division amounted to 44 officers, 630 ORs of whom seven officers and 115 ORs were killed. Prisoners captured totalled 30 officers and 2378 ORs and enemy casualties must have been very heavy.

General Dempsey also sent his congratulations: "I appreciate the splendid way HD fought during the recent operations."

36
Operation Ascot: 14th - 21st November
"real heroes of war"

On 7th November after a few days out of the line HD moved to Het Eind, a much-battered village 12 miles south-east of Eindhoven. 5th Black Watch were first in Helvoirt then in Leende. Liberty trucks were popular for visits into Eindhoven and the Div Hot Baths Unit, mobile cinema, ENSA and the Balmorals all helped morale.

Major Benson 2i/c 1st Black Watch carried out a satisfactory barter deal. The RAF wanted to borrow a wheeled Bosch generator that the BW had 'acquired'. In return the RAF agreed to send a plane back to Inverness to collect 48 cases of Scotch whisky, 12 cases for each battalion in 154 Bde and 12 cases for Brigade HQ. The sergeants got their share too - the amount was only a few weeks supply! 7th Black Watch had good billets in Vught and on 9th moved to Ospel on the Noorder canal to relieve 5th Seaforth. 5th Camerons in Someren were subjected for two days to a bombardment of German propaganda shells with leaflets depicting the Americans as shameless war-mongers. The Gordon battalions in Vught were shown the terrifying concentration camp and moved to Leende and Heeze where the Pipers played Reveille in the streets. Most of the time the weather was vile, cold with driving rain.

All battalions practised assault boat crossings jointly with carrier tanks and assorted 'Funnies.' Alastair Borthwick described Ospel where 5th Seaforth arrived on the 8th:

> It was a sad village. No house was undamaged. It was a muddy grubby little hole full of slates, broken glass and tattered curtains. A badly chipped church at the crossroads. The outlying farms lay in countryside flat and

waterlogged. A thin drizzle fell over everything and the mud on the road was ankle deep.

This sums up HD's autumn and the winter to come in the Dutch campaign.

Operation Ascot was the next battleground - the assault crossings of the Wessen and Noorder canals. They link at right angles just east of Weert and form two sides of a triangle. The third side - the ultimate objective - was the river Maas (once again) running south-west from Venlo to Roermond. In the first phase 152 Bde would establish a bridgehead over the Noorder, and 153 Bde over the Wessem canal. In phase two, 154 Bde would establish crossings near the lockgates at the junction of two canals at Nederweert and Hulsen. The countryside was flat, waterlogged by dykes and canals. The only cover was from a few woods. The weather was bad and it was going to rain every day. Lt Col Ralph Carr, CRE: "All this entailed a major engineering problem. 12 Corps made available 621 Field Sqn and 756, 262 Field companies with bridging equipment including three Bailey assault and culverted bulldozer bridges." If all went well in phase three 154 Bde would exploit to the south-east and capture Heijthuizen and Roggel seven miles to the east.

The enemy's substantial counter-attack on US 7th Armoured Division had enlarged their bridgehead west of the Maas and before it was contained posed a threat to Army HQ in Eindhoven! 15th Scottish and 53rd Welsh division were also taking part in Ascot on the northern flanks, the latter attacking across the Bois Le Duc canal towards Roermond. A German warrant officer who had deserted claimed that *394 Assault Gun Regt* with 27 SP guns had arrived in front of HD south of Nederweert. As the enemy could oversee the rear side of the canal banks for a full mile, East Riding Yeomanry tanks towed the assault boats on special sledges. Other troops were carried in Buffaloes or actually on tanks.

153 Bde set off at 1600, nearly dusk, on 14th November behind an HE and smoke barrage to hide their advance south from Nederweert towards the canal, 5/7th Gordons on the left and 1st Gordons on the right. It was bitterly cold and the Germans were dazed by the intensity of the barrage and the flame-belching Crocodiles. Nevertheless 1st Gordons lost three officers and 32 ORs killed or wounded. Major Martin Lindsay 2i/c, already back with the battalion from hospital watched the companies moving up to the FUP (Forming up point):

> Each man as usual was heavily loaded, carrying arms, ammunition, small pack and pick or shovel. They were always very quiet and solemn when going into action: intense, approaching the grim. Those were the real heroes of war. The men who actually went right up to the enemy position and through the doorway: they and the officers who led them. At one time

in the 1914-18 war the average life of a platoon commander was ten days. Now it was about a month. There was not very much difference.

A fox hunting staff officer at 153 Bde HQ had issued code names Grafton, Blazers, Garth, Fernie, Quorn, North Berkeley and South Berkeley. The 35 casualties to 1st Gordons from 'B' and 'C' Coys were mainly from two heavy long distance mortar bombs landing as boats were being carried forward. 5/7th Gordons' crossing went well. Sgt Molyneux, 'A' Coy helped dispose of 21 Germans out of the 80 killed, wounded or POW. Their action was watched and recorded by the BBC and the American Life magazine. Chester Wilmot who was present (at a distance) sent in a glowing report. 5th Black Watch followed through but despite the sappers blowing the canal banks their Buffaloes could not climb the steep banks. By 2345 the battalion was across and had taken their objective woods inland. Tom Renouf's platoon sergeant was Reubens Cooper.

> He proudly displayed his new third stripe at Schoor before the attack. 'A' Coy made the assault crossing of the Wessem Canal under the dreaded Spandau machine-gun fire. We were completely exposed in the assault boats with the fearful noise of battle all around. The cover of darkness gave us no protection, all adding up to fill us with a dreadful terror. By morning Sgt Cooper had been killed having worn his new stripes for barely two days. [Tom Renouf]

Sappers constructed a Class 9 bridge over the canal and 154 Bde came through at 1000 on 15th. 152 Bde crossed the Noorder canal successfully. Capt AW Lee acted as 'Beachmaster' for 5th Camerons as he organised the boating parties. Sledges towed by tanks were a great success used by 'B' Coy, whilst Piper Maclean played 'C' Coy on the left over in Buffaloes. On their right were 5th Seaforth who found their Buffaloes were excellent, the carrier-borne boats adequate and the sledges unreliable. 'C' Coy were happy with the first, but 'A' Coy had many sledge tow-ropes broken so that only a third of their craft arrived on the bank. 'B' had assembled boats on Brengun carriers. The Die Hard platoon Vickers did their best but the defenders had blown a lockgate, and lowered the level of the water down to yards of thick black mud. Men were stuck fast in it and had to be rescued with ropes. The supporting tanks arrived late over the swampy polder and fired blindly through the smoke, scattering and wounding some of the Seaforth. Despite all these hazards all objectives were taken by 1800 hrs taking 35 POW for the loss of 16 casualties. Brigadier Cassels had told his assault troops during Guy Fawkes:

> I've just been promised a new beast called a buffalo. I don't know how it works, its an amphibious tank affair. You let down a door, drive in a Bren carrier or a truck or a couple of anti-tank guns [or 24 men] and it whistles them across in no time. Or so they say! We're taking no chances, so the

rafts will stay!

2 Seaforth then followed up and through. Now 154 Bde had three tasks. Initially hold a firm base north of the Noorder canal; make an assault crossing for tanks at the lock gates and lastly exploit to Leveroit. 7th Argylls crossed the canal at the lock gates at 1700, and supported the Avre bridge team, but an enormous number of the dreaded Schu mines (many shaped like ordinary bricks) caused casualties. Major Joe Corcoran then led 'D' Coy and mopped up resistance in Hulsen. Major General Rennie must have been happy with the first day of Ascot - every objective taken with minimal casualties. The next day 1st Black Watch in Kangaroos crossed over one of the four new bridges and advanced to Leveroit, with 7th Black Watch taking Heyjthuisen. 'A' Coy suffered from heavy shelling but the town's population in deep cellars below the school and other public buildings were overjoyed and greeted their 'liberators' with enthusiasm.

On the 153 Bde front 5th Black Watch passed through the Gordons and on 16th 1st Gordons reached Roggel in their Kangaroos thence to Vlaas and a carrier patrol to the Zig Canal. Meanwhile 5/7th Gordons occupied Ophoven and Bromholt. General Rennie visited Lt Col Cumming-Bruce and Major Martin Lindsay in a very cold and draughty farmhouse HQ. He told them about 154 Bde's casualties with the new wooden Schu mines. Every isolated farm house was a potential target. 153 Bde HQ mortar platoon had fifteen casualties with two direct hits upon 'their' house. 1st Gordons had Lt Charles Morley killed inspecting the Zig Canal lock gate. "We were now reduced to only two rifle platoon officers instead of the twelve we should have. So Harry [the CO] had a long talk to the Brigadier about the shortage of officers."

5th Camerons sent out a patrol on the 15th in which Canloan Lt Ross Le Mesurier accounted for two Bazooka teams personally. The next day they moved to Stokershorst and were astride the main road south of the Zig Canal bridge at Ruggleshe by last light. The main bridge was blown but by 0830 on the 17th 'C' Coy dashed across the collapsed bridge and dug-in as fast as possible. The opposition were initially slow to respond but heavy fire came down at 1130 with enemy charging behind a smoke screen. Major Mainwaring took 'A' Coy over to reinforce 'C' and the 128 Field Regt FOO Capt Douglas Tilly called down medium artillery and his own field artillery DF fire. The enemy were decimated and withdrew at 1300 but both Cameron companys were getting short of ammunition. At 2230 2nd Seaforth passed through and another night crossing by 1st Gordons further down the canal relieved the enemy pressure. When early on 18th Sappers erected a Class 40 bridge over the Zig canal it was named 'Cameron bridge'.

It was a gallant Cameron action with 38 casualties and the Corps

Commander General Ritchie wrote: "Had not 5th Camerons held on to their foothold on the east bank of the Zig Canal, the advance of the whole Corps might well have been delayed for an appreciable time." The battalion crossing was driven in between two German Corps, possibly causing some confusion! Major JL Melville OC 'C' Coy was awarded the DSO, Major Munro (acting CO) and Capt Cameron each the MC. Sgt D Carlin was awarded the MM when his platoon commander was killed and he took command. In their final action in Ascot on the night of the 17th to cross the Zig Canal, the Flail tanks and carriers carrying boats bogged down. 'D' Coy had a stiff battle but by dawn the blown bridge area was secure. 49th Polar Bear division took over on the 19th. On the same day the Balmorals played to 5th Black Watch in a barn converted into a theatre near Roggel. A welcome rest from 72 hours of rain and mud, mortaring and shelling and the horrible Schu mines in a wooden frame designed to look like a brick or a stone.

Some HD experts reckoned that enemy shelling on the 17th was the heaviest since the Bois de Bavent actions in the bridgehead in late June. Divisional artillery fired their first salvo into the Fatherland on the 19th, a target recorded as 'Mike 1944.'

154 Bde from Roggel, Neer and Onder were now ordered to make a final advance on Baarlo. 1st Black Watch started from Helden, then to Bong where an SP gun gave 'A' Coy some trouble but supported by artillery, smoke and HE Baarlo was occupied by the 21st. Minefields, heavy shelling and well-handled German SPs caused casualties but the enemy fell back towards Blerick to the north. HD had now completed 'Ascot' successfully and 15th Scottish and 49th Polar Bears now came up to squeeze out the final German bridgehead opposite Venlo. Lt Col Ralph Carr CRE wrote home:

> The old 51st has done it again a 'left and right' this time. We launched the 2nd Army offensive before anyone else - on the evening of 15th November. This was by far the trickiest canal crossing operation we have had yet because there were four separate canals which came together at one junction like a crossroads. The trouble with these Dutch canals is the water level. They are all locked and inter-connected in a most complicated way. When the enemy holds half of the locks, both sides can play about with the water level. If he blows his locks just as you attack, the water will all run away and leave you with a great ditch full of mud and rushes, so floating bridges are bit risky... We once more over-ran the enemy and the main difficulty was physically getting jeeps and carriers through the mud. We got another assault bridge down at a lock, a floating bridge and a bulldozer crossing behind this bridge, so they could exploit next day whilst we built a Bailey... The Corps and Army Commanders were both staggered when we got across this canal - in spite of the ghastly weather. I must say I take my hat off to the Jocks - the worse the conditions, the more they are asked to do, the more grimly cheerful they become...

37

On the Island: Operation Noah
27 November - 4 December

After the tragedy of Market Garden, the area between Arnhem and Nijmegen, a flat desolate polder region some six miles west to east by four miles north to south was called for obvious reasons 'The Island'. Surrounded by fast flowing rivers it was held mainly by British (recently the Polar Bears 49 Div) and American units. The northern sector quickly became German occupied and patrols from both sides tried to dominate the other. Most of the unfortunate Dutch civilians had left their fruit farms and villages. Now HD were ordered to relieve the gallant 101 US Airborne division to the left flank of the 50 Northumbrian Div. It was thought likely that the Germans might destroy the dykes further upstream by blowing holes in the high protective 'bund' and the waters of the River Waal would submerge most of the Island and make defence positions untenable. The contingency plan to evacuate the Island was of course called 'Operation Noah'. Since troops leaving the island would mainly use the massive Nijmegen bridge, (a target for underwater frogmen) it was an obvious target for long range German shelling. All units had to check the water level on the 'Island' three times a day and report to Brigade. Villages such as Andelst, Valburg, Zetter, Randwijk, Heteren and Opheusden, usually empty and battered offered shelter. Isolated farmhouses were occupied by standing patrols from both sides. Nijmegen still with 50,000 civilian population provided a satisfactory divisional base with bathhouses, cinemas, ENSA shows and very friendly Dutch families. Lt Col James Cochrane, OC Div Signals admired the 101 Division full line layout: "The first time we came into touch with the US Signal Corps. As field line routes laid weeks ago were now under water 'C' Section in boats made sure that all routes were poled." That is, miniature telegraph poles.

Lt Col Cumming-Bruce was promoted to command 44 Bde in 15th Scottish Division and Lt Col Grant-Peterkin now commanded 1st Gordons. "We had to hold a square mile of flat country with two small villages each side of it, Randwijk and Opheusden. The latter was a horrible place, our American allies said, for it was full of Schu mines which had blown off six American feet. The whole area," wrote Major Martin Lindsay, "was flat ground, broken up by a few farmhouses and avenues of trees and overlooked from beyond the Rhine. The river nearly a mile wide was very swollen. One could expect about 30 shells a day in the Battalion area."

Sgt Jack Cheshire, with the 1st Gordons anti-tank platoon had been warned that the Germans sent out patrols to capture and identify their opponents:

> Supporting a rifle company in a farm during hours of darkness we heard a scuffle and screams, obviously a guard being assaulted. Out we all ran and heard an English voice shout 'don't shoot'. The Battalion mortar support section had two Sgts (Bramley and McCoy) with years of service and knew all the tricks of the trade! They had just killed a pig! Freshly killed it provided us with a slap-up dinner. We were 'hors de combat' for 48 hours!

Heteren was the temporary home of 5th Seaforth. The American paratroopers they had relieved had suffered only five casualties in the last six weeks and the Seaforth IO Alastair Borthwick recalled:

> Moreover, they had left vast quantities of rations behind them including chocolate and every platoon had a furnished house. The Germans were a thousand yards away across the river Leck and bullshit was reduced to a minimum. A surprising number of pigs and fowls flung themselves to their deaths beneath the tracks of passing carriers. We grew sleek, and the odour of rich cooked meats was heavy on the air. We balanced great zinc tubs on the stoves and brewed ourselves baths. The gin ration arrived. The Great Egg Crisis (ie lack of) was solved. The Battalion snipers had captured all the hens, locked them up in a bedroom and were fattening them up for Christmas on a diet of corn and hot potatoes.

154 Bde in reserve had 7th Black Watch around Lienden (then to Andelst) 1st Black Watch at Valburg and 7th Argylls near Herveld, 5th Black Watch were less fortunate. On 26th November Capt Herbertson, the IO and Sgt Taylor were blown up by Schu-mines. Two days later a V-2 rocket in Antwerp killed Majors Wright and Monro whilst on leave and on 1st December Major Smith-Cunningham 'A' Coy was ambushed on a Recce and captured, and Lt Scott was wounded.

But leave parties now went frequently to Brussels, 's-Hertogenbosch, Eindhoven and perhaps dangerously to Antwerp. Lt Col Douglas Renny CO 5/7th Gordons and Major Martin Lindsay 2i/c 1st Gordons went to Brussels. On the way in Louvain they stopped for a hair cut, shampoo, "I ate a pound of luscious grapes. After supper we went to a nightclub. The girls were as pretty as birds. The saxophones gulped and shivered, retched and heaved. Oh the joy of central heating and a private bathroom."

The NAAFI ran the Hotel Plaza for officers leave parties. It was very popular partly because captured Wehrmacht gin and brandy was sold at three francs, a twentieth of the price outside. The Gordons officers went to the races (two on the flat, two over hurdles, two steeplechases), then played golf at the Waterloo Golf Club. 1st Black Watch sent a 'Champagne Patrol' to Rheims to purchase large quantities of fizz.

Early in the morning on 3rd December, the Germans burst a dyke of the river Leck in the 2nd Seaforth area. Operation Noah came into play. Trucks and transport were packed and off the Island by 0500. The marching troops evacuated their positions by 1400 and finally waded knee-deep to relative safety. Nijmegen bridge was under fire and 5th Camerons crossed the river to the mainland in outboard motor boats in a sleet storm, thence back to Oss.

Rafts and Dukws were used by 5/7th Gordons and their transport came across at Slijk by ferryboat. The next day Mary of Arnhem the English speaking German radio announcer told how the brave Germans had wiped out the British on the 'Island', all drowned or shelled.

154 Bde were left to hold the southern fringe of the 'Island' but by 7th December only 1st and 7th Black Watch remained north of the Maas, but were relieved on 19th December by 152 Bde. The first snows of winter appeared on the 9th and most of the HD had a peaceful, even enjoyable two weeks out of the line.

Better billets were available. 5th Camerons in a large RC Monastery and schools in 's-Hertogenbosch settled down for their happiest fortnight spent on the continent. Out came the Regimental flag, the quarter-guard, kilt and best battledress. The monks were most hospitable and friendly and every Dutch family 'adopted' one or more Highlanders. A Fete of Liberation was held back at St Valéry-en-Caux with the Divisional Pipes and Drums playing and representative parties from all units duly attended.

Decorations and awards were made known on the 6th December and later the recipients would be photographed shaking hands with Monty at the investiture. 7th Black Watch had MCs for Majors Small, Peck and Lowe and Lt Donaldson. Their CO Lt Col Cathcart received a bar to his DSO. 1st Gordons received two MCs and four MMs and 5/7th Gordons a DSO to Major Dunn, a MC, a DCM and four MMs. 5th Camerons received a DSO for Major Melville, plus two MCs and Sgt Carlin the MM. All units of course had their quorum of officers and men whose bravery was appropriately recognised. On the 15th Monty visited HD at Heeswijk St Michiels Gestel and other locations for the investiture.

Div HQ was at Hooge Hei, a village near Uden. Two brigades at a time were out of the line. Lt Col James Cochrane: "A 48 hour Brussels was like a fairly tale. Tea in bed before breakfast, baths, the shops full of perfume and silk stockings at a price, visits to Waterloo and L'Opera and hundreds of cafes to be investigated."

Lt Col Ralph Carr, CRE out of the line on 12th December in a comfortable caravan converted by his sappers: "I was clad in sheepskin from head to toe, with a 'balaclava' helmet and mitts. I even had soap, cheroots and books." With his 16 bore shotgun and 200 cartridges he shot pheasants, a rabbit and possibly everything that moved!

38
The Ardennes: Christmas and the New Year

In great secrecy General Von Rundstedt launched his great *Panzer Armée* offensive in the Ardennes on the 16th December on the unsuspecting American troops. HD were in training for the next major offensive, Operation Veritable. Three days later the GOC, General Rennie briefed his brigadiers about their future role in the attack through the Reichswald to clear the German forces west of the Rhine. But the best laid plans of mice and men... Perhaps a trifle reluctantly General Eisenhower asked (ordered) Monty to take command of the US

The Ardennes

9th Army, and the US 1st Army and to halt the *Panzer Armies* (*6th, 5th and 7th*) who had reached Hotton, Marche and Laroche. With his system of brilliant young liaison officers, Monty was at his best. The author's 29 Armoured Bde (11th Armoured Div) collected their discarded Shermans and by forced march reached Namur. They were followed by 30 Corps consisting of Guards Armoured, 43rd Wessex, 53rd Welsh and now 51st Highland Division who were moved to the Louvain - St Trond area. On 23rd December enemy tanks were reported only 12 miles east of Dinant. By Christmas Day Monty had sealed off the enemy offensive along the line Elsenhorn - Malmedy - Hotton - Marche - St Hubert and Bastogne.

HD Div HQ moved south via Beeringen, Louvain to north of Maastricht coming under command of 9th US Army. But urgent orders came through at 0900 on Christmas Day for a move to Liege to come under command of 1st US Army. General Rennie and all his senior staff officers had the great fortune to have a splendid Christmas Dinner with American rations.

It had been a week of almost total confusion of order, counter order and some disorder. The fog of war had descended over the main battlefields and only lifted on the 22nd enabling the RAF and USAAF to inflict terrible damage on the Panzers. General Rennie sent a

Christmas message to HD:

> I am afraid Christmas will not be as organised as it might have been, but I hope the food and drink turn up and that you will all have as happy a Christmas as can be under the circumstances. The present German offensive has been, to a large extent, established, and the flanks of the break-through are firm...

Div HQ settled down in Tilff, a small town south of Liege on the river L'Ourthe. Lt Col James Cochrane, Chief Signals Officer:

> The streets were packed with delighted Belgians who seemed terribly pleased to see us and who all wanted to put up 'a soldier for Christmas.' The people seemed to go out of their way to make us feel welcome, the first British troops seen since 1918. The next fourteen days while the Division stayed in this area were among the happiest days of the Campaign. We were again in Army Reserve with counter-attack roles in the event of a penetration on the fronts of two American Army Corps. Our delayed Christmas dinner took place on Boxing Day when General Rennie visited the men's Messes and wished them all the compliments of the Season. With traditional ceremony the New Year was seen in a few days later. The old songs of Scotland and the sound of pipes as the Jocks brought in 1945.

Flying bombs, V-1s, were a drawback as the Germans fired them towards Liege and on average 30 landed daily within a three mile radius of Div HQ. The 'Chasse de Sanglier' took place in the forests by

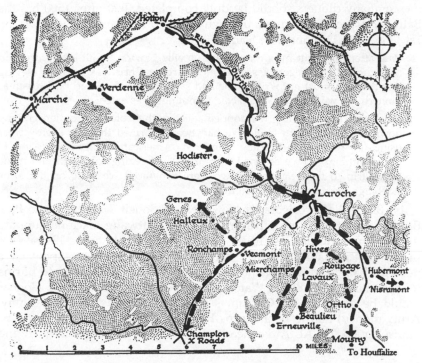

the river as the CRA and GSO1 and assorted beaters pursued errant wild boar. Signals HQ was in the Hotel de Casino whose owner was a noted Parisian chef whose 'Crepe Suzette' was superb! 5th Camerons had their Christmas Dinner in Grijze Grubben and moved that day to Chaud-Fontaine, a resort town east of Liege. 5th Seaforth arrived in Aalbeck on the 23rd and on Christmas morning the Padre held a service at 1030 with dinner due at 1230. At 1145 the advance party was ordered to move immediately. "They gulped their roast pork, roast potatoes, Christmas pudding in ten minutes flat, grabbed their bottles of beer and fled to the trucks and by noon were on their way to Les Cours, south of Liege," wrote Alastair Borthwick. Snow started falling on 28th December and continued until 2nd February. New Years Eve was a night of iron frost and the Hogmanay dinner for the Seaforth (and for HD) was tinned turkey, Christmas pudding and an excellent selection of sweets, nuts, chocolate, beer and cigars. "The RASC and PRI had done us proud. Col Walford, RSM and 'Pipie' visited the companies who were all very hospitable. Only the Colonel and the Pipie lasted the course!" 5th Black Watch were at Urmond and their Christmas service took place in the local Calvinistic Protestant Church. The language was in Flemish but the hymn tunes were familiar. During their Christmas dinner orders to cross a start point at 1400 hrs were received. With great aplomb Colonel Bill Bradford insisted that all the company dinners should be duly completed. Just after 1500 hrs the Battalion were on the move through Liege to Plaineveux and again on 1st January to Dorinne near Sciney.

> Well after midnight my officer, Capt Neville Lawton Smith brought round cold chops, cold vegetables and cold wartime Christmas pudding saying that the men must not write home and say that they had had no Christmas dinner! We were too tired, too cold so nothing was eaten!

> On Boxing Day morning we stopped a jeep with 4 coloured soldiers coming down the frozen farm track. We had been informed that the enemy were using every trick including captured American uniforms, down to underclothing. So we escorted them into our freezing cold shed and made them strip to their pants until we were convinced we were on the same side! [Sgt Jack Cheshire, 1st Gordons]

1st Black Watch celebrated New Year in Soheit Tinlot and the Pipe Band played to the accompaniment of the Luftwaffe machine-gunning the neighbouring unit. A successful concert was held and a liberal rum punch for all ranks ensured that New Years Day was spent in a peaceful haze. The 2i/c Major Benson left the Battalion to go to Burma to command 2nd Black Watch. "A special consignment of Cognac would be available for Christmas. Indents and cash (in the 'funny' Army money) had to be at Corps HQ by midnight two days later." So Staff Captain 'Q' AL Aitkenhead went off with the last indent in and money counted, driving on icy roads alongside canals. On arrival:

My opposite number said 'Well just count the cash' - The cognac arrived in due course but the event was spoiled - the Battle of the Bulge took precedence. Army Catering Corps led by Captain 'Sandy' Dunlop produced our dinner, [and Haggis for St Andrews night] but it had to be taken 'on the hoof'. The ACC excelled at General Rennie's pre-Battle Conference, magnificent repasts known as the 'Last Suppers.'

5th Camerons celebrated Hogmanay. Lt Ross Le Mesurier, his CO Lt Col Derek Lang, Major Donald Callander and the Adjutant, Capt Tommy Lamb were in a jeep heading off to an officers party in a local café. At a road block, the rather nervous American sentries asked pertinent questions 'What's the capital of California?' 'Who won the World Series [baseball]?' "I piped up from the back of the jeep 'The St Louis Cardinals beat the St Louis Browns four games to three.' The GIs at the roadblock were baffled by a Canadian in a Scottish battalion with drafty kilts, etc. However we were passed through and all started the party with a double Scotch!"

Many senior officers of HD were on leave, some in the UK when the real battle for HD started on 7th January. Lt Col Grant Peterkin was away, and Major Martin Lindsay again commanded 1st Gordons. Lt Col Renny left 5/7th Gordons to command 9th Brigade in 3rd British Div. HD were ordered to relieve 53rd Welsh Div and their first objective was the high ground south of the main Marche-Hotton road. 153 Bde would attack on the right, 154 on the left and 152 Bde would pass through to capture the high ground west of Laroche while 164 Bde cleared the main road and the valley of the river L'Ourthe towards Laroche. H-hour was 0900 on 9th January. Snow and ice made all movement, except on foot, an impossibility. The Middlesex had great difficulty getting their medium machine-guns and mortars up into position near the front line.

Little tracked 'weasels' and jeeps were the only vehicles that could be relied on and sledges were used to ferry up ammo and rations. The tanks of 33rd Armoured Bde had special gripping snow studs fitted to their tracks. 1st Gordons led the attack from Verdenne under Major Lindsay. His adjutant had just showed him the battalion's casualty list since D-Day of the four rifle companies. Their combined officer strength was twenty; to date 9 had been killed and 30 wounded. Their OR strength was 500 and casualties had been just that - 149 killed and 351 wounded. Lindsay had visited the RWF Battalions holding the front until HD took over. They recommended a constant supply of dry socks and hot tea. From the Chauvaimont farm 'C' Coy led into the snow girt valley but were held up by minefields inside the woods at the top of the ridge. In due course 5th Black Watch and 5/7th Gordons passed through towards Hodister. The country was hilly, the roads small and twisting and deep snow drifts, road blocks, AP and anti-tank mines slowed down the advance. But by nightfall Warizy Cheoux and Hodister and all objectives were occupied with little loss, and Lignières (known as Lingerie) was occupied by 1st Gordons.

127 Field Regt RA gun position in the Ardennes (Capt M V Sim)

On the left flank 154 Bde were making their way up the main road along the valley of the river L'Ourthe towards Laroche with Derbyshire Yeomanry armoured cars scouting ahead. From Waharday 1st Black Watch found Cheoux and Hampteau empty and so by dawn on the 11th, was the key small town of Laroche.

"We occupied Laroche village littered with German corpses from an artillery shelling. In the sub zero temperature the bodies looked fresh and still alive. We were ordered [Pte Stan Whitehouse 'B' Coy 1st Black Watch] to deal with SS men still holding out." In front of their eyes two platoon commanders were shot by snipers. "Once again we were without an officer. Platoon commanders were snipers prime targets, a lesson we had learned in Normandy, but a new breed of officers coming through made the enemy sharpshooters' task so much easier by flaunting themselves in the front line with map boards, binoculars and other trappings of rank." 'B' Coy pushed on through the town occupied the high ground beyond allowing 7th Black Watch to move towards Hives and Lavaux, 7 Argylls on Thimont and Roupage.

The road to Hives was up a steep hill and 7th Black Watch were heavily shelled but despite mines and an obstinate Panther, the village was taken with 35 POW. The Battalion stayed there until the 18th despite being mortared and shelled by an SP. 152 Bde had been despatched over the hills to occupy Halleux and Vecmont and main

Div HQ moved down to Rendeux Haut to control the final phases of the battle. Lt Col James Cochrane OC Div Signals:

> The cold during this operation was most intense and the Jocks during the many night moves and battles had to undergo many hardships. There was little or no shelter as villages had been devastated in the original Boche advance. No 19 sets froze up as did the electrolyte in the wireless batteries.

The Derby Yeomanry had now lost half a dozen armoured cars blown up on mines or knocked-out by anti-tank guns. The enemy from *3rd Panzer Grenadier Division* with *116 Panzer Divisional Artillery* were now retreating fast leaving small but determined rearguards. On 12th June 5th Black Watch moved to take Roupage from Warizy, now under command of Brigadier Oliver's 154 Bde. Panther tanks and Spandaus caused casualties, as unfortunately so did supporting artillery airburst. Major Pilcher's HQ had six casualties during a long hard, bitter day. Bren guns froze up and men became so cold that movement was difficult. Hot food could not be brought up that night with over 32 degrees of frost. By the 15th at the end of their battle 5th Black Watch had lost six KIA, 30 wounded and 42 sick with frostbite and exposure to the intense cold.

5th Seaforth in the Ardennes

5th Seaforth had occupied Genes on the 10th, 2nd Seaforth moved to Halleux and 5th Camerons to Ronchamps making the 152 Bde advance for the day of three miles. But on the 11th with Major Jim Powell now commanding 5th Seaforth, the next objective of Mierchamps was to prove difficult. Beyond three parallel ridges, and out of sight the

Germans were waiting and pasting the living daylights of Ronchamps now held by 5th Camerons. As the crow flies Mierchamps lay 2000 yards south with a mined road, a blown bridge over the little river Brouze and a winding road through thick woods up and over a ridge. But the Seaforth craftily zigzagged under a huge barrage and by 1900 hrs to everyone's surprise Mierchamps with 180 half frozen Panzer Grenadiers POW was captured. Major HJ Decker the Seaforth FOO, a former bookmaker, had laid odds of 50:1 against such an astonishing success. Alastair Borthwick was sitting in front of a stove to hard boiled eggs, bread, fresh farm butter and a pot of coffee before nightfall! The Seaforth casualties were 21 and they stayed in Mierchamps for a week. On the same day 2nd Seaforth attacked and captured Ronchampey but suffered casualties from heavy shelling.

The Argylls, ordered to capture Beaulieu, were held up by Spandau, mortars from the woods west of Lavaux, and Panthers caused 'A' Coy casualties. Private AC Jenkins:

> Our first section headed on down the road into a shallow valley. As the leading man reached a stone hut at the bottom there was a burst of machine-gun fire and the crump of exploding shells which killed and wounded several of our men. Some struggled back despite being badly hit. A scout car from the Derby Yeo spotted two dug-in Panthers on the high ground ahead. Our Coy comander Major [Peter] Samwell MC ducked behind the lead tank of Northants Yeo Shermans to report back via the telephone link at the Sherman's rear. A blinding flash and a shower of sparks and metal as a Panther's shell struck a glancing blow. The Major fell in a hale of metal fragments, some hitting L/Corp McCormick just in front of me. He was the bane of the Sergeant Major's life and at 33 seemed almost a grandfather to us mere 19 year olds. Understandably the rest of us legged it back to the barn as fast as we could.

By the time the Argylls had taken Lavaux, Beaulieu and Cens on the 13th they had lost 38 casualties to enemy action. For Major Lindsay, commanding 1st Gordons. "13th January was an unlucky, unpleasant day." From Laroche his Battalion was ordered to go through Hubermont. "The 5th Black Watch are just about there now," said the Brigade Major, "and then occupy Nisramont." The 20 Germans still in Hubermont put up a fight. The Black Watch inadvertently wounded Lt David Scott-Moncrieff, and Panthers in Nisramont, knocked-out four friendly tanks and SPs. Frank Philip, their FOO was badly wounded and during the uncomfortable day 1st Gordons suffered 20 casualties. Every vehicle was shot at by the hostile Panthers but by nightfall the enemy had quit Nisramont. "General Rennie came to see us next morning. It was one of his many engaging characteristics always to visit his battalions after a battle," recalled Lindsay. On the 14th came the end of the Ardennes battle for HD when they linked up with 84th

US Division advancing northwards. And on the 16th the US 1st Army met the US 3rd Army at Houffalize, seven miles east of Nisramont.

The Fuhrer's brave audacious *Panzer Armée* attack had caused confusion and chaos to the American defenders. Losses on both sides were estimated at about 120,000 men but 600 German tanks and SPs had been knocked-out. If they had reinforced the long length of the Siegfried line the war might have dragged on for several extra months.

> The margin between success and failure was perhaps narrower than one might imagine, with tired troops and war weary NCOs who did not feel up to taking the responsibilities of officers. Of course, it is easy for a man to avoid taking part in the dark; he can say he fell asleep at a pause or lost his way. I talked to Ewen Traill our padre who always, of his own choice, went into battle with one of the companies. He said what a small degree there was between sticking it and breaking down. When going forward under fire, it only needed one man to shout 'This is murder, I'm getting out' and he would take half a dozen with him. [Major Martin Lindsay, 1st Gordons]

On the other hand Private Whitehouse, 1st Black Watch wrote:

> I began to experience more acute symptoms of 'bomb happiness' or 'shellshock', I had been in the line now, almost continuously for more than six months and as week succeeded week I was having to dig deeper and deeper into those innermost resources of resolution, endurance and zeal to combat the growing, nagging fearfulness that filled my waking and often sleeping hours. I had long forsaken that spirit of adventure, that devil-may-care attitude that had sustained me in the early days [Whitehouse was part of No 6 Beach Group who landed on D-Day on Sword Beach], when mates all around me were being killed and horribly maimed and the whiplash of the murderous Spandau and the crunch of the mortars had men quivering in the bottom of their 'slitters'. A couple of our lads went 'on the trot' and as usual they were newcomers. So far we older hands had resisted the temptation to desert.

But SIW (Self Inflicted Wounds) were not uncommon. Indeed Whitehouse for a moment considered it as a solution.

39

Operation Veritable
"Hitler Youth fighting like demons"

1st Canadian Army with an enlarged 30 Corps under command was entrusted with the immense task of destroying all the German forces west of the Rhine. General Simpson's 9th US Army advancing from the south would cross the river Roer and advance north in Operation

Grenade to link up with 30 Corps. Lt General Brian Horrocks decided to attack with five divisions in line, 3rd and 2nd Canadian in the north, 15th Scottish in the centre, then 53rd Welsh (to clear most of the Reichswald forest), and 51st Highland on the right and south. Behind were 43rd Wessex, 11th Armoured and Guards Armoured Divisions plus two armoured brigades and most of the fearsome Funnies of 79th Armoured Division, backed by an immense artillery force of 1400 guns. 30 Corps was 200,000 strong and it was a tribute to Horrocks that Montgomery had chosen him to command Operation Veritable.

The strong defences of the original Siegfried line had been extensively developed into three zones, linked by minefields, A/Tank ditches, trenches, fortified farms and houses in this frontier area turned into concrete strongpoints. General Sclemm, GOC *1st Parachute Army* had all round defences in which he had placed *84th German Infantry Division* backed by three parachute units. In reserve was a strong mobile force with no less than three Panzer divisions plus two more parachute divisions.

HD's task was to clear the south-west corner of the Reichswald on a 5000 yard front advancing eastwards towards Kessel and Goch from a start line on the edge of woodland east of Nijmegen down to Mook. After the Ardennes intense training was resumed with Div HQ at Iteghem and then at Grave barracks. 30 Corps HQ was at Boxtel.

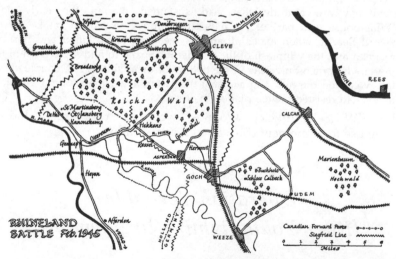

7th Black Watch moved to Boisschot near Mechlin, then on 22nd January to the villages of Haps and Mill near Rijkevoort absorbing new, mainly very young reinforcements. A Brigade discussion was held on the problems of cold weather fighting. The 5th Battalion moved to

Turnhout and on 22nd their Pipes and Drums beat Retreat, before moving to Haaren. Lt Col Bill Bradford their CO unveiled a memorial built by the local population in memory of HD men who had fallen liberating the town on 27th October. The 1st Black Watch arrived in Herenthaals near Brussels with their carriers making heavy weather of the glassy ice bound roads. Besides leather jerkins, patrols were issued with white snow suits. Don Rs (Despatch Riders) had fur lined waistcoats and many great coats were converted to Shanks pattern by kilting up the great coat by buttoning it with four buttons, turning it into a ¾ length coat in which it was possible to march *and* fight! On 22nd the Battalion moved to the Beers/Groot Linden area. 5th Camerons at Vught exercised in wood-clearing under realistic conditions, but managed some football matches and evening entertainment. On 20th January 5/7th Gordons gave a dance for the nursing sisters of the Canadian hospital at Turhout and by boarding a tram the Gordons could go to a cinema or variety show, before moving up on 23rd to Oisterwijk in Holland.

Sgt Jack Cheshire was, "musically involved that winter in the Gordons concert party entitled the 'London, Midland and Scottish' because of the non-Scottish reinforcements in the Battalion."

Privates Stan Whitehouse and 'Shorty' Shorthouse, 1st Black Watch were now experienced veterans but always reluctant - for various reasons - to accept a 'stripe'. Before Veritable, then at Grave, they decided to accept their company commander's urgent plea for them to become NCOs:

> The majority of reinforcements had been living in comfortable camps with showers and regular meal times. Others had been winkled out of half forgotten hidey-holes. Most of them had forgotten all the infantry tactics, how to dig in, camouflage, recognise minefields and booby traps and try to stay one step ahead of the well trained disciplined and conniving enemy. The standard of newcomers had generally deteriorated and invariably after an attack or patrol one or two went missing.

So for their survival, Stan and 'Shorty' became lance-corporals 'an unpaid and often thankless job.'

Alastair Borthwick had been IO to Lt Col Jack Walford, CO 5th Seaforth since D-Day, who now, whilst on leave, was appointed to command 9th Seaforth in Scotland:

> Towards the end most of us I think became superstitious about him. We believed that if we stuck close to him we would not be hit. He was always up with the forward companies. Miller his batman and Ibister his wireless operator were unscathed. He exposed himself constantly in his determination to know everything and see everything which attracted large numbers of shells while so doing...

Lt Col John Sym succeeded him. He had escaped twice from the

Germans in Italy and was soon to escape for a third time.

Brigadier Roddy Sinclair was home on sick leave so Lt Col Grant Peterkin was acting OC 153 Bde. Lt Col Man was promoted to AA and QMG in 15th Scottish Div and was succeeded as CO 1/7th Middlesex by Major DG Parker. The Corps Commander, General Horrocks visited every HD Battalion and said how pleased he was to have them under his command for Veritable. The Die Hards were particularly pleased to see him as they were his old regiment. General Rennie gave all his commanders a final briefing followed by a sumptuous 'Last Supper'. TAC HQ was in a game keepers hut in Bisselt woods south of Mook.

1/7 Middx Die Hards: Sgt Jeff Hayward MM and mates, Limburgh
(J Hayward)

The Divisional plan of attack - on the 8th February was for Brigadier James Oliver's 154 Brigade to 'break in' to the defences on the western edges of the Reichswald. 152 Bde in reserve behind would pass through into the main forest and clear the southern 'track' in an easterly direction. 153 Bde were to assist with widening the 'break in' and move parallel to 152 Bde later, but along the southern edge of the forest. Initially 5/7th Gordons were 'lent' to 154 Brigade to strengthen the 'break in.'

"126 Field Regt left the Ardennes on 18th January for Boom near Antwerp. The thaw had started, roads gripped by severe frost broke up and torrential rain added to the general discomfort," wrote Captain WJ Brown. A few days of Belgian hospitality then a move to St Anthonis. "Preparations were made for fighting under the worst conditions -

supplies of windproof clothing, rubber boots, white camouflage nets and sheets and oil stoves were ordered and tents and bivouacs issued on a reasonable scale." On 3rd February all three Divisional Gunner Regts moved to the ghost town of Mook with the 25-pdrs hidden amongst the ruins of houses and barns, 3000 yards from the enemy FDLs. No formation signs were permitted and the great build up was carried out in total secrecy. Before dusk on the 8th February the gunner regiments had fired 630 rounds of HE and 65 of smoke per gun.

As part of the immense 'Pepperpot' 1/7th Middlesex were joined by 1st Middlesex and their 72 Vickers guns were lined up together and fired over seven million rounds of ammunition. In the thick dense woods of the Reichswald it was difficult for the Die Hards to give close support.

The next horrible 17 days of intense close quarter fighting in the forests were to be an infantry slogging match. The armour were destined to be bogged down and unable to provide appropriate support. But after the PBI the sappers and the signallers were the heroes of Veritable. After the battle Major General Thomas Rennie wrote to his CRE:

> My dear Ralph, please congratulate all your sappers from me for their performance in Veritable. It has been largely a sapper battle. To have completed the Kessel bridge under constant shelling with very tired men was a magnificent performance. I believe it was the finest bit of work the HD sappers have ever done.

Lt Col Ralph Carr was awarded a bar to his DSO.

The main tracks and rides in the Reichswald forest ran north-south across the general line of advance. The rapid thaw coupled with heavy rain, demolitions and bombardments had turned every path and track into a quagmire. Corduroy road work was essential and tank routes had to be separated from wheeled tracks. The CRE had additional units under Command. 239 Field Park Coy mechanical equipment, 16 Bridge Platoon, two sections RASC tipper lorries, 222 Assault Sqn RE, 210 Field Coy and 1642 Bridge platoon - all from 30 Corps. Later on during Veritable the sappers of Guards Armoured Div were placed under command. For the initial attack the three axis of advance were through Breedeweg, north of Grafwegen; another through Bruik and a third, a track north of Bruik. Lt Col James Cochran, OC HD Signals:

> One long slog through this thick forest with desperate and often hand to hand battles by the infantry night after night. The ammunition and supply columns did wonderful work in replenishing the units up one axis, which after the first days fighting became a sea of mud and water, of signals linesmen working day and night to keep the main axis and its satellite arteries through, of special wireless layouts for the difficult traffic problem and the great spirits of the Jocks of the infantry battalions which kept them

on top of these desperate German soldiers, Hitler Youth and Paratroops fighting as infantry and also like demons, never gave them any rest and dislodged them from one defence position after another.

The Break In

Behind an enormous bombardment and 'Pepperpot' from medium machine-guns, LAA, tank guns, even exceeding the famous Alamein barrage, at 1045 Lt Col Cathcart's 7th Black Watch advanced. They were screened by 2" mortar smoke, crossed an anti-tank ditch and got into Breedeweg without much difficulty. But snipers killed Major KA Lowe and two platoon commanders of 'D' Coy, and the Battalion suffered 34 casualties that day. 1st Black Watch led by Major Peter Taylor reached all their objectives, the high ground on the west of Reichswald, taking 100 POW for the loss of 17 wounded. The tremendous counter battery artillery programme had subdued the enemy for the time being. 1st Battalion claimed they just beat 7th Battalion for the honour of being the first HD troops into Germany.

During one of the many long delays Lt Bernard's No 6 Platoon 1st Black Watch was shelled by friendly smoke bombs falling short.

Private Stan Whitehouse then saw 'little Mac' felled by a burst of gunfire from their neighbouring platoon and Corporal Aitchison blown up by a Schu-mine. "His Sten flew out of his hands and on landing set off another mine. Bastard things, I thought." A 'friendly' shell dropped short on Company HQ and Whitehouse was ordered back to collect a Bren and mortar from wounded men behind. "I was horrified to see Ken Ware, eyes glazing over, his face creased with pain and his limbs shattered. Blood, a strange light brownish colour was bubbling out of his legs - Larry Crowther, his best mate, lay nearby, in an equally hopeless condition. Ken and Larry two of the most gentle, lovable chaps ever born, now lay in bits and pieces." 7th Argylls in reserve entered the forest at 2300, through 1st Black Watch but as the tracks were now a muddy quagmire had to abandon all their transport.

Both 154 and 153 Bdes had to use the same route, so it was the turn of 152 Bde at dawn on the 9th to push through deeper into the forests. Brigadier Cassels sent in 5th Camerons behind 5/7th Gordons on a one company front. A large crater held up their tank support but 'D' Coy soon took 80 POW before being held up. Major Callender led 'B' Coy right flanking and Major Jim Melville (who had already earned an immediate DSO) was wounded, led 'C' Coy in a bayonet charge in which Sgt M'Lew won the DCM. Their tank support had now arrived, fired HE point blank into the enemy dugouts causing terrible casualties. Lt Col Lang ordered the advance on at 1600 and at a crosstrack half a mile ahead Capt Beaton 'C' Coy led another successful bayonet charge for which he was awarded the MC.

Lt Ross Le Mesurier, Scout Platoon was attached to 'B' Coy 5th Camerons:

> Without tank support which had become bogged down, machine-gun, snipers and mortars took their toll throughout the morning of the 9th. My head was creased by a bullet, then a piece of shrapnel hit my back. Later on another fragment hit my upper left arm which stiffened up. The day dragged on, progress was slow and darkness came early. It also started to rain. Our company wireless operator was badly wounded in great pain, his uncontrolled moans seemed to draw gunfire. My company commander, Major Donald Callender yelled out, 'For God's sake, Ross, do something.' The wind was blowing towards the Germans, so I cocked a phosphorous grenade to throw it. It was hit by a bullet or a piece of shrapnel and burst in my face which was covered with blobs of burning goo. One lens of my glasses was covered. I rubbed handfuls of snow mixed with mud on my face to stop the burning. Some Germans began advancing towards us. Our firing forced them to go to ground. A few of us charged them firing from the hip. My Sten gun jammed so I freed my shovel. They started to run and we chased them. I hit one with the shovel blade in the neck. He hit the ground in a heap. I swung at another but he ducked and it glanced off his shoulder. I was a little in front of my boys so I decided to go back to my platoon.

When the Seaforth came thorough the next morning Le Mesurier was evacuated to hospital in Ghent and convalescent depot at Knokke-sur-Mer.

During the night 9/10th, 2nd Seaforth took over the lead, encountered determined paratroopers of *7th Parachute Division* and were held up. Two Crocodile flame-throwers then helped 5th Camerons to penetrate and turn the opposition and continue the advance on the 10th another two miles before darkness fell. 2nd Seaforth mopped up behind. 153 Bde's main task was to cut the Mook-Gennep road on the southern flank, led by 5th Black Watch on 8th February. Major Eric Mathew led 'A' Coy to Pyramid Hill and by 1930 Major Sandy Leslie took 'B' Coy towards a causeway and bridge which the enemy was using to escape southwards, capturing and killing 50 in the process. The night was confused. Corporal Andrew Dow:

> Settle down to wait. Butterflies in stomach. Sound of voices shouting as they came down the track. No need for Password, all shouts are in German. One grenade each, pins out. On command 'Throw' - heads down.... count five... heads up... Chaos, shouts, screams, sound of men running back up track keep silent, keep down. Silence for hours, then sounds of movement again down the track... German voices... repeat of last time... more chaos. The Germans don't know which way to run but none got past our section.

Private Jack Easton, 5th Black Watch:

We were led into action to capture a bridge led by a brand new ginger-haired officer christened Blood Nut. (Ginger hair of course), in his first action. 'Bash on' he said. Our Sgt said we should wait for 'A' Coy after taking our objective. 'Bash On' led across the fields and a watery ditch to another farm and mansion. The ten of us were then cut off by 70 Germans on 'A' Coys objective. We should not have been there. Our artillery put over a stonk. If ever I thought there was a God, it was that night. We escaped all the shells that fell. Give our officer his due, he was very brave that night. We held off all night and helped clear the enemy position in the morning.

By the morning of the 9th the Battalion had taken 76 POW, and captured 4 guns.

1st Gordons left Groot Linden with a two mile march to the Mook bridge and then another two miles to their assembly area at about 1300 on 8th February. But Major George Dunn commanding 5th Black Watch ahead of the Gordons told Major Martin Lindsay, CO 1st Gordons that all tracks ahead were hopelessly blocked by trees felled by enemy demolitions and HD artillery fire. 5/7th Gordons also gained a hold of the high ground east of Breedeweg, passing over smashed trenches, pillboxes and fallen trees. By midnight despite 30 casualties all objectives were reached. 'C' Coy in the darkness and confusion found themselves at a crossroads in the midst of an enemy relief! In the melée that followed 5/7th Gordons took 150 POW and only had one man wounded themselves.

Two companies of Gordons were now sent to work forward outside the edge of the forest towards St Jansberg and linked up with 5th Black Watch. At dawn supporting tanks towed up jeeps and carried on top cooked breakfasts for the Gordons. Soon St Martensbeg and Grafwegen were mopped up and 'B' Coy took 150 POW. Major Frank Philip their FOO put down a regimental target to help 'D' Coy but 'C' Coy had difficulty securing Del Hel, and 'A' were held up by a strong point on the vital Mook-Gennep road. "I knew that both the Divisional and Corps Commanders were waiting for news that 1st Gordons had opened up the road. Failure was unthinkable." The 5th Black Watch had reached this road at Kanonskamp and cut it, but it was not yet open as a key axis. So Major Martin Lindsay now led 'D' Coy in a night attack which despite being ambushed took the enemy strongpoint in the rear. "We've got to take this position now, cost what it may. Get all the Bren guns up in line. Fire rapid for one minute and make as much noise as possible. I don't believe the sods will put up much of a show. As soon as the Brens stop firing we'll rush the place." Major Danny Reid and Coy did just that and "a column of Huns, 71 in number, came running out with their hands up." Now very close to the Cameron Highlanders of Canada, Lindsay ordered his Gordon Pipers to play 'Cock o'the North' and the Canadians responded with 'Piobaireachd Dhomhnuill.' 1st Gordons lost nine KIA and 17 wounded but the crucial road was opened. Lindsay was appropriately awarded the DSO for this fine action.

Major Pearson took a Recce party of 9 men including Sgt Howard to Recce a position for 'C' Coy of the Die Hards on the 9th. Held up by a minefield the Recce party made a detour into two companies of German infantry. He 'borrowed' four Churchill tanks and with two Vickers guns in carriers, took on four enemy pillboxes. Sgt Dollin was shot dead by a sniper. A Spandau sent a burst of fire between Sgt Howard's body and arm without wounding him. The two Vickers teams withdrew by stages to join up with 5th Black Watch near Grafwegen who resumed the attack. Capt Pearson earned a bar to his MC and Sgt Howard, the MM. Corporal Sleath, the other Vickers commander had already earned the DCM.

The small town of Hekkens lies astride a crossroads of the main Cleve-Gennep and Goch-Kranenburg roads and was now a key objective for 152 Bde. The main Siegfried line defences ran through the town in front of which was a deep and difficult anti-tank ditch.

On 10th February 2nd Seaforth led with tank and artillery support but met heavy defensive fire and dug-in 600 yards west of Hekkens, taking 35 POW. 5th Camerons advanced at 1530 to avert a German counter-attack and at 0100 on 11th, 5th Seaforth in heavy rain had a sticky ten minutes when Capt Russell Ferguson led 'B' Coy head on against a counter-attack. He and Pat Grant were hit by a Spandau burst, the former was killed and Grant seriously wounded. "The wireless died and a runner had to be sent for the tanks. We [Capt Alastair Borthwick] heard them rumble forward, the sound of their heavy Besas cutting clear above the rattle of the other machine-guns. The Germans stood only two or three bursts and fled. Major Hamish Paterson with 'C' Coy went through with the tanks, caught the counter-attack still trying frantically to form up on the road and scattered it. Once again there was silence." 5th Seaforth was a thousand yards further into the Reichswald than anyone else in a 200 yards square. For the whole of the next day the Seaforth were shelled and mortared including 150 huge rocket bombs.

The MO, Farquhar Macrae had no cover and lay in the open binding up the wounded. The two gunner half tracks were hit and put out of action. Eventually during the night of the 10th, 5th Seaforth quietly slipped through the darkness southwards to link up with 5th Camerons. But worse was to come. The German paratroopers with fixed line, Spandaus, mortars, 88mm guns pinned down the Seaforths for a whole day in a deep anti-tank ditch protecting Hekkens. Lt Col Sym was wounded, as was Major Forshaw-Wilson, the 2 i/c and in the two days of close quarter fighting 5th Seaforth lost 19 KIA, 65 wounded. The attack on the Hekkens crossroads was abandoned, but 154 Bde later made a wide detour and succeeded.

General Rennie arranged for 30 Corps artillery to put a concentration on the paratroop defenders of Hekkens for the 154 Bde attack which started at 1530 on the 11th. 7th Black Watch were on the right flank. 1st Black Watch on the left advanced south for a mile and a half with 7th Argylls protecting the left (eastern) flank behind a barrage of fourteen field, four medium Regts and six heavy RA batteries! The village and crossroads down to the Niers river was captured, with 120 POW emerging from the immensely strong concrete bunkers and long lines of entrenchments. Casualties were very light indeed, 18 between the two Black Watch Battalions. The brutal artillery concentration forced the defenders to stay in their deep bunkers and found the Jocks in them before they could man their defences. 7th Black Watch collected a further 70 POW in the woods bringing their tally for the day to well over 200.

Just after the crossing on 13th in Buffaloes over the river Niers, Pte Stanley Whitehouse's (1st Black Watch) platoon commander Lt Bernard and his company commander were wounded. Whitehouse fired a PIAT bomb at a strongpoint and later looked inside it at three dead paratroopers killed by the blast. Two huge Corporals Lock and Lockie were found dead in a wood, both shot in the back. Stretcher-bearer Tom King went out to collect their bodies and explained the difficult choice he had to make when several wounded men needed attention at the same time. A man calling 'stretcher bearer' got priority over one crying out for his mother. The latter was usually severally wounded and was probably dying anyway. "I often heard wounded Germans calling out 'Mutter, Mutter' and it was often the last word they ever uttered."

During the night of 10/11th 153 Bde received orders to capture Gennep two miles due south of St Jansberg well outside the Reichswald. As 'A' Coy 5/7th Gordons approached the town, the bridge over the river Niers was blown and their patrol had to be withdrawn under cover of smoke. 'C' Coy with tank support occupied Ottersum, half a mile to the east. Next Major Donald Beales led 'D' Coy 5th Black Watch in a silent night crossing of the river and Major Sandy Leslie's 'B' Coy spiritedly attacked the bridge, church and hospital area. Sgt John Johnstone and his section were involved in savage house clearing and cut down two small counter-attacks. By the time 1st Gordons came thorough, 5th Black Watch had taken 174 POW in Gennep. But the defenders in the railway station and a large factory on the south side of the town held out. Snipers and Spandaus caused casualties but the Gordons tackled one side of a street at a time working through the back gardens from house to house. The fighting went on throughout the 12th involving both Gordon Battalions and 5th Black Watch.

"In the Reichswald Forest the enemy armour kept their distance", recalls Sgt Jack Cheshire, 1st Gordons, but at Heyen south of Gennep enemy tanks and SPs appeared. Capt Neville Smith the anti-tank platoon commander layed himself a 6-pdr anti-tank gun and fired four rounds to the nearest SP jinking about behind a hay stack. The SP won. The 6-pdr was knocked-out and Capt Smith got a large shell splinter through his Tam O'Shanter for his pains! "When we were moving forward fast our role was of firing into buildings, machine-gun emplacement and OPs." Wrote Jack Cheshire, anti-tank Platoon. "At close quarters a 6-pdr shell makes quite a mess." Lt Col Ralph Carr, CRE:

> That night 12th February we successfully launched and completed a 110 foot triple single Bailey bridge. Direct observation by the enemy coupled with self propelled guns firing had effectively prevented bridging operations until dusk fell.

The Die Hards with six platoons of Vickers machine-guns carried out successful shoots near Ottersum. Sgt Hayward 10 Platoon

> 11th February. We are into Gennep under intense enemy fire. The Fallschirm Jager (paratroops) fight for every yard. The Black Watch and Gordon Highlanders take heavy casualties.

It took 153 Bde three days of determined fighting to clear Gennep and Heyen; 1st Gordons had 34 casualties and only 17 effective officers survived and 5/7th Gordons 31 casualties. 5th Black Watch suffered badly too. Major Donald Beale, Lt JR McDonald and Lt Alan Foster killed in action with many ORs killed or wounded, but they took 259 POW in revenge. Sgt Albert Hinchcliffe led 'B' Coy with magnificent courage and destroyed two enemy posts in central Gennep for which he was awarded the DCM. The next key objective was the town of Kessel, five miles east of Gennep, on the south side of the river Niers now in full spate. General Rennie ordered 154 Bde to attack the high ground south-west of Kessel. The key bridge over the river was blown but assisted for the first time by a dozen troop carrying Buffaloes, 7th Black Watch crossed on the night of 13/14th from the Zelderheide area. The RAP of 7th Black Watch managed to arrive first at a group of enemy occupied houses in Villers, only just making a strategic retreat! 'B' Coy cleared the village of Kapelle with 50 POW and 'D' Coy captured Villers with its large flour mill with 100 POW, but suffering 31 casualties. Enemy fire had now destroyed most of the Buffaloes but 1st Black Watch got across the river and came through the 7th only to run into trouble around Hassum. Capt Hogg, their RA FOO led a charge on one strongpoint and later received the MC. But ammo supplies were now low, the 18 sets were not working and enemy infiltration captured a standing patrol. An enemy counter-attack with two SPs surprised and took a platoon of 'B' Coy. So some withdrawal was necessary with the loss of 48 casualties, two anti-tank guns and two carriers lost. Typhoons blasted the enemy for an hour, heavy DF was brought down by divisional artillery in front of Kessel and 5th Camerons lent anti-tank guns, ammo and wireless sets. 1st Black Watch were shelled heavily all of the 14th and most of the 15th. Bridging was thus difficult. "As a result of previous experience at Gennep, I [the CRE, Lt Col Carr] thought it essential to use the confusion just after a night attack and the ensuing hours of darkness to launch a Bailey before first light so that enemy artillery fire could not prevent bridging operations."

Mine clearance and bridge Recce parties from 274 and 275 Field Coys RE filtered forward and dumping started. The Recce party in an assault boat reached the far bank but all except one became casualties to Schu-mines. Eventually a double single class 24 (ton) Bailey was launched across the 110 foot gap, named 'Shackleton Bridge' after the sapper subaltern killed in the action. 'A' Coy led by Major Johnny Sloan and 'D' Coy under Major Joe Corcoran of 7th Argylls passed through the Black Watch battalions. By the morning of 15th February Kessel had been cleared with 70 POW taken. The next day the Argylls were heavily mortared, fended off a counter-attack and on the 16th with Churchill tanks cleared more dugouts with another 70 POW. At the same time 1st Black Watch with some tanks and Crocodiles of 1st Fife and Forfar Yeomanry, under a huge concentration cleared Hassum station and the woods around collecting 112 POW. Shelling on 'A' Coy killed Capt Walton and wounded Capt Molteno, a North African veteran, and 13 ORs. The main village of Hassum only fell the next day to the Welsh Guards. The Die Hards fired another 'Pepperpot' to help the Argylls take Kessel and 'B' Coy broke up a determined counter-attack on them.

*   *   *

The HD main objective was Goch but on the way from Kessel were three more defended villages. General Rennie now ordered 152 Bde into action after their difficult five mile advance in the Reichswald forest. 5th Seaforth were directed on Asperden, 5th Camerons on Hervost and 2nd Seaforth on Grafenthal.

On 16th 'D' Coy 2nd Seaforth started from Kessel and soon captured a crossroads 1500 yards down the Goch road; 'B' Coy then took two woods 500 yards beyond, and finally by 2245 'A' had captured Grafenthal monastery. At the same time having absorbed 60 new reinforcements 5th Camerons under a powerful barrage crossed the river at Hekkens and advanced on Hervost, taken without much difficulty. Helped by the waddling deadly Crocodiles six large pillboxes were then seized. 'C' Coy threw .36 phosphorous grenades down their ventilators and 'B' dealt with another trio called 'Shem', 'Ham' and 'Japhet.' In the woods around Hervorst on the night of 17/18th 'A' Coy cleared three more strongpoints called 'Faith', 'Hope' and 'Charity' with a total bag of 230 POW.

The obvious route to Goch was through Asperden and Alastair Borthwick, 5th Seaforth watched, "several mattresses of rockets went over, each weighing ten pounds, equivalent to a medium 5.5 inch shell. They made a sound like rushing water as three mattresses each with 300 rockets passed overhead into Aspenden." Led by Lt Col Sym on 'a midnight steeplechase,' the battalion followed the barrage and entered the village almost unopposed.

Alastair Borthwick described the technique of dealing with the 60 foot square enormously thick concrete pill-boxes heaped over with earth. "Infantry and supporting arms dealt with the trenches outside. The casement was the weak point but even 17-pdr anti-tank shells simply bounced off. But AVRE Churchill tanks with a 40 lb 'dustbin' bombard, thrown by a petard, would blow the steel shutters out of the casemate. Then a Crocodile would come up, squirt unignited fuel through the casemate for half a minute, then fired one ignited squirt after the rest. The garrison died instantly and horribly. Quite soon the German defenders realise that their supposedly 'impregnable' Siegfried line pillboxes had become a death trap."

*　　　*　　　*

The way was now clear for the main attack on Goch, which was a very strongly fortified town, part of the Siegfried line with many pill boxes with an anti-tank ditch on three sides and a river on the fourth. Five key roads and a rail line Cleve-Weeze ran through it. 43rd Wessex Division had advanced to the escarpment just to the east of Goch by the 16th February; and it was the task for 15th Scottish to attack from the north east and HD from the north west. 153 Bde would make the main attack after 2nd Seaforth (152 Bde) had made a crossing over the A/Tank ditch with an AVRE bridge, allowing 5th Black Watch to lead into the town. 275 Field Coy RE made crossings for two way traffic. The CRE, Lt Col Carr wrote home. "Ten long days and nights of incessant battling. However we are getting on and the other side is in very poor shape. HD have taken over 2000 POW and they seem to be coming in more easily now."

The Allied Forces and artillery concentrations had destroyed most of the town. This of course hampered the advance! The streets were blocked to tanks and wheeled traffic and the house debris was ideal cover for snipers, Spandau and bazooka teams. The enemy were well dug-in, in the gardens, behind buildings and most of the cellars were occupied by the defenders. H-Hour was set for 0100 on the 19th.

"The plan was fairly simple," wrote Major Martin Lindsay, 1st Gordons:

> 5th Black Watch were to start by taking all the main parts of the town south of the river, up to and including the big square. Then 5/7th Gordons were to pass through and take on beyond the square as far as the railway. 1st Gordons objective was the area just south of the 5th Black Watch/5/7th Gordons boundary. This included the beginning of the main road to the south-west [Thomashof] with two road junctions, a school, a factory and several largish buildings in the area.

Seven new officers joined 1st Gordons, making twelve in two days. One Lt Harrison was only 18, another, Ventris was wounded five times in the course of the battle for Goch. "It was fun while it lasted," he said as he was carried away on a stretcher. 5th Black Watch found many Germans either asleep or sheltering in their cellars. 'D' Coy captured a crossroads, then 'B' another, 'C' a factory and 'A' a street in the suburbs. Sgt Maxie instead of throwing grenades into cellars found that a large stone produced similar results! The CO Lt Col Bill Bradford sent patrols into the main square and ordered 'D' to secure the church and hospital. Major Brodie and Lt Ian MacDonald using Sten fire and grenades persuaded the German OC troops in Goch, a major, a lieutenant and 18 shaken ORs in the hospital cellars to emerge and surrender. Major Alec Brodie OC 'D' Coy 5th Black Watch a man of outstanding bravery won a DSO on 20th February. Although twice wounded in the attack after Spandaus had checked the advance, he dashed forward and shot dead two Spandau gunners in a house, using revolver and grenades. His company followed and put 37 paratroopers into the bag. In the nearby orchards and buildings he led further charges and was wounded twice more. Although weak from loss of blood he made sure 'D' Coy saw off a dawn counter-attack with two SPs and infantry.

At 0730 5/7th Gordons entered the fray and were soon committed to a day of hard fighting and by dark three rifle companies were involved in the struggle to dislodge the enemy from ruined buildings and rubble heaps. Very strong resistance and 'Moaning Minnies' pinned them down.   1st Gordons then came through to attack towards the south-west of Goch towards Thomashof. Major AJ Thomson 'A' Coy was shot through the head. Both 'A' and 'D' were pinned down, so Major Lindsay at 1600 deployed 'B' and 'C' with Crocodile and smokescreen support into the large housing estate in the western suburbs. "The rest of the day was perfectly bloody. It just could not have been more unpleasant," noted Lindsay. CSM Morrice said that the enemy shelling was the heaviest since El Alamein. Brigadier Sinclair then ordered a dawn attack on the 20th to take Thomashof, a hamlet of farm buildings half a mile south.

Medium artillery shelled the objective throughout the night. Due to a shortage of officers, Lindsay decided to take charge of the attack which moved off at 0600 with 'A' Coy leading under Capt Bill Kyle, "a stout hearted lad but not very experienced." At first all went well, but with no R/T or line communication to Battalion HQ, Lindsay and his runner went back to summon 'B' Coy up with tanks. Just before they started, survivors from 'A' Coy came in to say they had been overwhelmed. It was a disaster. 1st Gordons lost in the battle for Goch three officers KIA, seven wounded and one missing; 21 ORs KIA, 59 wounded and 48 missing. 'B' Coy under Major George Morrison (who later received the DSO) finally took Tomashof, taking 80 POW, but losing ten men KIA. Lt Col Grant-Peterkin returned from commanding the brigade back to 1st Gordons. Poor Major Lindsay, "depressed beyond words, I thought this disaster was my fault. Typhoons if available might have helped, but tank support had been negligible. 'D' Coy area was a shambles, houses burnt out, armoured cars and carriers blown up. Two new officers got hit on their way up to join their companies. I had not met them. Now I probably never should."

"As we pushed through the Gordon's positions along a track busy now with vehicles we saw a four foot high pile of bodies, neatly stacked, head to toe and still being built: there must have been a dozen corpses in the pile. 'That's how I like to see the Jerries - piled high' said Beachy [Pte Les Beach] to the Gordons who were standing about, looking sullen. 'Trouble is,' said one of them, 'they're our lads.'" [Pte Stan Whitehouse, 'B' Coy 1st Black Watch]

Before the end of February reinforcements poured into HD including ten officers and 230 ORs for 1st Gordons. When the German defenders withdrew on the morning of 21st 5/7th Gordons had 133 casualties including seven officers wounded. To add insult to injury the RAF mistook Goch for Weeze and twelve Mitchells unleashed a stick of bombs in Goch. Lt Col Ralph Carr the CRE was badly wounded and evacuated and 7th Argylls had 23 casualties including four ORs KIA.

Finally, 154 Bde were brought into the fray directed on the south eastern suburbs. 7th Black Watch under Major Monteith attacked at 2300 through the housing estate occupied by 1st Gordons. There 'D' met intensive shelling and mortaring and 'B' was cut in half by an unexpected counter-attack with infantry and three SPs. At dawn Crocodiles appeared to flame the enemy held barracks and eventually the Battalion reached its objectives whilst 7th Argylls advanced through the southern edge of town. The Black Watch had 44 casualties in their night operation.

For a few more days HD mopped up around Goch whilst 53rd Welsh passed through to attack Weeze. 154 Bde tackled Boyenhof,

Winkel and the muddy stream area called the Kendel. On 26th in a night attack 7th Black Watch accounted for 100 enemy but lost 29 casualties. Two members of Bde HQ were killed by mortar fire, Lt D Colquhoun and Sgt Hewan CMP. 1st Black Watch, 7th Argylls and 7th Black Watch took part in the same operation before being relieved by 52nd Lowland Div on the night of 27/28th February. During Veritable 1st Black Watch had 125 casualties and the Argylls 121. 152 Bde were also involved with 5th Camerons capturing Boeckelt on the 25th with 200 POW.

The Seaforth Battalions also had one more task, to capture Siebengewald held in strength and protected by the meandering river Kendel and dominating the Gennep-Goch road. Through a Kapok bridge laid by the Guards Armoured Div, 2nd Seaforth tried to take two well-defended farmhouses near the river. Alastair Borthwick, 5th Seaforth:

> It was a bad night for morale [26/27th]. We had crossed the bridge behind 2nd Seaforth expecting to advance in an hour or so. Instead we lay until long after midnight hearing nothing but sounds of strife from the base of the isthmus, alarming rumours and the groans of 2nd Seaforth wounded as they were carried back over the bridge. There were a great many wounded. Every now and then the fighting flared up, Spandaus and Brens rattled, flashes dotted the distance and stray bullets whipped overhead.

Eventually Lt Col Andrews, 2nd Seaforth and Lt Col Sym, 5th Seaforth, "retired to the nearest ditch to hatch a plot." A heavy artillery concentration was put down on the farming hamlets and a joint Seaforth attack went in. They surrounded the stout-hearted paratroopers who decided that enough was enough and surrendered. 2nd Seaforth lost 141 casualties during Veritable.

Although their FOOs found it difficult in the Reichswald to pinpoint targets for their hungry guns, once outside many targets were called down. Capt WJ Brown 126 Field Regt:

> All the time the guns were firing - countless programmes laid on by telephone and fired at short notice in support of small attacks made by the infantry. Move ammunition. The vehicles were never still. Backwards and forward between the ammunition point and the gun positions, over roads hourly becoming more and more impossible, sticking in thick mud, digging, pushing, winching, finally carrying the load, box by box across hundreds of yards of muddy morass to the gun pits. 300 rounds per gun was the average daily expenditure. The guns were hard task masters during that time.

At one stage 126 Field Regt were deployed in uncleared minefields and the battery commanders' vehicles of 297 and 298 Batteries were casualties. The RASC were praised for the way their vehicles in dreadful 'road' conditions hauled their precious cargoes of ammo and

rations up the line. The Divisional Signallers too had a difficult time.
Lt Col James Cochrane:

> The combination of cold, wet weather, very bad country and a high
> incidence of cable breaks owing to the large number of vehicles using the
> few available roads, the increased enemy fire and the large number of
> formations under command from outside the Division, all of whom
> required lines, were the causes linesmen usually averaged only four hours
> sleep in 24 hours and were constantly on the move.

General Horrocks wrote to GOC HD:

I have seen 51st Highland Division fight many battles since I first
met them just before Alamein. But I am certain that the Division has
never fought better than in the recent offensive into Germany. You
breached the enemy's defences in the initial attack, fought your way
through the southern part of the Reichswald, overcame in succession
several strongpoints of the Siegfried line such as Hekkens and then
finally cleared Goch, a key centre in the German defensive line. You
have accomplished everything that you have been asked to do in spite
of a number of additional German reserves which have been thrown in
on your front. No Division has ever been asked to do more and no
Division has ever accomplished more. Well done, Highland Division.

Operation Veritable was over.

40

Preparation for the Rhine Crossing
Operation Plunder

General Dempsey on 18th March explained to Alan Moorhead and
other journalists the master plan - Operation Plunder:

> We will cross the Rhine on the night of the 23rd. Four Corps are under my
> command. Thirty Corps will cross in the north near Rees and continue
> northwards for the capture of Emmerich. Twelve Corps will cross in the
> centre at Xanten while the Commandos turn south to capture Wesel. On
> the following morning the 18th USA Airborne Corps with the 6th British
> Airborne Div under command, will drop near the Issel river on the opposite
> bank of the Rhine and secure the bridges there. Finally, Eighth Corps will
> follow through and I cannot yet tell you how far they will go. The Ninth
> American Army will also attack on my right flank and proceed eastward
> along the Ruhr.

Moorehead asked. "This might well be the last battle?" General
Dempsey answered "Yes." General Horrocks commanded 30 Corps on
the left and General Neil Ritchie, 12 Corps (including HD) on the right.

The 51st attack would be on a two brigade front, 154 to cross near Honnopel and 153 to cross downstream from Rees. 152 Bde would then exploit northwards towards Isselburg. 2nd Seaforth would be attached to 153 Bde.

7th Black Watch on the left, 7th Argylls on the right would lead the 154 Bde assault, and 5/7th Gordons on the right, 5th Black Watch on the left, lead for 153 Bde. The German *8th Parachute Division* was clustered opposite around Rees with *6th* and *7th Parachute Divisions* on their flanks. In reserve were *15th PZ* and *116 Panzer Division*. For nearly three weeks most of the British Army, elements of the Royal Navy, and the Airborne Divisions prepared for the great leap forward into the heart of Germany - across the river Rhine. Major Martin Lindsay, 1st Gordons:

> The initial crossing was to be made by the two Scottish divisions, ourselves and the 15th, and it was a great honour. Montgomery was supposed to have said that Scottish troops were best for assaulting.

152 Brigade enjoyed a rest for a week around Nijmegen. Alastair Borthwick, 5th Seaforth: "There the houses had roofs and windows and there were such things as theatres, cinemas and baths. The baths were best of all." The 1st Gordons, 1st Black Watch and 7th Black Watch spent a week in Goch, 5/7th in Hervost and on 4th March HD sent representative officers and men to Grafenthal where in cold wet weather the Prime Minister, Field Marshal Montgomery and the CIGS addressed them on the progress of the war. The massed Pipes and Drums beat Retreat. The Pipe Majors of all the Battalions came together to play 'The Flowers o'the Forest' in memory of all ranks who had fallen. Winston Churchill's last words were: "The reconstituted Division has fully avenged the old 51st in 1940 and it is second to none in the British Army." Field Marshal Alan Brooke wrote in his diary: "We finished up with a visit to 51st HD who are out of the line and produced their Pipes and Drums. It was interesting to, at last, see this Division on German soil. I first came in contact with them when I took over the remnants after St Valèry, when I returned to France subsequent to Dunkirk. They were next under my orders when I commanded Home Forces and I visited them twice in Scotland, then again after their arrival in Egypt and ready to move to the defence of Cairo against Rommel and in Tripoli after Rommel's defeat to the invasion of Sicily, and now at last in Germany." Brigade Major Alan Daglish recalled that just after the Reichswald battle, Monty sent a signal to say he was coming to award a decoration. Major Daglish mounted a parade. Then there was a delay and the parade was dismissed. The Field Marshal eventually arrived at teatime to meet "a pretty ragged line of officers drawn up to meet him. Monty asked each of them how long he had been in HD. Answers were "Actually I'm not

I'm from RA Recce." And 'Actually I was just going through the village and the chap told me to get into the line," and "Sir, I vas Dutch, I am no officer, I no speak English goot," and the ADMS was no Scotsman. He came from Northern Ireland!

The HD then moved on 8th March to the Maesyck area for special training in assault crossing in stormboats and Buffaloes. 33 Armoured Bde Shermans who had marched with HD since Normandy would be handling the Buffaloes and the Royals were going to be in charge of communications on the west bank. New No. 46 sets with crystal control had been issued to the infantry Battalions and No 68 sets to the RA observation post parties. Major Salter was OC 102 Beach Sub-area Signal Section to assist in communications for traffic marshalling areas and traffic and control on the river banks. A signals planning office was set up at Stamproij under Major Fraser to co-ordinate the signal plan for signals throughout the division. On 14th, 15th and 16th March full scale divisional exercises in assault crossing were carried out over the river Maas. Field Marshal Montgomery observed the daytime exercise and actually crossed the Maas in one of 'A' Coy 8th Argylls Buffaloes to see for himself his Highlanders at work. But in the afternoon local leave was granted to Hasselt, Eindhoven, Maesyck and Brussels Leave camps. The Balmorals put on concerts and football competitions were run.

1st Gordons had a regimental reunion, started with a football match, then Retreat played by the massed bands of the 1st, 5/7th and 2nd Battalion which was stationed nearby. All the special Gordon tunes were played, 'Marquess of Huntly,' 'Captain Towse VC,' 'My Highland Home' and the 'Cradle Song' and after tea the Gordons danced reels. Lt Col Lang 5th Camerons ensured that kilts were now worn and 5/7th Gordons had their pre-war white spats, diced hosetops and hairy white sporrans for their Pipe Band!

Reinforcements arrived and so did a number of HD veterans wounded in previous engagements Major George Dunn DSO MC 2i/c 5th Black Watch who had been in every battle since Alamein to Goch, was promoted to command 2nd Seaforth.

On 19th and 20th March first the seniors and then every officer in HD was briefed on their role in the assault crossing with maps and up to date aerial photographs available. A huge blanket smoke screen covered from 22nd, the whole western bank of the Rhine, much of which was under direct and accurate mortar fire from the German held eastern bank. Meanwhile the immense build up for ammunition for the artillery barrage went on. Strange nautical craft appeared on the roads as well as scores of pontoons. 3rd British Division were guarding the left bank. To minimise dust on roads and tracks their signs read "Ashes to Ashes," "Dust to Dust" and "Your Dust turns us into Ashes."

41

Across the Rhine
"Rennie was a great leader"

General Brian Horrocks wrote: "The 51st Highland Division had been earmarked to carry out the first crossings. Just before 9pm [23rd March] I climbed into an observation post on high ground overlooking the Rhine... I could imagine the leading buffaloes carrying infantry of 153rd and 154th Infantry Brigades lumbering along their routes, taped out and lit beforehand and then lurching down into the dark waters of the Rhine... then at four minutes past nine precisely I received the message for which I had been waiting - in its way a historical message because it was from the first British troops to cross the Rhine - 'The Black Watch has landed safely on the far bank.'"

The 7th Black Watch had moved to their marshalling area east of Calcar by nightfall on the 21st and in liaison with the Bank Unit, marshalled control parties, D-D tanks and were issued with Mae West's, ration packs, shell dressings and the other vital components for a river assault at night. To their amazement they saw the Prime Minister and CIGS moving about among the troops wishing them 'God Speed' for the crossing. General Horrocks received his vital message at 2104, but the Buffalo crossing took only 2½ minutes. There were casualties mainly to Schu-mines and nearly all the Unit Landing Officers party were killed or wounded. By dawn on the 24th four villages and 70 POW had been taken, and a counter-attack the next day fended off with nearly 50 paratroops dead or wounded. The Adjutant, 7th Argylls, Captain Angus Stewart wrote:

> The surprise for Plunder was achieved by a double ruse, a short barrage (four hours and an assault after dark in the evening rather than our favourite time - two hours before dawn. At 8pm we got into our Buffaloes, ponderous, clumsy creatures looking like the original tanks of 1916. About 8 feet high on dry land, driven both on land and water by great tracks which travel round the whole perimeter of the vehicle instead of on bogies as on a modern tank. They carry a platoon of men or a small vehicle like a jeep or carrier. At nine o'clock the Argylls entered the water and chugged across, none failed, none sank, all landed our men where we wanted them.

The Argylls captured Ratshoff taking 100 POW, but when 1st Black Watch passed through to Kleine Essenden and Speldrop opposition hardened. 'B' Coy sustained heavy losses and its OC Major Boyle killed under heavy mortaring. In confused fighting Speldrop was taken, lost and retaken. Enemy SPs knocked-out the supporting Staffordshire Yeomanry tanks. Lt Bernard took command of the battered 'A' Coy and 19 year old Lt Henderson 'C' Coy won an immediate DSO when his patrol was cut off in a blazing house attacked by bazooka and Spandau fire.

15 Platoon 'C' Coy under Capt Coates and Sgt Les Johnstone was defending a large farmhouse against bazooka and SP gun attacks. 'Dusty' Miller and Pte JW Mitchinson guarded the doors. Corporal McArthur who was wounded in his back was treated in the cellar by a German MO and his staff. Amongst their patients were two expectant mothers. During the 'siege' a son was born to one and twin daughters to the other. When the HLI of Canada finally rescued the Black Watch platoon 35 enemy dead were counted around the farmstead. In their first 24 hours fighting in the bridgehead the Battalion had 81 casualties including five officers.

153 Bde's main objective was the town of Rees. 5th Black Watch crossed the 450 yards of the Rhine in buffaloes manned by 4 RTR. Major JD McGregor:

> The noise was deafening. The dark overcast sky was lit by searchlights, red tracer bullets... Morale was high and excitement at fever pitch. Someone started to sing and the singing spread from group to group. The Padre led with 'Onward Christian Soldiers' but the unmistakable 'Ball of Kirriemuir' was heard despite the fearful din. Then the company Pipers took over and 'Scotland the Brave' echoed across the scene.

The crossing went smoothly and by midnight all objectives had been taken and contact made with the Argylls. Esserden was cleared despite Spandau posts needing house to house clearance. 5/7th Gordons also made their crossing on the right flank but were checked by the Alter Rhine defences, a backwater east of Rees. Despite a smoke screen and barrage their assault boats on the 25th were beaten off with a loss of 44 casualties. 1st Gordons followed 5th Black Watch to attack Rees itself from the west, led by Major Morrison's 'B' Coy. By dawn on the 24th they had reached the Rees-Speldrop road, cleared a housing estate and bund and were established in a cemetery with 70 POW taken. Rees was in a state of ruin and chaos and defended by two Battalions of paratroops. Major Lumsden took 'C' Coy and cleared the northern suburbs. Fighting went on throughout the 24th. At dawn on the 25th 'D' captured a strongpoint in the cathedral, 'B' cleared the river bank and 'A' Coy the town centre. 5th Black Watch closed in on the railway station and by then sappers were starting to bridge the Rhine. General Horrocks came to Rees at 1030 to congratulate 1st Gordons who had suffered over 70 casualties including their CO Lt Col Grant-Peterkin wounded by a burst of shellfire. 5th Black Watch had 56 casualties and took nearly 400 POW after two all night battles. Sgt Robert Fowler 'C'

Coy distinguished himself and won the DCM for conspicuous gallantry.

But HD suffered a terrible tragedy on the 24th as Capt Angus Stewart, adjutant 7th Argylls related:

> It was a finely conceived operation though casualties were moderately heavy. They included General Rennie killed in a mortar stonk just after wishing me luck. I was taking six carriers up the road in a convoy. As he was passing us the mortar bombs came down and he was caught by an unlucky splinter. His death rather shattered us. He was known so intimately and was held in such regard by everybody.

And General Horrocks:

> I have always felt that Rennie had some foreboding about this battle. He and I had fought many times together but I had never seen him so worried as he was over this Rhine project. He hated everything about it and I couldn't understand why, because the actual crossing was fairly plain sailing compared with other operations which he had undertaken quite cheerfully. Like so many Highlanders, I believe he was 'fey'. All three brigades were involved in heavy fighting so I crossed the Rhine in a buffalo and summoned the three brigadiers to a conference. They were very upset by the death of their popular commander. No wonder because Rennie was a great leader. It was thanks largely to him that the division had recovered after a somewhat inauspicious start in Normandy.

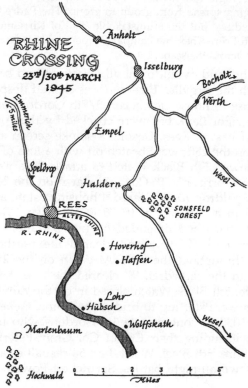

> Horrocks appointed Brigadier James Oliver, OC 154 Bde to command until, "Macmillan of the Argylls, a most able and popular officer, known throughout the Army as 'Babe' arrived. A fortunate choice because as commander of 152 Bde in Sicily he was a familiar figure to all the Jocks."

Major Lindsay, 1st Gordons:

> This was a terrible blow. It was especially sad as he had gone so far with us and had now been killed

on the last lap. His death was not so very surprising in view of the risks he took. You cannot dice against the law of averages and get away with it for ever. He was a great man and a great figure, one of the tallest men in the Division and quite unmistakable to any Jock as he stood at the roadside and watched them moving up into battle. He always wore a naval duffle coat, his hands in the two large front pockets. On his head a Tam O'Shanter with the red hackle of the Black Watch. No wonder the Jocks loved him. He had undoubtedly made the Division what it was at the time, the best in Second Army.

Lt Col John McGregor in *Spirit of Angus* recalled how Thomas Rennie as CO 5th Black Watch had addressed the Battalion before D-Day: "A Soldier must face the possibility of his being wounded or killed in action, but if that was the ultimate price to be paid then he should face death in the knowledge that he had done his duty to King and Country... As a soldier, I can expect to die in battle and I do not ask for any other fate."

Major General GH Macmillan had been commanding 49th Polar Bear Division and immediately on joining HD, crossed the river with Lt Col Leslie, GSO1 to ensure that 30 Corps directives were being carried out. On the morning of the 24th the huge fleet of air transports carrying 1st Airborne Corps was seen flying Stirling-towed gliders to their dropping area in front of 15th Scottish Division. That afternoon the funeral of General Rennie took place at Appeldorn attended by Lt General Horrocks and Lt General Symonds GOC 1st Canadian Corps. Main Div HQ was established in the battered town of Rees, crossing over the sapper bridges called Westminster (outgoing) and Waterloo (returning traffic).

By the time 152 Bde came to cross during the early hours of the 24th only a dozen of the 30 storm boats originally available were still servicable. Enemy guns and mortars were strafing them as they lay against the west bank; 5th Camerons landed at 0330 hrs, two hours behind schedule. At first light they moved through 2nd Seaforth who had captured the main road bridge over the anti-tank ditch and a large factory, beyond Essenden taking 250 POW. Mittelburg with several large brickworks on the main axis north of Rees was a key objective for 5th Camerons. Their first attack was not successful with Staffordshire Yeomanry tanks being knocked out by enemy SPs. 'C' Coy leading lost 34 casualties and Lt Le Mesurier, their Canloan officer was severely wounded. A second attack at night was successful although the German paratroopers fought to the last. Major AW Lee was awarded the MC and Sgt L Toogood, the MM. Lt Col James Cochrane, OC Div Signals had ordered his 'C' Section to lay cable across the fast flowing river to the HQs of the assault Brigades:

Two DUKWs were given to the unit. In each was fitted a tripod capable of taking a seven pair cable drum in diameter some five feet. On these drums was wound 500 yards of double carrier quad... from air photographs it had been calculated that 500 yards would do the crossings. Under command of Major Henderson and Capt MacLaughlan the cable was laid by hand down to the bank of the river.

The first DUKW was holed by a shell splinter and abandoned. The second was successful and by 0330 hrs field cables had been laid to each TAC Bde HQ. Line parties patrolled their lines, often cut by mortar fire and friendly tracked vehicles. Major Henderson was awarded the DSO and Signallers Clark and Reilly, Military Medals for their signal laying operation under fire.

After the huge supporting barrage, the divisional artillery FOOs went across the river with the leading companies. Red smoke shells were fired frequently to indicate targets for the rocket-firing Typhoons. 126 Field Regt crossed on Lambeth bridge on 26th and came into action at Esserben, an area overlooked by the tall enemy held tower of Millingen church.

In his book *Sans Peur* Alastair Borthwick, 5th Seaforth describes two consecutive and very difficult battles: "Groin was the hardest village fight the Battalion ever fought." At 0100 on the 25th Groin a hamlet of a score of well-defended farmhouses and outbuildings had to be cleared, and then the hamlet of Hollands Hof. 'A' Coy started the action and Lt Col Sym ordered 'C' to take out the right hand group of houses. Major Hugh Robertson:

> Peter Stone's men had been badly shot up. A 'tattie masher' landed three yards from me. There seemed to be Boche firing from the hip all over the landscape, men coming full belt at us about 30 yards away with muzzle flashes coming from their middles, shouting 'Komm, Komm'. We went, scattering back across the fields to our firm base.

Later Robertson sent Sgt Goldney's platoon into the centre of Groin. "It was terrible. All the buildings were on fire. Roofs were caving in and sparks were flying all over the place. Cattle were trapped inside. The stench sickened me. In the firelight I could see both the Boche and my own lads dodging about." Capt Jock Gardner led 'D' Coy in just before dusk. Corporal J Purchase and Pte J Gray, the Brengunner of No 5 Section charged trenches and ditches held by paratroopers with three Spandaus. L/Corp Green:

> Of course they were hit. They were hit all over. We were mad when we saw them lying there. We didn't know what we were doing. We yelled at the Boche to come out. And so help me they did. A wee white flag came over the edge and then an officer, and then two or three and then the whole issue. Forty-six of them." Pte Gray survived and was awarded the DCM. Corporal Purchase died of wounds and was mentioned in despatches. The next afternoon Hollands Hof was taken with the loss of 27 casualties; two

sections of 17 Platoon were wiped out. Lt Bill Flynn was killed by fire from a big hospital and Lt Bill Manson was wounded. The supporting tanks shot HE at point blank range. "As the shelling stopped [Lt] Evans went in with 17 Platoon HQ and bits and pieces of the other two Platoons and with a supreme effort stormed the house. They fought in the rooms and cellars and when the last German had been killed, only Evans, two NCOs and thirteen men of the company were left on their feet." The one tank was blown up by a bazooka. Corporal Stevenson and Pte Hall the 38 set operator hauled the tank crew out. Eventually after a desperate fight 'D' Coy had to withdraw with four men killed and twenty three wounded, to Groin to reorganise but after dark 'A' Coy found Hollands Hof deserted. "The para-boys had run." Jock Gardiner was awarded the MC for his leadership in this bitter action.

Meanwhile the Camerons had taken Isselburg on the night of the 28th with 145 POW - almost unopposed. So 5th Seaforth then had to fight a very difficult battle capturing two bridges over the Astrang between Anholt and Dinxperloo. After a cautious night advance Major Hector MacKenzie's 'A' Coy dashed across the river to capture two bridges. One was blown up as Sgt Elliott and 8 Platoon were crossing. "There was a terrific explosion and a bit of a flash and a wave of blast. I was lying on my face in the middle of the road with all sorts of stuff coming down round me, stones, earth and bits of iron." The second bridge was half blown up. Unfortunately the supporting tanks did not arrive at first light and 200 German infantry arrived marching smartly in threes in peacetime formation. They swamped Battalion HQ. "Col Sym and part of Battalion HQ that most mattered, were marched off to a house. The situation was chaotic. Germans were still flooding into the area. Ammunition on both sides was running short. We were firing captured Spandaus and some Germans were using Brens. Both sides were taking prisoners." Their FOO and the Battalion 3" mortars brought down fire on the Battalion HQ area. Major Hugh Robertson:

> About 0900 hrs I saw British tanks in the distance, the best sight I'd seen for many a long day. White flags began to pop up all along the bank on both sides of the first bridge and from the buildings beyond. It was all over.

Over 200 POW were captured and at least 50 were killed. All the captured 5th Seaforth were re-captured, but casualties in this frenzied muddled battle of the Astrang bridge were 14 KIA, 40 wounded.

L/Corporal HJ Bagshaw was a section commander in 5th Seaforth: "We were all determined to try and end the war as quickly as we could. I was a veteran of the battle of El Alamein and the Sicilian campaign like so many men from the famous reformed HD under 'Big Tam' Wimberley. As we approached the town of Isselburg at night, it was alight like something from Dante's Inferno." Later on the 28th: "We ran quickly to reach the narrow bridge, minus its wooden flooring. My section had the task of holding the bridge that was nearest to Coy HQ. We consolidated at 1230 am. During the enemy shelling of our position, four of my section had deserted into the night. At 230 am some 200 odd Germans started to attack on the far end of the two bridges wiping out the other section." The Brengunner Pte Kavanagh was mortally wounded. Bagshaw fired his captured Schmeisser but was hit badly in his left arm. Back at the RAP under heavy mortar fire: "our wonderful Padre Capt JI Simpson MC covered me with his own body while the heavy mortaring lasted. A fine and fearless man nicknamed 'Ironside' by the men of the 5th Seaforths."

When 5th Camerons moved on 30th March to the unspoilt village of Schuttenstein they held a memorial service at the Divisional cemetery for the 33 officers and men killed as well as 119 wounded during the Rhine crossing operations.

2nd Seaforth under Lt Col GW Dunn had cut the German line of retreat north-east from Rees by the capture of a large factory on the main road, eventually taking 250 POW. They then resumed their advance on 28th and forced a bridgehead over the Oude Issel river. Rocket firing Typhoons were called up to destroy enemy holding out in 'Buttercup' Wood. Then the hamlets of Hohenhorst, Hagesfeld, Sielhorst and Bramhamp were taken with tank and artillery support with another 160 POW. In the battle of the Rhine 2nd Seaforth lost 11 KIA, 40 wounded or missing.

Isselburg was the main objective for 153 Bde after their two day battle for the capture of Rees. As late as the 26th, 5th Black Watch were still discovering more prisoners, 70 in a deep cellar and then a complete machine-gun company with officer and weapons. Major Sandy Leslie found that many POW and arms taken were of a mature vintage, some rifles with long barrels dating from the 19th century! 1st Gordons moved from a wood near Empel on the 27th, crossed the autobahn at night and occupied a factory area. The next day they took possession of Konigshof and two other hamlets. 5/7th Gordons moved up parallel, cleared the main road south of Issselburg towards Werth and the woods along the Anholt road. 'D' Coy took 70 POW as Lt Col Irvine returned from leave.

Pte John Tough 5/7th Gordons recalls how on 28th just south of Isselburg:

> we got quite a hot reception with air burst and mortars. Pte Bleesby was killed in the action. Typhoons shot up a German AFV. Three or four men were on the road or hanging out of the top, all dead and badly burned. It was not nice to witness.

But 152 Bde had already occupied Isselburg on the 28th, so 153 Bde moved over the border to Enschede where both Gordons battalions found comfortable billets with very friendly Dutch families. 5th Black

Watch stayed in Isselburg until 5th April and reinforcement officers joined them from LAA, Suffolks, Argylls, Duke of Wellington's, West Yorks, Durham Light Infantry and more Canloans. "They all proved excellent Black Watch officers as if to the manner born," wrote Lt Col John McGregor in *The Spirit of Angus*. 1st Black Watch rested in Dinxperloo having captured 120 POW of *104 Regt* of *15 Panzer Grenadier Division*. The CO also captured some Volksturm (elderly Home Guard) sheltering in the Command Post cellars. Total casualties in the Rhine crossing battle were 25 KIA, 99 wounded including six officers. And in three days of fighting in the Empel area 7th Black Watch had lost 32 officers and men killed and 89 wounded including two of their best platoon commanders, Lts Jack Niven and Ivor Butcher. 'A' Coy had a desperate struggle to keep the village of Empel and its key bridge intact. Dinxperloo was a small town, half Dutch, half German on the frontier border and was taken without much trouble by 154 Bde on 30th March. The Guards Armoured Bde swept through to start their armoured drive. Major Innes left to command 7th Black Watch as Lt Col Charles Cathcart was posted back to the UK. Their Pipe Major played a new march, 'Lieut Colonel Cathcart of Pitcairle.' Major Landale Rollo was also urgently recalled to the UK - to resume his duties as a parliamentary agent! He too earned a march, 'Major Rollo across the Rhine.' Reinforcements rolled into every infantry battalion. 7th Argylls, after a two battalion attack with 1st Black Watch across the Rees-Isselberg road, received drafts totalling 136. By then their casualties in Plunder were 143. Major Joe Corcoran DSO MC lost a leg in the capture of Dinxperloo and CSM E Wildman DCM and 28 others were killed in action.

Two key problems had faced the British Army since entering the Fatherland - looting and fraternisation. Looting has been endemic in every army, and the probability is that the British Army looted slightly less than others. But in Germany the opportunities and the motives presented greater problems. Division and Brigade sent down urgent 'rules of engagement'. Nevertheless any kind of food or drink 'appeared' on the menu. Strange cars (and senior officers in particular were seen in shiny Mercedes), cameras, field glasses, shotguns were in theory 'verboten'. Every Jock had extra watches and much else that was portable. Strict guidelines were laid down about fraternisation with the enemy, which were doomed to failure. Food and chocolate for the children and considerable attention to the more comely 'frauleins'. Pte Stan Whitehouse 1st Battalion Black Watch wrote during Veritable:

> Our lads rushed forwards slinging their weapons over their shoulders to free both hands for ransacking the prisoners. The 'prisoners' threw themselves on the ground whilst others emerged from cover and mowed down the Jocks. Some squaddies were consumed by the desire to loot

prisoners, stopping at the height of the battle to take watches, rings, money and other valuables.

On 31st March Sir Mike Dempsey, 2nd Army commander sent a message to HD: "Now that the Battle of the Rhine has been won and the breakout from the bridgehead is well under way, I would like to give you [Major General Macmillan] and your magnificent division my very sincere congratulations. Yours was one of the two Divisions which carried out the assault crossing of the river, defeated the enemy on the other side and paved the way for all that followed.   A great achievement - and I am sure you are all very proud of it." When Major Martin Lindsay, 1st Gordons visited his old CO, now Brigadier Harry Cumming-Bruce, with 15th Scottish, he was told "How much fresher they all were than us, as the result of not having had the desert campaign before this one." On 1st April a Memorial Parade service was held at Isselburg for General Rennie and nine Battalion pipers played 'The Flowers of the Forest' HD were now out of the line in Corps Reserve. Div HQ was near Isselburg, other units around Dinxperloo, Empel and Anholt - for five days.

42

The Last Swan: Operation Eclipse

The writing was on the wall. "In the month from 5th April to 5th May, main Div HQ moved no less than sixteen times which gives an indication as to how the enemy were on the retreat. That month took the Division from Isselburg, some five miles from the Rhine to Eversdorf on the outskirts of Bremen," wrote Lt Col James Cochrane OC Div Signals. The magnificent armoured divisions (11th, 7th and Guards) and the indomitable armoured brigades (4th, 8th and 33rd) were pushing and hustling the German defenders inexorably back - a bloodstained 'sandwich' with the Russian armies advancing on Berlin and the American armour streaming through the Ruhr. The issue was never in doubt and everyone now knew it. The problem was that a roadblock defended by school boys with panzerfausts, the Volksturm with a Spandau or Schmeisser, an occasional well-manned SP gun, or 88mm gun and mines and booby traps inevitably - day by day - took their toll. There were to be no more set piece divisional attacks and rarely a brigade action involving more than one Battalion.

30 Corps advance was directed on Bremen and Bremerhaven some 160 miles away and via Enschede, Salzbegen, Lingen, Quakenbruk,

Vechta, Wildeshausen and Delmenhorst. For most of the way 2nd Derbyshire Yeomanry led with their scout cars and carriers reporting back, pushing, probing and harrying the defences.

152 Brigade

5th Camerons made a long road move to Enschede on 7th April. Their two day stay ranked with the welcomes received in Vught and 's-Hertogenbosch. Five days later they moved without TCVs to Vechta in their own few vehicles, on tanks, flails, on 17-pdr SPs. They advanced in 24 hours, 28 miles and took 200 POW in Oythe, Amerbusch, and Visbek. They then had a two day rest until the 18th with the Pipes and Drums played at 1615 hrs. 'B' Coy 5th Seaforth was reformed in Enschede before moves to Altlingen a pleasant village on the Dortmund-Ems Canal, to rich farming country at Acht. The IO Lt Alastair Borthwick led the battalion on a pitch dark night towards Vechta:

> ...steering by faith, a sense of smell and a 1:100,000 scale map to help me. It was a good joke. Here we were streaming along the road past woods containing goodness only knew what towards a village about which we knew nothing. Our tanks could not join us for hours and most absurd of all, we were enjoying ourselves. The whole business was too crazy to be taken seriously. It was exhilarating after all the months of creeping forward.

In Goldensteht 184 POW were taken. HD were fortunate that their centre lines did not include the Teuton berger Wald, or forcing the Dortmund-Ems canal and the rivers Weser and Aller, where the German army cobbled together ferocious defences.

153 Brigade

From Enschede on 5th April 1st Gordons moved to Gildehaus and 5/7th to Bentheim, passing through 5th Black Watch to Emsburen. Progress was slow due to craters and firing from front and flank caused 14 casualties. The fortunate Gordon battalions then halted at Leschede and Emsburen for four days, fished, played football and 'obtained' transport of one kind or another. The advance was resumed on 12th, 1st Battalion to Ankum, Hoskensburg and Brettorf, despite fire from well-handled SPs which caused casualties. Mines killed people every day. Despite sandbags Pte Morrison's jeep was blown to pieces and he was killed instantly. Major Lindsay found two sappers lifting more mines and saw the mutilated body of a man by the side of a road crater. A booby trap was set off by a string tied to an igniter to the bank on the other side of the road.

> This advance of two or three miles [towards Wildenhausen] caused us to lose more good men. Howett was blown up in a carrier, an elderly subaltern nearly 40. He and his brother joined us together on 14th

February. Charles was killed four days later and now Jake was dead too. Sgt Hares was killed shot through the head. Donald a stretcher-bearer in 'C' Coy since El Alamein was lost to a piece of metal from a tank, itself hit by an SP gun.

5/7th Gordons reached Amerbusch on 13th and the next day to Wildeshausen which they and 5th Black Watch combined in a joint attack. 152 Bde were on the left and 1st Gordons on the right. In artificial moonlight a silent attack went in. Huge craters had to be filled up under shellfire and at dawn flail tanks helped the Gordons in. In the ensuing mêlée many Germans were killed and captured and 5/7th were lucky to lose only ten men.

On the 15th and 16th 5th Black Watch had a fight on their hands near Wildeshausen. Their supporting tanks went up on mines and enemy SP guns caused 42 casualties to 'B' and 'C' companies with three officers killed or wounded. Lt Wood was killed. Major Graham Pilcher and Major Sandy Leslie were badly wounded. The Recce Regt took over the crossroads and 5/7th Gordons took Dotlingen without trouble.

154 Brigade

HD had taken over the Lingen bridgehead on the 8th and mopping up went on around Altenlunne. 1st Black Watch acquired a German bulldozer from the TODT organisation to repair craters beyond the new Dortmund-Ems canal bridge. In Badbergen, Battalion HQ had tea on the lawn of a pleasant house near the church. Their pioneers showed great skill in constructing a class 3 (ton) raft to ferry their jeeps and anti-tank guns across small rivers and an improvised ferry from a tarpaulin and bales of straw! The Burgemeister of Dinklage surrendered the village after a stonk by mediums and the Battalion had a pleasant rest there until the 16th. 7th Argylls from Elbergen moved over the river Ems to Furstenau and on the 11th were given the task of clearing Ankum, thence to Badbergen, Dinklage and Lohne where a hospital was found with 250 German wounded. In Vechta the Argylls collected 111 POW, liberated some wounded British POW and another German hospital was found with 2500 wounded. On the 16th from Harpstedt to Ippener where a hostile SP caused five casualties. 7th Black Watch crossed the river Ems on 9th, reached Mundersum, Messingen, Furstenau and Quakenburg. Here they found three German military hospitals, and their prisoners included policemen, firemen, postmen and the local sanitary inspector! Near the Lagerhase stream, Spandau fire caused six casualties, then to Lohne and a comfortable stay in Vechta until 16th April.

*   *   *

The Die Hards had a minor action at Quakenburg on 12th and moved through Dinklage on the evening of the 12th, Vechta on 13th, Holtzhausen on 14th and Wildeshausen on the 15th. The speed of the advance was such that on 11th April 126 Field Regt occupied three action positions in one day ending up near Badbergen. Harassing fire was the order of the day and many small programmes were fired as the infantry and tanks winkled out the stubborn rear guards.

*   *   *

The Wehrmacht in its dying days put up a determined defence of Bremen, not in the devastated city, but in the outskirts to the west and south. No less than four British divisions were converging on the city. Delmenhorst to the west was the key objective given to HD. Moving from their concentration area around Ippener, 152 Bde were to lead the attack. 2nd Seaforth had been in action on the 19th near Adelheide and 5th Camerons had an unpleasant action around the bridges at Adelheide losing 30 casualties to mines and bazooka teams. 'B' Coy who suffered most were awarded a bottle of Scotch whisky by a grateful sapper officer. Grateful because the Camerons had captured the bridge intact!

Two days were spent in clearing the approaches to Delmonhorst, and the divisional artillery and Die Hards fired many concentrations. But on the morning of the 20th patrols of the Derbyshire Yeo reached the northern outskirts of the town and reported it clear. 153 Bde then secured the northern suburbs while 152 Bde moved north-west to capture Ganderkese where 2nd Seaforth had a brisk action on the 21st. The Burgomeister of Delmonhorst informed HD that there were no less than 15 hospitals in his town full of German wounded.

HD suffered a great loss on the 20th as Lt Col James Cochrane wrote:

> The CRA was blown up on a mine while out on a Recce in his jeep. Brigadier Jerry Sheil was a great gunner and sportsman and one, who in the four years he served with HD made friends and followers with everyone he came into contact. His wave of the hand and cheery grin will long be remembered by those who served with him. His good humour, his pawky personality which made him the perfect foil to General Rennie will be remembered by all.

On the 21st April 5/7th Gordons beyond Delmonhorst were again under shell and mortar fire. Pte John Tough with 'D' Coy:

> We came to a wood under quite a bit of Spandau fire. The order was given to fix bayonets. (I was on the Bren) and in open formation we moved forward. Most of the Germans started to surrender as we went towards some houses. L/Corporal Kilgallon was in charge and was in line with me when the Spandau hit him on the side and hip. He saved my life, otherwise I would have copped it on the side of the head. He went down screaming for stretcher bearers.

When they arrived the Germans ceased firing having seen the red cross on their arms. Eventually 16 Platoon got into the shelter of the houses ahead. "Suddenly about ten Germans appeared beside us who had been hiding down in the cellar. Just as well they decided to surrender. They could have taken us by surprise." 'D' Coy gathered in 40 POW that day.

When HD crossed the river Weser with large numbers of German vehicles, army and civilian which had been 'acquired' in the last month, a special check point confiscated the looted cars.   The huge consumption of petrol and time spent on vehicle repairs were the prime reasons. Probably the GOC was not happy with the HD sign appearing on Mercedes and Volkswagens.

43
Victory in Europe

Major Martin Lindsay 2i/c (and often commanding) 1st Gordons calculated that up to 27th March, 102 officers had served with his Battalion. The average strength was usually about 30. The average service of the 55 officers commanding the twelve rifle platoons was 38 days or 5½ weeks. Just over half had been wounded, a quarter killed, 15% invalided home and 5% had survived. "Everybody had a prejudice against being killed in the last month of a six years war. So people were playing for safety..."

And Alastair Borthwick wrote of the advance to capture Bremervorde on the way to Bremerhaven: "I believe this attack was the most miserable one we ever did... People who had fought in twenty actions seeing their friends drop one by one, began to think that once more would be once too often." No wonder the HD divisional cage harboured nearly 200 men on charges of desertion. Many were veterans who - poor devils - had simply exhausted their store of courage. Many others were 18 year old reinforcements poorly trained and disciplined, new to the 'game', who were just completely out of their depth. A third group were from rear lines of communication units who had been hauled out of comfortable jobs and thrown into the 'sharp end' of the campaign.

On the 25th HD had a grandstand view of the final, terrible bombing of Bremen and the Burgomeister, several generals and admirals surrendered the next day. So, by-passing Bremen HD continued its advance northwards into the tongue of land between the rivers Weser and Elbe.   Volkersen was reached on the 27th, the river Oste was crossed on 2nd May and Bremenvorde captured against slight opposition. The German navy had supplied not only marines and seamen for the Bremen defences but also 'material'. Magnetic sea mines were buried a yard below the surface of the road or fastened to trees by the side of the road. Set off by the approach of a vehicle they made a very big hole indeed. The Luftwaffe had been active on other divisional fronts particularly at the river and canal crossings and bridgeheads. On 2nd May four enemy jet propelled fighter bombers appeared, dropped a few bombs and did some token strafing. Although the radio reported the death of the Fuhrer and the Russian armies fighting in the centre of Berlin, 5th Black Watch encountered heavy shelling near Bremenvorde on the 1st. The old enemy ahead was the *15th Panzer Grenadier Division*, proud and indomitable who had not the slightest intention of surrendering - yet. Indeed 'B' Coy 1st Gordons attacking Bremervorde were themselves counter-attacked from front and flank. The Gordons also had two carriers towing 6-pdr anti-tank guns captured and a third knocked-out. When 5/7th Gordons moved towards Ebersdorf on the evening of the 2nd they had to fight for each house along the road, under 'moaning Minnie' mortar fire and shells from captured Russian heavy guns. 154 Bde finally subdued the Ebersdorf garrison after artillery concentrations and tank support was required. Many Germans were killed and 300 POW taken for the loss of seven Gordon casualties.

5th Black Watch captured 'Brake'. 'Bolt', 'Ostrich', 'Bonnet' and 'Wire' and objectives around Hipstedt where they were shelled by 88mm LAA Flak guns and 20mm guns. They captured 100 POW, a troop of 105mm guns and several 88mm, LAA guns. The Luftwaffe AA troops had been trained to fire their guns into the sky and were rather shaky on ground targets. Even as late as 4th May 7th Argylls were shelled from Beorkesa. In heavy rain 7th Black Watch moved into Westertimke and found three large POW camps containing several thousand British, American and Polish prisoners. Five HD prisoners from St Valèry were also rescued and duly entertained. When 1st Black Watch arrived on the outskirts of Bulstedt near Otterstelt and Vorwerk, the CO and a company commander moved to the edge of a wood to recce Bulstedt which had produced a hostile SP gun and several Spandaus. They were approached from the village by a Jock who on being questioned informed them that his platoon commander had sent him into the village to collect as many eggs (and he produced a basketful) as possible and to get them appropriately boiled for his friends by the hitherto hostile natives of Bulstedt. He did admit that he had not encountered any uniformed enemy in the village.

From Ganderkesee where Major General DN Wimberley paid a brief visit, 5th Camerons, moved to Holtum and Otterstedt saw finally a small action in Glinde. Single-handedly Captain DK Beaton took on and knocked-out a tricky SP gun. Later he was awarded the MC.

On the morning of the 4th representatives of *15 Panzer Grenadier Division* arrived at Battalion HQ 7th Argylls in Lintig. Negotiations for surrender went on all day. The German GOC was not only a proud man (Major General Roth) but he made it clear that his division although weakened was still well-equipped and a well-disciplined fighting formation which would sell its life dearly. He was also unaware that Field Marshal Busch was about to surrender all his troops facing 21st Army Group in north-west Germany. Indeed about 2000 hrs the BBC news announced the capitulation of forces in Holland, North Germany and Denmark - amid great rejoicing, and much firing of tracer and Verey lights. One formation even fired their PIAT bombs.

The village of Ringstedt became neutral territory for HD and *15th PZ Div* negotiations, and a temporary truce was agreed. Eventually at 1035 hrs 5th May Lt General Rasp, Commander Corps EMS, Major General Roth, a Naval representative and several staff officers arrived at the RV, and the terms of surrender agreed between the two old adversaries. The 'old' *15th Panzer Division* had surrendered in Tunisia in May 1943. There was no doubt that the sad story of St Valèry had been well and truly avenged. And that night a tremendous party was held to which many officers from Brigade HQs were invited and amid the noisy jubilation the Senior Chaplain of HD, Major WCB Smith conducted a Thanksgiving Memorial Service.

7th Black Watch Victory Parade, Bremerhaven

Envoi

On 8th May HD moved to a concentration area in and amongst the German units of *15th PZ Div*, 152 Bde was at Bederkesa, 153 at Bremerhaven and 154 Bde in Bexhovede. Div HQ was in Schiffdorf, a village outside Bremerhaven. All ranks found comfortable billets in houses and flats. Guards were also needed for the docks and warehouses to prevent looting by the Displaced Persons (DPs) of all nationalities. 5/7th Gordons 'A' Coy area included a food store filled with luxuries for provisioning submarines. On 12th May a Victory parade was held at Bremerhaven when HD marched past Lt General Sir Brian Horrocks GOC 30th Corps, played past by the Massed Pipe Bands of the division. 5th Cameron Highlanders supplied the only fully kilted contingent on parade. General 'Babe' Macmillan himself led his division. Private Ian E Kaye, Bde HQ watched the parade:

> From far, far away in the distance we heard a faint command 'Pipes and Drums, By the left... Quick March' and the skirling of the bagpipes could be heard all over the town. As they came into view with kilts and sporrans swinging in unison and the glitter of silver and brass in the sunlight it was quite breathtaking; the smart drum majors, each swinging his mace with immaculate precision and the famous 'bearded Piper' Ashe of the Seaforth Highlanders who stood out on every parade. As they marched past the General, the sound of the pipes just seemed to lift you, and we cheered our heads off. One by one the regiments passed us, and it was a blaze of colour with all the different regimental tartans on display. The sound of 'Highland Laddie' echoed round the chimney pots.

HD had made prisoner in North-West Europe almost 24,000 and during the whole of WWII (except the BEF tragedy) the division had suffered 16,469 casualties, including 3084 killed in action. 1st Gordons had fought some 36 actions and suffered nearly a thousand casualties in north-west Europe. "I shall never get over the sadness of these losses. To the day of my death [Major Martin Lindsay] I shall remember David Martin, George Stewart, Arthur Thompson, Donald Haworth, the best platoon commander that ever was; Albert Brown our doctor; Glass the young Canadian, Jimmy Graham, my first servant; 'Carrots' Chamberlain for so long my signaller and Sgts Dunlop and Coutts, together with General Thomas Rennie and many others, as gallant and lovely Highlanders as have ever been." Lt Col John McGregor, author of *The Spirit of Angus* recalls some of the 25,000 miles travelled by 5th Black Watch from Butterburn School, Dundee to Bremerhaven:

> From the heather of Scotland, the woods and fields of England, half way round the world to the heat, dust and flies of Egypt. The baptism of fire at

Alamein, across the deserts of North Africa, to the mountains of Tunisia. The brief respite on the sun soaked beaches of Algeria, then through Malta to the sultry plains of Sicily. Back across the winter seas for a few precious months at home and preparation for the Normandy landings. Then from the treachery of the small fields and woods of Normandy, across Northern France to the waterways of Holland and Belgium, the bitter cold of the Ardennes, and the bloody battles in the Reichswald, before the Rhine and the advance into the strongholds of Germany. An epic journey full of incident, endeavour and triumphs for the Battalion.

*   *   *

We remembered friends who were dead. It had been a long time. Sometimes we [Alastair Borthwick, 5th Seaforth] could not remember their names. We talked of drought in Africa and floods in Holland and how the 88 had come down on the olive grove at Sferro. We argued about which truck had sunk on Nan beach and whether or not there had been a rum ration after Francofonte... it seemed strange in the following days to find the same drab landscape outside our windows. This, we felt, was not the way wars should end. We should feel suddenly different. Perhaps we were too tired. Perhaps the abnormal had become too much our second nature. The war had just petered out and left us, disillusioned and weary in a world where even peace had lost its savour. There was nothing left but anticlimax.

Eclipse was over and on 14th June Field Marshal Lord Montgomery visited HD to present medals to his Highlanders.

THE END

Acknowledgements

In the making of *Monty's Highlanders* Lt General Sir Derek Lang KCB, DSO, MC, DL has given me much encouragement and advice. Major Neil Wimberley MBE has kindly given me permission to quote from his famous father's wartime journal, as has Alastair Borthwick from *Sans Peur*, Lt Colonel Angus Fairie from '*Cuidich 'a Righ*, Lt Colonel John McGregor MC and the Regimental Trustees of 5th Battalion Black Watch from *Spirit of Angus*; Hutchinson & Co for Lt Col Martin Lindsay's *So Few Got Through*, Stanley Whitehouse for *Fear is the Foe* and Jack Didden for *Operation Colin, the Highland Division in Brabant*. Andrew Black and David Sclater have produced key books, listed in the comprehensive Bibliography.

In addition, I would like to thank the following for their help and advice: Lt Col Leonard Aitkenhead MBE TD DL, Eric Atherton, HJ Bagshaw, Peter Bacon MBE, Jim Blackman MM, Captain WJ Brown MBE TD JP, C Fraser Burrows, Jack Cheshire, Denis Daly, Geoffrey Durand, Jack Easton, Roy Green, Jeffrey Haward MM, AC Jenkins, Leslie Meek, Ross Le Mesurier, JW Mitchison, Peter Parnwell, Dr Tom

Renouf MM, Capt MV Sim, Angus Stewart, John Tough, KEA Wilson, George Wagstaffe and James Younic.

This book is written in tribute to the finest infantry division in the British Army during WWII who, commanded by General (later Field Marshal) Montgomery, fought from El Alamein to Bremerhaven. They left over 3000 young Highland soldiers who died and were buried beside the long dangerous centre lines. The total casualties were 16,469 of which officers 1546 and ORs 14,923.

If there are errors of names, places or dates, they are mine alone.

Bibliography

Felix Barker: *5/7th Gordons in N Africa and Sicily* (1944)
Lt Col J E Benson: *War Diary 1st Black Watch NW Europe* (1996)
Alastair Borthwick: *Sans Peur, 5th Seaforth in WWII* (1946)
Capt W J Brown: *126 (H) Field Regt RA* (1946)
Ian C Cameron: *7th Bn Argyll & Sutherland Highlanders* (1946)
Ralph Carr: *A Sappers War* (CRE 51st Highland Div) (1944)
Lt Col J Cochrane: *History 51st HD Signals, NW Europe* (1945)
Saul David: *Churchill's Sacrifice of the Highland Division* (1993)
Jack Didden: *Operation Colin: Highland Div in Brabant* (1944)
Geoff Durand: *History 128 (H) Field Regt RA* (1989)
Lt Col A A Fairrie: *Cuidich 'a Righ, History Seaforth Highlanders*
Roderick Grant: *51st Highland Division at War* (1977)
Historical Records: QO Cameron Highlanders (Blackwood 1952)
PK Kemp: *Middlesex Regt 1919-52* (1952)
Eric Linklater: *51st Highland Division 1940-41* (1942)
Lt Col Martin Lindsay: *So few got through* (1949)
Lt Col John McGregor: *Spirit of Angus. History 5th Black Watch* (1983)
Neil McCallum: *Journey with a Pistol* (1959)
Leslie Meek: *Brief History 51st Highland Div Recce Regt* (1991)
Wilfred Miles: *History Gordon Highlanders*, Vol V (1961)
Major D F O Russell: *War History 7th Black Watch* (1948)
J B Salmond: *History 51st Highland Division* (1953)
Jerry Sheil: Diary as CO128 Field Regt RA (1942/3)
Captain M V Sim: 127 (H) Field Regt RA (Notes) (1996)
Stanley Whitehouse: *Fear is the Foe* (1995)
Lt Col M H G Young: *Transport and Supply Column ASC* (Journal)

Index